Who Needs Care?

SOCIAL-WORK DECISIONS
ABOUT CHILDREN

Jean Packman
with
John Randall
Nicola Jacques

Basil Blackwell

© Jean Packman, John Randall and Nicola Jacques 1986

First published 1986

Basil Blackwell Ltd
108 Cowley Road, Oxford OX4 1JF, UK

Basil Blackwell Inc.
432 Park Avenue South, Suite 1505,
New York, NY 10016, USA

British Library Cataloguing in Publication Data

Packman, Jean
  Who needs care?: social-work decisions about children.
  1. Child welfare—Great Britain—Decision making
  I. Title II. Randall, John III. Jacques, Nicola
  362.7'0941 HV751.A6

  ISBN 0-631-14374-2

Library of Congress Cataloging in Publication Data

Packman, Jean.
  Who needs care?
  Bibliography: p.
  Includes index.
  1. Child welfare—Great Britain. 2. Social work with
  children—Great Britain. 3. Family policy—Great Britain.
  I. Randall, John. II. Jacques, Nicola. III. Title.
  HV751.A6P224 1986 362.7'042 85-26670

  ISBN 0-631-14374-2

Typeset by DMB (Typesetting), Oxford
Printed and bound in Great Britain at
The Camelot Press Ltd, Southampton

Contents

Acknowledgements

Thanks are due to the Department of Health and Social Security for funding the research project on which the book is based, and to Miss June Gilbert and Mrs Jenny Griffin for their support throughout.

We are especially grateful to the staff of the two social services departments who welcomed us into their midst with great kindness – the managers and advisers at every level, and, in particular, the social workers, who discussed their child-care work with such courage and honesty and who enabled us to make contact with so many families. We are also immensely grateful to the parents of the children concerned for sharing with us their thoughts and feelings on what were often difficult and painful events in their lives.

Many people have helped, and, sadly, most must remain anonymous. However, we mention Jill Farwell, who provided us with an excellent start through her work on the pilot study, and the Dartington Social Research Team, who gave invaluable help in all manner of ways – not least with computing, and the accompanying tea and sympathy! They, and many others – Professor Roy Parker and his colleagues, Glyn Roberts and his fellow-researchers, Mrs Barbara Kahan and the indefatigable Bill Jordan – also provided generous advice and lively criticism. We hope that the end result reflects this, but in no way hold them accountable for it! Finally, Alex Allan deserves our special gratitude for her own pertinent comments and for the outstanding skill and good humour she has shown in typing the many versions of this long account.

PART I

Introduction

1

The Background

The research study which is described in the following pages concerns social-work activity at the gateway to the local-authority child-care system. It explores the basis, the process and some of the outcomes of decisions which determine whether children are admitted to care or not, and does so through the eyes of two groups of major participants – the field social workers and the parents of the children concerned.

It is probably no accident that we were originally asked by DHSS to look at this area of decision-making in the late seventies. There had been mounting concern about the quality and quantity of public care for children throughout the decade, coming from all directions and expressed with varying degrees of alarm. Most obvious and strident were the media, their interest alerted·by the public inquiry into the death of Maria Colwell[1] and sustained by succeeding scandals. Maria's death raised a host of questions, not least those of whether, once in care, she should ever have been returned to her natural parent or whether, having been restored, she could have been readmitted in time to avert the tragedy that occurred. The wisdom and competence of those who had made the decisions about her were called sharply into question.

Public inquiries do not, of course, just happen, but are a manifestation of interest and anxiety on the part of politicians as well as the public. It has been persuasively argued[2] that the setting up of the Colwell inquiry, which elevated a private tragedy to the status of a public scandal, occurred not only because child abuse had, by then, become an internationally recognised problem, but because the case fitted neatly into contemporary theories of a 'cycle of deprivation'. Conservative-government strategies for breaking that cycle were hotly debated at the time, and the fundamental problem of the state's role in relation to families – and in particular to poor and deprived families – was at issue.

The mushroom growth of pressure groups in recent years – some on behalf of children and families who are the consumers of child-care services, others on behalf of foster and adoptive parents, who are some of the *providers* of care – also reflects widespread, though not always compatible, concerns. Finally, researchers and commentators from within as well as outside the child-care system have been increasingly critical of the lack of effective planning for children in care[3] – a lack which reflects failures in decision-making at many stages of the children's care careers and at many levels in the responsible social-services departments. Indeed, the seventies can be said to have generated at least as much disquiet over public child care as was evident in the 1940s, when a new child-care service was eventually created, in the wake of scandals and public inquiries. There are, in fact, echoes of the famous Curtis Report of that period in the findings of the working-party on the care, welfare and education of children separated from their families, which were published in 1980; and some similar areas of concern are apparent in the 1984 Report of the House of Commons Social Services Committee on Children in Care.[4]

It is worth looking at some of the facts which lie behind these widespread expressions of alarm and discontent with current child-care practice, for they form the background to the present study. One is the growth in the number of children in local-authority care. Despite the rhetoric of prevention and the passing of two major pieces of legislation (the Children and Young Persons Acts of 1963 and 1969), part of whose aim was to divert children from care, the number and proportion of children in care rose, almost without interruption, for twenty years. In 1962 there were 63,500 children in care in England and Wales – a rate of 5.1 per 1,000 of the eligible population under the age of 18 years. By 1971 there were over 87,000, or 6.5 per 1,000 under 18 – a rise only partially explained by the absorption of offenders into the mainstream of child care, by means of the Children and Young Persons Act 1969. In 1978, when this research project was first being planned, the figure was well over 100,000 and the rate had risen again, to 7.6 per 1,000. It was only at the very end of the decade that there was any sign that the upward trend was flattening out, and then only in terms of absolute numbers. The figures for 1979, 1980 and 1981 showed a modest decline to just over 97,000 but the rate per 1,000 under 18 remained at 7.6.[5]

Rising numbers bother a number of interest groups, including central and local government, because they conjure up all sorts of undesirable things – not least the spectre of rising costs. To the critics of public care they also mean a growing number of children exposed to the damage that poor standards and stigma can inflict. To defenders of family rights they imply an unacceptable increase in state intervention; and to those who emphasise family responsibilities they represent disturbing evidence of the failure of families to cope and look after their own. Whatever their standpoint, in fact, many regard children in care – and, more especially, a rising number of children in care – as a sign of failure on the part of families to care for their children; on the part of social services, to prevent admissions; or on the part of both.

Our own standpoint is rather different. 'Failure' expressed in these terms appears too narrowly defined and the rights and wrongs of admitting children to care seem artificially polarised. Deprivation, isolation, poverty and unemployment have obviously increased in recent years and all have long been recognised as key contributors to the ranks of needy and vulnerable children. The increase in one-parent families alone would probably be sufficient to explain the increased number of children in care over this period – notwithstanding any shortcomings in parental commitment and standards, or in the preventive strategies of social-services departments. The real issue, in our view, is not therefore numbers in care, and how to make them shrink, but the nature and purpose of care and its appropriateness as a means of meeting the social needs that give rise to it. 'Care' is, in any case, potentially a number of different things. It can be the provision of short-term relief, a supplement to parental care, or permanent substitution for it. Professional decision-making is therefore concerned, not simply with whether children shall be admitted or not, but also with how to offer care appropriately to those needing relief or supplementation and how to remove and plan for children needing substitution.

This brings us to a second trend in child care that has been apparent for some years, and which forms another part of the background to this research. This is the steady increase in the use of compulsory powers, at the expense of voluntary child-care arrangements – a trend which has certainly fostered the growth of family and children's rights movements, by way of protest and resistance, as well as contributing to the growth in numbers that we have just outlined. (Children admitted compulsorily tend to remain in care a long time.) Less than half (47 per cent) of all children in care in 1962 had been removed from home by means of a court order, or had become subject to local-authority resolutions, assuming parental rights over them. In 1973 the proportion had risen to 61 per cent - a rise not fully accounted for by the addition of committed offenders under the Children and Young Persons Act 1969. In 1980, the proportion had reached 74 per cent - three out of four of all children in care.

A parallel growth in the use of Place of Safety Orders (POSOs) - the emergency power to remove children from home, under compulsion, with only subsequent recourse to the courts - is another aspect of the trend away from voluntarism. Four years after the Maria Colwell Report was published, the rate of POSOs had more than trebled and the rise continued, though less dramatically, until the end of the decade.[6] Changes of this nature and magnitude are highly significant and require exploration. We have therefore looked quite closely at the use of different routes into care and have examined some of the consequences of this new emphasis. It raises the question of whether such trends reflect changing needs, or changing perceptions of the decision-makers - a question that is not easily answered, but one which it is nevertheless important to ask.

A third fact of importance is the enormous variability in rates of children in care (and in the use of voluntary and compulsory powers) between one local authority and another. As a phenomenon it is not new, but has been evident ever since there were published child-care statistics. In 1978, for example, when this study was being planned, rates ranged from 27.2 per 1,000 in care at one extreme, to 2.9 per 1,000 at the other. Differences of this order have always given cause for concern. If they cannot be accounted for by equally dramatic differences in indicators of social need - and a considerable weight of evidence suggests that they cannot - then they indicate a degree of variability in practice that requires explanation and may, indeed, be unacceptable.

Behind all the facts and figures, there is also the continuing debate in social work about how children's needs can be most appropriately met; the importance of the blood tie, the nature and timing of psychological bonding, and the possibilities of achieving permanent substitute care through legal transfer of parental rights at any stage in childhood.

Such vital professional concerns have also to be seen in the wider context of state-family relationships. There is the question whether the primary function of government is, or should be, to identify 'not good enough' parents and to transfer the child's care and parental rights to 'good enough' substitutes; or whether its main task should be to identify disadvantaged parents, in order to supplement their care. This is not just a professional question, but one which has deep political implications in an era of cutbacks that affect the welfare state as a whole, as well as the personal social services.

It is against this background that the present research was undertaken. It was one of three studies which were initiated and funded by the DHSS and which were clearly seen as complementary. The National Children's Bureau was to examine the factors contributing to the different lengths of time that children stay in care. How long children stay obviously affects how many are in care at any one time – the longer they stay, the greater the cumulative effect on numbers. Decisions about length of stay are also a vital ingredient of child-care planning. The Dartington Social Research Unit was to explore the ways in which the links between children in care and their families are (or are not) maintained. Previous research has shown that the maintenance of links is an important factor in enabling children to return to their families, so this project, too, had implications for accumulating numbers in care as well as the quality of the care experience itself. In contrast, our own study was to examine the decisions of local authorities at the point of entry. How are decisions to admit children, or to refuse admission, taken? What evidence is there of variability in practice and on what basis do such variations rest? What are the consequences of admitting or not admitting children? Taken together, the three studies clearly represent a research response to some of the major anxieties and puzzles of contemporary child care.

Each project was able to draw on previous research of relevance, and our own was no exception. In the early sixties one of us had attempted to explore and explain variations in numbers of children in local-authority care,[7] and this earlier study proved a useful jumping-off point. The approach then had been to select a very large sample of authorities (48 in all) and to take account of a number of potential contributory factors. It was therefore a large-scale, wide-ranging and inevitably 'arm's length' study, heavily dependent on published and unpublished records and statistics and the administration of postal questionnaires. In the process, at least three sets of factors emerged as having some bearing on the variations. One group concerned differences in the perceived 'need' for care. Not all families are equally well placed to bring up their children without aid or intervention, and certain social indicators - of poverty, poor housing, mobility, illegitimacy, family disruption and so on - showed some positive correlation with admissions of children to care. Clearly the environmental conditions, class structure and population mix within different local authorities were themselves variable factors, and in this sense the 'need' for care could also be said to vary. This begs the question of who identifies and defines need in these circumstances[8] - those who experience poor home circumstances, those who look on or perhaps refer them to social services, or the social-services departments themselves; but, whoever applies the label, the circumstances to which it is regularly attached are certainly not evenly spread throughout the country as a whole.

A second set of factors which was considered was the tangle of services which lay beyond the public child-care system, but whose activities were clearly related to it. A range of statutory and voluntary services existed (and still exists) whose role in supporting, referring on or substituting for families in difficulties could thereby help either to steer children into care, or to keep them out of it. Variations in the spread and effectiveness of these services clearly have an effect on statutory child-care caseloads.

Finally, the role of the public child-care authorities themselves was considered, in terms of their resources, policies and practice. It became evident that children's departments, as they then were, were not all equally well resourced in terms of the numbers or qualifications of their staff, the amount and range of their accommodation for children in care, or in the money available for the service as a whole - hardly a surprising finding. It was also clear, however, that attitudes to the child-care task itself, and the assumptions on which they were based, were also far from uniform, and that there were identifiable differences in the policies pursued over admission and discharge, for example, which resulted in significant variations in practice.

It is upon this last set of factors that the present study is primarily focused. Rather than replicating the earlier research (which we believed would take us no further forward in our understanding), we decided to concentrate upon only one group of influences upon the admission of children to care, and to view these in close-up. This meant studying a very few local-authority social-services departments (in fact, just two!) and doing so at first hand. It meant viewing decisions about admissions not only in retrospect and in aggregate, but individually and at the time they were being made. Furthermore, it was essential to understand not only what authorities *did* do, but also what they did *not* do, so we needed to take as much account of cases where the decision was to leave a child at home as we did of those where the child was admitted to care. This took us back a stage in the decision-making process, to a point where serious consideration was being given to care as an option but where the outcome had not yet been determined. It also led us to consider an (in research terms) hitherto neglected group. Very little has so far been recorded[9] about the characteristics and circumstances of children who might have come into care, but didn't – yet, without such knowledge, the picture is incomplete. It is important to know, for instance, how like or unlike the in-care group they are and therefore how difficult or arbitrary decisions have to be. We need to know, as well, whether some children remain out of care because of forms of help and support which could feasibly be extended to others, to prevent unnecessary admissions. Knowledge about the 'not admitteds' may also tell us more about differences between practitioners or their authorities – about where they draw the line, and why they differ. And it should also reveal more about the quality as well as the quantity of child-care 'need' as presented to the social-services departments.

We began with an assumption (shared by the DHSS) that local authorities were, to some extent, masters of their own fate. Notwithstanding the varying degrees of pressure on them to admit children to care, the powerful social and economic factors beyond their control, and the different levels of support services on which they could draw, our earlier research had suggested that they still had some room for manoeuvre and choice, and that admission rates were therefore partly of their own making. It was this area of choice that we wished to explore.

This focus dictated that we should be looking at decision-making very much from the *inside* of the departments. For instance, we wished to understand their organisational structures, to determine who were the key decision-makers and where they were located; to look for internally generated policies and to understand how and why they were formulated and disseminated and with what effect on practice. In the event, we found that much of our time was spent with field social workers, who are clearly the prime gatekeepers of the child-care system.

This concentration on the roles and views of the *providers* of child-care services was deliberate, but we wished our self-imposed blinkers to sharpen our perceptions without blinding us to other, important influences. To balance the view from the child-care services we included another vital perspective – that of the families who were involved. In this we were concerned not only to explore consumer views for their own sake – an essential ingredient in any evaluation of a service – but also to understand better the complicated and often protracted negotiations over care which the deceptively simple term 'decision' actually involves.

One further dimension to the study concerned outcomes. What happened to the children (and their families) who were kept out of care, compared with those who came in? What changes did they experience and what, for them, stayed the same? Were there any indications that those who came in fared any better than those who stayed out – or vice versa? Obviously there was an attempt here at a crude *evaluation* of the decisions we had studied.

This last aspect, though only a beginning, was important because views about the merits or disadvantages of having children in local-authority care often conflict and are generally passionately held. Yet the evidence on which they are based is often partial and lopsided, because we know much more about children in the care system than about those outside it. As we have already indicated, we therefore endeavoured from the start to maintain a neutral stance over the issue, resisting the temptation to assume that admitting children to care was, *per se*, a good or a bad thing. We hope we were aware of our own prejudices in the matter and that we have either subdued them appropriately or, where necessary, have declared them with sufficient clarity and honesty. Obviously we have not been that improbable animal, the 'value-free researcher', but we have tried, by arguing amongst ourselves, to avoid the worst excesses of those who discover what they wish to find!

Given such a concentrated, even microscopic study, we were anxious to avoid the dangers of myopia – of looking so closely at one narrow, though vital, area of decision-making within a pair of social-services departments that we failed to appreciate its relationship to wider child-care practice, to what happened elsewhere, and indeed to issues far beyond child care itself. In fact, as we explored we were repeatedly reminded of the wider relevance of much that we were trying to describe and explain.

Regional variations in welfare services

Variation in rates of children in care, which had prompted the study in the first place, was a major factor in our choice of sample authorities and a focus for many of the comparisons we made between the two authorities and the different areas within them. Yet such variability is not peculiar to child care, but appears in all branches of the social services, whether administered by local government or not. Indeed, a search for the cause of and cure for unacceptable variation in levels and types of service has been a major theme in social policy since the Second World War, and it has played a significant part in generating the massive exercises in reorganisation that have taken place in local government and social services alike.

An important reason for the frequent attempts to redraw administrative boundaries and to restructure social-services organisations has been the pursuit of 'territorial justice' - which allows for variability in response to local needs, but seeks to eradicate otherwise unjustifiable degrees of inequality. The concept itself, and the many manifestations of its stubborn refusal to be captured, are massively documented elsewhere, in research studies and in the annual reports and statistics of the social services.[10] Our understanding of variations in child care can only be enriched and put into a better perspective by being viewed against this wider background.

Social need

The thorny concept of social need also had to be grasped. For instance, we wished to highlight any differences in policy and practice, and one way of doing so was to attempt to hold need constant and to make comparisons between what different authorities and practitioners did in similar circumstances. To do this we relied on well-tried social indicators, especially those that appeared to be associated with child-care admissions. We were aware, none the less, that there were probably many equally significant factors which could not be so neatly measured and which we might not even recognise, so we were under no illusions about the crudeness and partiality of many of our measures.

Social need is also very much in the eye of the beholder, and there was a danger that by concentrating so hard on understanding how the professionals within the social-services departments defined it we should neglect other perspectives. As social workers ourselves, we were also in danger of colluding with this service eye view – and our choice of questions and selection of data may indicate how far this was the case. Here again, inclusion of the families' views was an attempt to check too much one-sidedness, whilst equal attention to the circumstances of children who came into care and some who stayed out, in search of likenesses between them, gave us a comparative dimension. In trying to pin down 'needs' we were joining a large army of fellow researchers, not to mention the policy-makers themselves.

Professional discretion and managerial control

Our small-scale study also raised issues of wider relevance in organisational terms. In seeking to understand who made the policies and who made the decisions in social-services departments and what the connection between them might be, we recognised that one of the central dilemmas was that of autonomy versus control; or, more precisely, how the considerable discretion vested in the fieldworkers could be 'managed'. Despite the formal hierarchies, the bureaucratic organisation charts and the social workers' own perception that they crouched at the bottom of a very heavy heap, cramped and restricted by rules and regulations, the picture, as we understood it, was very different. What we saw were workers with considerable potential autonomy, at least in so far as decisions about child admissions were concerned, and the power that comes in part from being the prime holders of vital information – vital to the organisation as well as to the consumers of its services – and also from working at the boundary between the organisation and the outside world.

In this, social workers seemed to us to belong to the species 'street-level bureaucrat' identified by American sociologists[11] and to be found not only in social-welfare organisations, but also in the police force, in teaching – in all branches of public service, in fact. In common with face-to-face, ground-level workers in other public agencies (the transatlantic 'street' imagery was a shade too urban for our English tastes!) they appeared to possess a degree of freedom that, though often unrecognised, was inevitable. The complexity of the situations they were required to assess and to respond to defied detailed regulation or prescription, and room for manoeuvre was very important if the service was to be truly individual and personal. But this posed the organisational problems of how to promote general standards of good practice; of how to safeguard clients from the quixotic or damaging exercise of discretion; and, indeed, of how to set about implementing *policies* at all. These themes quickly surfaced as we pursued our case-by-case study of decisions in the making, and it was both helpful and salutary to recognise that they were in no way unique or peculiar to the departments we were studying.

The tensions between freedom to operate at the ground level, where 'need' manifested itself, and control from above, which were evident to us in the social-services departments, were only rather pale mirror images of the wider struggle between the local authorities and central government – a struggle which was particularly acute at the time we were at work. Our study period coincided with a time when local authorities were being urged repeatedly to cut back on expenditure, when within one year they had been obliged to prepare three separate budgets, and when central government threatened dire penalties if they did not toe the line. (It was a period during which one of our sample directors gave a lecture entitled, with some feeling, 'Whatever Next?'). The gloomy national economic situation and the Conservative government's hostile attitude to public expenditure, with its implications for local autonomy, tended to overshadow any discussions we had of *local* policy within our sample authorities – neither of which was in any sense a 'rebel' in this regard.

Policy

The pursuit of 'policy' was indeed central to our study. Any naïve ideas we may have had at the outset that it could be swiftly identified and understood and that its effects would be readily traceable in the actions of operational staff were very quickly dispelled. Grasping 'policy', like grasping 'decisions', was a matter of trying to capture something that was multidimensional, constantly moving and, furthermore, something that often appeared ghostly and insubstantial in outline and detail. As we consulted committee minutes and departmental guidelines and memoranda, and as we discussed with managers and advisers at various levels, we sometimes felt close to understanding what some of the relevant local policies were, and why they had evolved. But at the operational level, when we sought to link policies with practice and to fit individual decisions into a general framework, we were much less confident. Social workers themselves were less than eloquent on this, and rarely made such connections. 'You tell me what the department's policy is – and I'll tell you if it fits', as one remarked succinctly.

It was with some relief that we came upon the analysis of implementing *central* government policies in the personal social services, by Adrian Webb and Gerald Wistow,[12] in which they conclude,

> The problem of integrating the components of service policies, and of service and resource policies, casts doubts on any simple approach to the problem of 'implementing' central government 'policies'; it casts doubt on the very notion of 'policies' being readily identifiable, let alone being the core influence on how services develop at the local level.

We were inclined to say much the same with regard to *local* policies, though our data will show to what extent that very negative view had to be amended and modified.

Care and control

Finally, the issue of care and control within social work was unavoidable. In monitoring decisions about admissions to care, it became quickly apparent that the question of *how* to admit a child to care was just as important as whether to admit the child or not. The two main routes into care – voluntary reception with parental agreement, via section 2 of the Child Care Act 1980, or compulsory *committal*, via a magistrate's or court order – neatly encapsulate the 'care' and 'control' dimensions of the role of personal social services in relation to families. The former suggests the offer of a child-care service, in partnership with parents. The latter depends upon publicly establishing faults in the parents, the child, or in both, and, in consequence, a take-over of the parental role by the local authority.

In considering care as an option, social workers often spent much time worrying about which route was the most appropriate to the circumstances; and, though it was sometimes in this area of legal interpretation that departmental guidelines were at their most detailed and explicit, this did not appear to make their decisions any easier. Feelings about the need to share, to protect or to control ran high and varied considerably as between individuals, teams, and areas.

The families were equally sensitive on this point, and were as eloquent about *how* children were removed as about the removal *per se*. To some, the compulsory admission, particularly in the form of the emergency procedure of a Place of Safety Order, was a nightmare version of state interference – the work of the 'SS' or the 'Gestapo' to an angry minority. It was also a symbol of betrayal on the part of workers whom they had often approached for advice and support, in whom they had confided, and who then seemed to have broken trust and used their confidences in evidence against them. Our study offers no easy solutions to this crucial dilemma and we certainly do not believe that it can be dodged or circumvented. What we can contribute, however, are some suggestions as to how social workers and their departments might handle these painful areas of conflict in the least damaging way for the children and parents concerned.

We have outlined the genesis of our research project, its main focus, and some of the key issues with which it is concerned. In the following chapter the sample authorities and the design of the study are described in more detail.

2

The Shape of the Study

In this chapter we first describe the two authorities in which we chose to work, and then the ways in which we set about our task.

The sample authorities

Social characteristics

The two areas which were chosen for the study are both in the south of England and they form distinct, middle-tier administrative units of the large local authorities of which they are a part. We called these authorities County and Shire. At the heart of each administrative area, and comprising the bulk of its population, lies a port - Clayport in County and Shiptown in Shire. These are towns of substantial size, the former having a population of over 200,000, the latter somewhat below that figure, at the 1981 Census. They are both, in effect, garrison towns, sharing a long history of close involvement with and dependence on the armed forces - the Navy in particular. They also have their share of summer visitors, though the tourist industry is not their prime source of employment and they bear little resemblance to conventional resorts, being larger, more heavily industrialised and more thoroughly 'urban' than the typical seaside town.

For social-services purposes, administrative boundaries at the time of our study stretched beyond the two cities; and here similarities broke down, for their hinterlands were in sharp contrast to one another. Shiptown is linked, administratively, to several barely separate built-up areas, one of which is a fast-growing small town which presents many of the features of a desirable suburb. Only small areas of countryside of a semi-rural, market-garden character are included beyond. We called this whole area Plainfields. Clayport is linked to a much larger area. Part of it is overspill and suburban sprawl, but the greater part comprises acres of wild and beautiful countryside containing two small market towns and a wide scattering of hamlets, villages and farms, and a population of sheep which outnumbers the people. This area we named Roebuck. The differences between Plainfields and Roebuck were a bonus, enabling us to look at decision-making in some sharply contrasting settings, and giving the study a wider applicability than it might otherwise have had.

The evident similarities between the two *ports* were, however, a major reason for selecting them for investigation, as we wished to concentrate upon differences of practice within areas that apparently shared similar levels of social need. Clayport and Shiptown are classified as being alike in several studies of British towns,[1] and the two ports clearly have a lot in common. Their population structure is broadly similar, with Clayport having the slightly larger child population, but population *trends* run in opposite directions. Clayport is expanding but Shiptown is on the decline – something which has been apparent since the Second World War at least. Yet Shiptown is still markedly more cramped and crowded, with an outstanding level of population density, while in Clayport there is a much greater feeling of space. Indeed, this is one obvious way in which the cities are in direct contrast to one another. The one seems tightly squeezed within its boundaries, its buildings close-packed, with very little green or open space between; the other spreads itself, with many wide roads, numerous parks and playing fields, and a general airiness which can be delightful in summer, but bleak and windswept in the winter months.

Both towns have surprisingly low proportions of local-authority housing – around a quarter of their housing-stock is council-owned, and both therefore have rather high percentages of privately rented accommodation and extensive 'tied' service quarters. In general, measures of quality show Clayport to be rather better off for amenities, such as baths and inside toilets, but worse-off in terms of overcrowding (ironically, the freedom to spread themselves *outdoors* is not reflected *inside* their homes!). On the other hand, because Shiptown is so densely populated some of its post-war housing has been in the form of tower blocks, with all their attendant disadvantages, but in Clayport there is very little high-rise housing.

When we turn to unemployment, it is Clayport which stands out. Throughout the seventies, and at the time of our study (1980-3), Shiptown's unemployment rate was about average but Clayport's figure exceeded the national rate by 20 per cent. By comparison with Shiptown it also suffers a scarcity of skilled jobs and average wage levels are well below the national norm, a feature it shares with County as a whole.

In contrast, some other stress factors affecting families with children appear rather more prominently in Shiptown. Its divorce rate was well above average throughout the seventies, and at the time of our study it was somewhat higher than in Clayport. Illegitimacy rates have traditionally been high in both towns but, at the 1981 Census, Shiptown had a slightly higher proportion of children living in one-parent families, and its juvenile-delinquency rate was also somewhat higher. Neither city has a large immigrant population, but Shiptown is marginally the more cosmopolitan, though both ports host a sizable and shifting service population.

Taken as a whole, therefore, the two towns at the centre of our study areas are alike in many respects, but their worst stress points are not the same. Unemployment and low wages stand out in Clayport; a cramped environment and various indicators of family disruption are more to the fore in Shiptown. Neither suffers the extremes of urban blight and decay which exist in some of our big cities, but nor is either in any sense a haven of privilege. They both have their share of chronic and acute social problems and as such are not atypical of many urban areas today. (Table 2.1 presents a comparison of characteristics of the two towns.)

Child care

In choosing our two authorities we were also concerned to compare patterns of child care, past and present. Although we aimed to select two authorities which had roughly similar social characteristics, we were also looking for contrasting child-care profiles in the hope that there would be differences in policy and practice to be investigated. On a number of criteria Clayport and Shiptown provided the desired contrasts - differences that can be seen most clearly in data concerning children in care at any one time.

Table 2.1 Some characteristics of Shiptown and Clayport

	Shiptown	Clayport
Resident population, 1981[a]	175,000	240,000
Percentage population under 16, 1981[a]	19	22
Percentage born outside UK, 1981[a]	5	4
Percentage households with 3+ dependent children, 1981[a]	5	6
Percentage children in one-adult households, 1981[a]	8	7
Population density (persons per hectare), 1981[a]	48	31
Percentage council housing, 1981[a]	23	27
Percentage private rented accommodation, 1981[a]	18	18
Overcrowding (more than one person per room), 1981[a]	2	3
Number of divorce petitions 1980[b]	2,124	1,594
Juvenile-delinquency rate (per 1,000), 1980[c]	40	34
Unemployment rate, 1982[d]	13	17

NB: All figures are rounded.

[a] Census 1981.
[b] County Court records 1980.
[c] Criminal statistics 1980.
[d] *Employment Gazette*, August 1982, Area Statistics.

In Clayport the rate of children in care (that is, the number in care per 1,000 of the population under 18 years on any one day) had been spectacularly high in the fifties, but had gradually declined so that at the time of our study it was somewhat above the national average, though unexceptional for an urban area. Shiptown's rate, in contrast, had climbed dramatically from a low point in the fifties to twice the national average by the early seventies and was still at that level, and comparable with many inner London boroughs, by the time we did our research.

Such figures are obviously the product of rates of admission and discharge and of the ratio between them. Admissions to the two authorities had been rather similar, and not much above average for several years before the project began, but Clayport's discharge rate had consistently outstripped its admissions over the same period, hence its declining numbers in care. So more children had been emptied out of Clayport's child-care system than had been put back in it, which was against the trends in Shiptown – and indeed in Shire, County and in the country as a whole, where lower rates of discharge have for some years accounted for accumulations of children in care. In their exits and their entrances and the balance between them, the two cities at the heart of our sample areas therefore provided some interesting contrasts.

The legal status of children in care in the two ports also differs. Three quarters of Shiptown's children in care are in care compulsorily (the national average); that is, they are there on a court order, or the local authority has assumed parental rights over them, following a voluntary admission. In Clayport, nine out of ten children are in that position – a proportion to which an exceptionally high (and historically consistent) percentage of parental-rights resolutions clearly contributes. But both towns, and the local authorities to which they belong, care for a similarly high number of children on matrimonial care orders as well.

Finally, the manner in which children in care are accommodated differs to some degree. The proportion of children fostered – always a popular measure of child-care practice – has been and remains well above average in Clayport and County, but is not outstanding in Shiptown and Shire.

This and some other child care data are summarised in table 2.2, which shows that in many respects the areas of special study and the two local authorities of which they form a part are 'ordinary' enough to promise a wider relevance to our findings but different enough from one another to invite investigation.

The social-services departments

The social-services departments which operate in our two rather similar local authorities were also organised on similar lines (though both were reorganised rather differently once our study was completed). At the time, both were based on a three-tier, hierarchical structure that was a mix of the 'functional' and the 'geographical'.[2] At headquarters was a relatively small staff, headed by a director, with several assistant directors who were responsible for various aspects of the department's

Table 2.2   Aspects of child care in the sample authorities

	County	Clayport	Shire	Shiptown	England
Rate of children in care per 1,000 under 18 (1980)	7.7	9.7	7.4	15.6	7.6
Admission rate per 1,000 under 18 (1.4.79-31.3.80)	3.2	3.5	2.2	3.8	4.0
Discharge rate per 1,000 under 18 (1.4.79-31.3.80)	3.0	4.0	2.2	4.1	3.5
Voluntary admissions as percentage of all admissions (1.4.79-31.3.80)	54	52	61	43	61
Percentage in care on court orders and section 3 resolutions	83 (1980)	91 (1980)	74 (1978)[a]	73 (1978)[a]	74 (1980)
Percentage in care on Section 3 resolutions only (1980)	25	34	20	20 (1978)[a]	18
Percentage in care on matrimonial care orders (1980)	10	14	15	11	6
Percentage fostered (1980)	59	59	45	48	45
Rate of POSOs per 1,000 under 18 (1.4.78-31.3.79)	0.51	unknown	0.46	unknown	+0.46
Rate of POSOs on under-fives per 1,000 under five (1.4.78-31.3.79)	0.97	unknown	0.65	unknown	+0.84

[a] These Shire and Shiptown figures for 1980 were not available at the time the table was prepared.

Figures derived from DHSS personal social-services local-authority statistics and from the research departments of the sample authorities.

work, together with consultants or advisers for different client groups. Child care was a conspicuous specialism in both departments. At the second tier (in our terms, the 'area') a similar pattern was repeated. Area directors were assisted by more than one level of variously titled specialists, some of whom were concerned with child care (fostering-officers, child-abuse specialists, intermediate-treatment officers, children's homes advisers, etc.). Whether these specialists or their counterparts at headquarters carried any executive responsibility or were occupying an advisory role, and to whom that advice was directed, was not always clear, and job descriptions depended upon who was answering our questions. In this we suspected that the departments were fairly typical![3]

The third tier we called the 'district', and this too was headed by a director with a small staff of clerical and administrative officers; but the majority of staff at this level consisted of teams of social workers (in some cases incorporating home-help organisers and occupational therapists), each led by a senior social worker (team-leader). We focused in particular upon three districts within one area in each authority. These were Plainfields, and North and Central Shiptown, in Shire; and North and South Clayport, and rural Roebuck, in County.

The broad similarity in departmental structure was probably a response to some similar problems. Both counties covered a large and varied territory and at local-government reorganisation in 1974 both had incorporated some previously independent county boroughs (not least, Shiptown and Clayport) with distinct traditions of their own and with strong feelings about the amalgamation that had been forced on them. The middle tier of administration was one way of allowing the boroughs some degree of continuing independence. The lower tier was no doubt an attempt to relate more closely to the 'community base' of the Seebohm formula for personal social services.[4] Coincidentally, the two areas chosen for study were both at a considerable distance from their county towns. The mileage was greater in County, but busy roads and bottlenecks out of Shiptown created a similar psychological distance between the area and headquarters.

There were differences in how these two apparently similar pyramids functioned in relation to child-care decisions, which we discuss in later chapters. There were also differences in how their teams of social workers were organised and in the sort of communities they served – differences that were deliberately highlighted in our choice of teams for special study.

In County, each team was clearly identified with a geographical 'patch' – albeit in some of the rural areas a very large patch indeed. Although the several teams that comprised a district all worked from the same offices and could therefore be operating at a considerable distance from their particular patch, each drew work from within clearly defined boundaries and there were overlaps only when there was a strong case for preserving continuity of social work with clients who had moved.

In Shire, generally (though not invariably) a cluster of teams in a district would each cover the whole of that district and work was divided up between them in ways not related to geography. In some districts they operated a rotating duty system, each team being responsible for all referrals occuring on a particular day. In one district, teams were distinguished by function. An intake team had been set up to deal with all new referrals and to handle work of a short-term nature, while two long-term teams concentrated on the cases where more prolonged involvement was judged necessary. The intake team and one of its long-term partners were clear candidates for inclusion.

We concentrated on a dozen teams (seven in Shire and five in County) that would reflect these structural differences and at the same time cover a wide diversity of catchment areas. One team (in Roebuck) covered a market town and a vast rural area; three others (in Plainfields) worked side by side in a small, fast-growing town surrounded by a smattering of villages and some fairly comfortable tracts of suburbia, and because their work was so interwoven we included them all. To the city teams, these rural and suburban areas were 'easy', 'a doddle', but those who worked in them held a different view. Roebuck social workers were sensitive to real problems of isolation, especially for newcomers without roots in the area. Teams in Plainfields complained of a lack of community spirit and supportive networks in the fast-expanding new estates.

Even the city teams worked with very varied communities. Only one (in Clayport) could be described as a relatively compact and homogeneous area, which happened to be the decaying red-light district at the city's core. The rest grappled with a range of private housing and local-authority estates of mixed vintage and variable reputation, where there was rarely an obvious centre and where child-care problems were perceived as being unevenly distributed. The population served by patch-based Clayport teams, for example, varied from 10,000 to 30,000. There were also particular teams in both authorities which complained of problem black spots in certain estates or clusters of streets – produced, it was alleged, by housing departments' 'dumping policies' in relation to 'problem families'.

Child-care caseloads reflected these differences. One outer-city Clayport team had 32 children in care when our study got under way, while the long-term team in Shiptown cared for well over 100. Numbers on 'at risk' registers and annual police referrals of children in trouble were similarly variable.

Not surprisingly, the size and composition of the sample teams, their premises and the style and atmosphere they conveyed were as varied as the areas they served. At one extreme were the tiny Plainfields teams of two or three social workers and a senior; at the other, some of the Shiptown teams were three times as large. Qualifications and years of experience varied between teams and the average age of staff ranged from 28 to 44. The stereotypical bunch of youthful, long-haired, left-wing social-science graduates were not much in evidence in either authority.

There were also some sharp contrasts in their working environment. The teams outside the two cities, in Roebuck and Plainfields, occupied comfortable, modern purpose-built premises, and in the latter the proximity of these offices to those of other services, such as the probation department, police, and health services, was thought to promote fruitful co-operation between them - something which did in fact show up in our data. The city teams were less fortunate. Social workers in the north of Clayport, for example, occupied the old workhouse, where even a certain amount of 'upgrading' and a tacked-on extension couldn't disguise its formidable proportions, basic decrepitude and some oddly nineteenth-century odours. Inner-city teams in both authorities were generally well located near bus stations and shopping-centres, but worked from equally unsuitable premises. South Clayport's teams operated from a sort of warehouse, two floors up, with no public lift, in one vast room divided by shoulder-high screens, and grimy windows set well above eye-level. Shiptown's equivalent was an old school building - a rabbit warren of stairs, nooks and crannies and demoralising interview rooms.

Finally, given the very different mixtures of personalities amongst team members, as well as the varied areas and conditions in which they worked, it was not surprising that we found that each conveyed its own peculiar atmosphere and style. Some were more cohesive than others, sharing both work and social life to a marked degree. Some seemed relatively peaceful working-groups, at least to the outsider, but others were hectic, boisterous - full of crises or broad jokes and banter. No doubt in reaction to their crude working-conditions, teams in one district adorned the lavatory walls with some equally crude and telling graffiti!

From time to time we were convinced that we had identified a team 'ethos' that was actually manifest in a common approach to child-care work and to the decision-making in which we were interested. Generally this seemed to arise when a team-leader was particularly forceful and when social workers were apparently influenced in a common direction. But it was an elusive notion in more senses than one. Not all teams were of one mind, and not all teams stayed the same. There were comings and goings throughout, and the composition of one team had changed almost entirely by the time we completed our field-work. Judgements made at a particular time could be misleading and, in due course, our data on decisions did not always bear out what we had thought we had understood to be a team's approach. Differences of attitude and emphasis were undoubtedly there; but they were fluid, inconsistent and sometimes individually rather than team-based.

If we were to summarise the differences between our two *authorities*, teams in Shire compared with those in County were generally larger, but with slightly lower proportions of qualified staff. The social workers in Shire were much more likely to have been trained locally (and were not infrequently born and bred there as well) and had a narrower working experience in terms of alternative social-services departments, though a somewhat wider experience of other forms of employment. So far as working-conditions were concerned, there was not much to choose between them. The so-called 'easy' areas in both authorities had the best offices; the rest made do with some unlikely premises. Variations in team styles, atmospheres and attitudes followed no apparent pattern but cut right across local-authority boundaries.

Other services

Finally, the social-services departments were not solely responsible for handling the child-care problems occurring in their territory. On the contrary, a vast network of other statutory and voluntary services offered help, support or control to families in difficulties in each area, and we attempted to take account of this from the outset. Our success in mapping out the full range of relevant services was only partial, but we gained a vivid impression of each authority's network.

Three points emerged from this exercise. One was that, despite many similarities (the presence of a lively naval welfare service in each authority was an obvious example), there was considerable variation in the number, strength and mix of related services, of which the National Society for the Prevention of Cruelty to Children (NSPCC), day facilities for the under-fives and residential establishments for children run by other statutory and voluntary agencies were all examples. Secondly, some services operated in different ways in the two authorities, the police force being a prime example. Thirdly, variations were apparent not only between the two authorities, but between different areas of the same authority. The apparent significance of some of these differences in terms of child-care decisions will be discussed in later chapters.

The research design: sources of information

Published child-care data for all local authorities in England and Wales[5] provided a useful starting-point for our study, but many strands of inquiry within the sample social-services departments fleshed out this skeleton. At an early stage we conducted a series of interviews with a whole range of social-services personnel, from staff at headquarters to ground-level workers. We attempted to explore with each in turn the structures and procedures, the policies and beliefs that impinged on child care in their departments, shedding some light on admissions to care in the process.

To supplement the interview material, we pored over relevant committee minutes, departmental memoranda, policy documents and practice guidelines. We also attended some advisory and decision-making bodies on a regular basis in order to understand their functioning at first hand. Indeed, one of us faithfully sat in on a weekly Children's Panel for more than six months and became its most conspicuously consistent attender in consequence!

Outside agencies were another source of data, providing a useful additional perspective. Officials from voluntary child-care agencies, psychiatric and education welfare services, the police force and others were interviewed and provided valuable written material. Some even kept special records of relevant child-care cases that they handled or referred on to social services during the period of study.

The heart of the matter was, however, a monitoring-exercise conducted in the twelve sample teams and designed to examine in detail all decisions about admissions to care that occurred over a period of twelve months, together with a follow-up inquiry six months after the decisions had been made. Definitions for and boundaries to this exercise were agreed after a year's pilot study. Every type of admission to care was included – voluntary receptions under the Child Care Act, and committals under criminal as well as child proceedings, in juvenile, divorce and matrimonial courts. We also included Place of Safety Orders – the emergency removal of children by police or magistrates' order – although in *law* they are not admissions to care at all. We did this because in *fact* they always involve the removal of a child from home – most usually to a social-services placement – and many children thus removed subsequently become the subjects of care orders. Even where they do not, they have always experienced temporary separation from home and often in a more dramatic manner than most other children who come into care. POSOs also now represent a very substantial minority of all removals from home. Such a wide and significant doorway into the ante-room of local-authority care could not be ignored.

In order to include children who might have been admitted but were not, cases had to be picked up before a decision was reached. For this purpose a working definition of a 'serious consideration' of a child's admission to care was established and cases were accepted into the study if one or more of the following applied: a parent, caretaker or child requested admission to care; a social worker, whether on referral from another agency or as part of his current work with a family, discussed the possibility of admission with his senior (team-leader) or recorded its consideration in the case file. This meant that new referrals as well as recent and long-established cases were all included, provided that admission was a conscious option currently being considered.

Our chief informants were the social worker who handled each case and the parents of the children in question. Once a case had been identified as being seriously considered for care, the responsible social worker was interviewed, whenever possible *before* a decision had been reached. (Obviously this was not the case with emergency admissions or where action had followed hard on the heels of an initial referral.) For such interviews we devised a long schedule of questions which ranged over the nature of the referral, family circumstances in terms of structure, finance, housing, health, relationships and history, and the particular circumstances and characteristics of the children who were being seriously considered.[6] We also asked for the social worker's views on the problems being presented and the preferred and available solutions to those problems. Once a decision had been reached, the worker was again interviewed to discuss how and why it had been taken, what influences had been brought to bear, what were the perceived links between this particular decision and any policies or rules of practice in the department, and what were the future plans consequent upon that decision. To arrive at this point in the proceedings it was sometimes necessary for the social worker to be seen several times, for some decisions were a long time coming. Researchers were therefore able to pick up something of the complicated and protracted process of decisions in the making. Where a case involved a case conference or other meeting (especially so in child-abuse cases), the researcher tried to attend, in order better to understand this particular aspect of the process.

At the first interview with the social worker, the possibility of contact with the family was raised. We relied on social workers to ask families whether they would participate, or to give us permission to make direct contact, and no approach was made if they or the families refused. The timing of family interviews depended on their own convenience and on the stage at which they had been approached and had given their consent. For some this was a considerable time after a decision had been reached, because of the social workers' anxiety about choosing the right time, but for others it was soon after the decision, and for a few it took place even before the eventual outcome was known. We interviewed the 'parents' - that is, the adult caretakers in the family unit under consideration, whether or not they were the natural parents of the children in question. Because there were so many one-parent families in our sample and because not all interviews could be conducted in evenings or at weekends when breadwinners were available, it was often only one parent who was interviewed, and this was more usually the mother than the father. Quite often we saw both, and sometimes the children were present, though we did not try to interview them in their own right. Our consumer perspective is therefore an adult's eye view.

Both family and social worker interview schedules covered very similar ground, and both relied heavily upon open-ended questions.

Despite the hard labour of coding the subsequent replies, we were not in a position to prejudge any issue and wanted to encourage those interviewed to speak freely and to range as widely as they wished in their answers. There was little difficulty in encouraging them to do so and we were pleased and grateful for the generous response from both sides of the social-services fence. In the interchange, researchers were sometimes asked for their opinion of events and occasionally their advice was sought about actual decisions. They did their best to remain engaged but non-committal. Naturally, hearing both sides of what were often painful or contentious issues posed problems of confidentiality. It was agreed from the start that nothing the families said to us would be passed back to the social workers, and vice versa, unless specifically agreed between them. Sometimes we sensed that families wanted us to relay their opinions or criticisms, but we resisted becoming the bearers of tales. Sometimes we learned things in family interviews which were unknown to social workers, and which they might have wanted to know. Only if we judged a child was seriously at risk would we consider passing on such information.

At this first stage the social workers and the families were warned of our intended follow-up and we asked permission to contact them again in approximately six months' time. There were hardly any objections, so the participation rate at the second stage was almost as high as at the first. Again, interview schedules for both parties followed similar lines, with the emphasis upon what, if anything, had changed in the intervening period. We looked again at family circumstances, at the problems that had been discussed earlier, at the solutions that had been tried (or neglected) and at the present state of affairs compared with what it had been before. We were especially concerned to trace the continuities and discontinuities for the children in question (an important point of comparison between those admitted and those not) and to obtain both a retrospective view of earlier events and an up-to-date account of how things had now developed. With the social workers we were also keen to see how early plans had matured or changed and to learn from families how well they understood or participated in the planning.

The monitoring and follow-up material are at the centre of our argument, but much derives from the many other sources we have outlined. The sum total of our data therefore varies from hard to very soft and from one-off encounters to sustained observations. We have tried to do justice to all kinds. What has been measurable has been computed, and, where we feel that even our most imaginative coding-frames have been unequal to the task of categorising answers full of feeling and variety, we have relied on what people said to bring some life to our figures and our tables.

PART II

The Monitoring Exercise

3

The Children and their Families: The Social Workers' View

In all, 361 children from 266 families were seriously considered for care in the sample teams during the monitoring year – 166 in Clayport and 195 in Shiptown – and the social workers described them and their family circumstances in some detail.[1] (For the sake of simplicity, 'Clayport' and 'Shiptown' henceforth refer to *all* participating teams – urban *and* rural – in the two authorities, unless we indicate otherwise.) The picture which emerged was characterised by deprivation, disruption and disadvantage, a professional view that was subsequently confirmed in most respects by the families themselves, whose perspective is described in more detail in a later chapter. It is a picture which marks them out from the child population as a whole, and which has much in common with that recorded in other child-care studies.[2]

Family disruption

The most striking feature of all was the degree to which the families were incomplete, disrupted, or restructured following earlier breakdowns (see table 3.1). The 'normal' family unit of a married couple with children from that and no other union was the exception rather than the rule. A whole range of data charts the dimensions and complications of the family structures involved.

Less than half of the children (43 per cent) were living with a pair of married adults, compared with nine out of ten of the total child population.[3] By the same token, almost as many (40 per cent) were living in a one-parent family, compared with one in ten of children in general.[4] The rest were with cohabitees, with other adults not married

Table 3.1   Family structures

	1980-1 (N=361) %	1962-3 (N=4,540)[a] %
The caretakers		
1 person (unmarried)	9	10
1 person (widowed/separated/ divorced)	31	30
2 persons married to each other	43	54
2 persons not married to each other	14	6
Others (e.g. juvenile mother +parents)	1	
No adult caretaker	1	
Unknown	1	
The natural parents		
Child with both parents	28	52
Child with neither parent	9	7
Child with natural mother	82	80
Child with natural father	37	65

NB: The unit of information in this earlier study was the family, not the child.

[a] From Jean Packman, *Child Care: needs and numbers* (Allen and Unwin, 1968), tables V and VI, pp. 44 and 45.

to each other, or were without any adult caretakers at all. Furthermore, less than one third (28 per cent) of the children were living with both their natural parents and 9 per cent were living with neither. Four out of five (82 per cent) were still with their mothers, but a minority (37 per cent) lived with their natural fathers. Comparison with figures from an earlier research study is revealing. Almost twice as many children considered for care in the early 1960s were living with both parents, and, although the proportion who were with their mothers was almost identical, far more were with their fathers a generation before. The rising illegitimacy and divorce rates since the 1960s are faithfully reflected - and magnified - in the contemporary figures.

Following marital breakdown, the family is frequently reconstructed by means of remarriage or cohabitation. One in five of our children were therefore living with step-parents or, to be more precise, with stepfathers (22 per cent) who had come to take the place of the many absent fathers. In contrast, stepmothers were rare (4 per cent) – an interesting sidelight on fairytale stereotypes and their wicked ways with children! (Even more rare were adoptive parents, who were present in only 2 per cent of cases). Alongside step-parents, children had often acquired step-brothers and sisters, or half-brothers and sisters had subsequently been born and now shared their home. In fact, only half of the children who were living with siblings lived with only 'natural' brothers and sisters. The other half had various mixtures of natural, step, half and adoptive relationships with the other children in the household. The picture is therefore of a high proportion of 'one-parent' family situations: or, where 'whole' family units exist, of many new family relationships superimposed upon previously fractured marital situations with bewildering effect. Again, some contemporary national comparisons can be made. According to the General Household Survey 1979, 84 per cent of dependent children were living with both natural parents, 5 per cent with a natural mother and stepfather and 9 per cent with a lone mother. Only 1 per cent were living with natural fathers (with or without stepmothers) and another 1 per cent were fostered or adopted. It is clear that our cohort of children magnify common patterns in family composition and accelerating social trends in a most vivid and exaggerated way.[5]

Behind this picture of the fragmented and complex families from which a high proportion of the children came, there is of course both a history of discord and disruption as well as many present strains and difficulties. No less than 56 per cent of the children were said to have lived through a marital breakdown in the past, and 22 per cent were in families where there had been marital violence. Further, for those children in households where a couple were still living in partnership (213 in all), social workers were asked for their opinion about the present quality of the 'marital' relationship. Their view was a gloomy one. We were able to group their answers under five headings: good, fair, fragile, poor and mixed. The 'good' were those rare partnerships where social workers perceived no serious problems and where positives clearly outweighed any negatives in the relationship. It was a label that they applied to couples in charge of only 14 per cent of the children in the study. The 'fair' were also judged as basically sound, though experiencing some difficulties and stress, and 19 per cent were assigned to this category. Taken together, therefore, social workers were prepared to say that a third of the marital relationships were fundamentally all right. This left almost half (47 per cent) where there was thought to be acute stress and danger of actual breakdown (fragile), or where chronic marital discord was perceived (poor). Conceptually the two categories were reasonably distinct; in practice, it was often difficult to choose between them, and they are better taken together, forming a substantial group that caused considerable concern. In a small minority of cases (5 per cent) social workers described the partnership in terms of extremes, containing strong negative *and* positive elements. For the remaining 15 per cent no categorical answer could be given.

Even where the children were in the charge of only one parent, the relationship with the absent partner was often very much 'alive' and in evidence and played a significant part in the family's functioning. 63 children lived with one parent who was still 'attached' to an absent partner in this way, and for four out of five of them this lingering attachment was said to be stressful and unhappy.

It has to be said that such an unrelievedly bleak picture was *not* shared by the parents themselves. True, many described marital disharmony of a extreme kind, as Chapter 7 will show. But there were often positives to balance the darker side, and their own evaluations were twice as optimistic as those of the social workers. Nevertheless, it was the latter's assessments that formed the basis for decision-making, and so far as they were concerned marital strain was a fact of life both in the past and in the present for a substantial proportion of children, whether or not their parents were together in an 'intact' family unit.

Social class

One-parent families and marital discord and breakdown occur right across the class spectrum (albeit not necessarily in the same proportions) but all the evidence suggests that children considered for local-authority care come disproportionately from the working class, and our own findings do nothing to refute this. Because social class is conventionally derived from the father's occupation, the large numbers of missing fathers in our cohort, and a high rate of unemployment amongst those who *were* present, means that we have very incomplete data. Only 131 fathers were working and occupational details were not available for all of them. What we *do* know is that at least two thirds were manual workers and 20 per cent were unskilled – more than three times the national proportion.[6] The other side of the coin was that non-manual and professional workers were very sparsely represented.

The housing and neighbourhoods in which families lived fills out the picture. Well over half (58 per cent) lived in council accommodation in two authorities where only a quarter of the housing-stock is local-authority owned. One in five (21 per cent) lived in poor, run-down inner-city areas. There were, of course, exceptions. There were some children of professional parents, living in attractive neighbourhoods. Because of the nature of our sample authorities, a high proportion of fathers (21 per cent) were in the armed forces and not all were 'other ranks'. However, the majority of children came from a section of society where economic hardship was common, and where social deprivation was evident in a variety of ways. Even where parents may have been comfortably off originally, the breakdown of a marriage and one-parent status or a restructured family had often depressed their living-standards to a marked degree.

Deprivation

Unemployment was one indicator of the high level of economic deprivation present. In the families which *had* a father figure, no less than 31 per cent were known to be unemployed, at a time when the national rate was less than half as large. That this was no transitory phenomenon was all too clear when we came to follow up the families six months later. The unemployment rate had remained stubbornly constant and a high proportion of these fathers (especially in Clayport) had actually been unemployed for at least a year. This chronic problem was reinforced by low employment rates amongst mothers. Only one in five of them worked and the majority of these were in part-time employment, so wages were inevitably small. Overall, 44 per cent of children came from families where there was no wage-earner at all. We did not ask for precise details of the families' income or expenditure, but, when social workers were asked if the families were in financial difficulties, they asserted (not surprisingly) that over half of them were, and they believed that 37 per cent were actually in debt. Asked to account for these financial difficulties, a low income was cited in the vast majority of cases, so, although 'poor management' was also blamed for some of their difficulties, it was generally their inability at managing to be poor that was being recorded.

Financial hardship sometimes went hand in hand with accommodation problems. One in seven (14 per cent) of children lived in dwellings where the structure and fabric was said to be in a bad state, and this was sometimes compounded by standards of housekeeping which were criticised as poor. Some flat-dwellers and families in rented rooms were without any outdoor space of their own (17 per cent), and a few were sharing living-space with other families (5 per cent). Social workers were particularly critical of poor standards, design and amenities in a number of estates and neighbourhoods from which large concentrations of their cases originated, and these criticisms were later echoed with much more vehemence by the families themselves.

Stress

To these environmental disadvantages were added parental health problems and handicaps, some of which were of a long-term kind. No less than 30 per cent of mothers were said by social workers to suffer from some form of mental disorder, and their descriptions ranged from what were probably mild anxiety states and neuroses to acute and chronic mental illness. (The equivalent figure for fathers was only 6 per cent, but there were large 'not known' categories in this, and in other data about the fathers.) Only 5 per cent of the parents of both sexes were identified as mentally handicapped to any degree, but physical handicap was slightly more prevalent (7 per cent for mothers and 9 per cent for fathers). Furthermore, one in ten mothers and a smaller proportion of fathers were thought to be in poor health, though it became evident when we interviewed the families themselves that their own poor health was seen as an even more significant disadvantage than the social workers apparently perceived.

We also anticipated that, given the amount of family disruption, there would be considerable family mobility and that supportive networks of kin and neighbours might be missing or under strain. The breakdown of a marriage often means a move for all parties.[7] Furthermore, the absence of informal networks of support can be a key factor in propelling families towards official forms of care, and mobility and rootlessness had appeared as significant factors associated with child-care admissions in our earlier study.[8]

There was some evidence that such factors affected at least a substantial minority of families, though data are incomplete and these were not necessarily things that social workers knew much about. Of those who *were* 'known about', a third of the mothers and half of the fathers originated from outside their local authority, though in our two areas only 5 per cent of the parents came from overseas. Recent, small-scale migration was also in evidence, one in five families having lived in their present neighbourhoods for less than a year and one in ten having moved more than twice within two years.

Knowledge of the whereabouts of the extended families was patchy. Maternal relatives were considerably better known than paternal kin (not surprisingly, given the many missing fathers); and grandparents were much more likely to be mentioned than uncles and aunts, who in turn were better known than any other relatives. What we do know is that at least half of the children had maternal grandparents who were living near enough to be readily accessible and that a third were in contact with them quite often. But proximity did not always equate with helpfulness, at least in the social workers' eyes. Positive and helpful relationships with kin were recorded for less than a third of the children (28 per cent), whilst for a substantial minority (roughly one in six) there was said to be little or no contact and poor or non-existent relationships with them.

Perhaps these rather depressing findings should come as no surprise. We have seen already the high levels of family disruption experienced, and marital breakdown not only affects parents and children but has repercussions throughout the family network. Furthermore, it was clear from questions about the past histories of both the children and their parents that there were many such disruptions in the past that may have caused a souring or severing of links with kin. For instance, social workers were aware that at least one in five (20 per cent) of mothers and one in ten of fathers had themselves been separated from their parents in childhood (figures that proved to be underestimates, once we had talked to the parents themselves). So ruptured relationships spread back in time as well as outwards to the extended family, and may have magnified the vulnerability of the families concerned.

Relationships with neighbours were also of interest as a potential source of help and support. In a quarter of cases social workers did not know whether they were good or bad, but on their reckoning only a minority were seen as potentially supportive. One in five were said to be 'good' and helpful but as many were rated 'poor' (21 per cent) and the rest were either distant and 'neutral' or a mixture of good and bad.

Thus, to summarise, in the view of the social workers the families of the children being considered were notable for the degree of marital disruption in the present and in the past; their strong working-class bias; the large amount of financial and material deprivation many of them suffered; and the considerable stress caused by ill health as well as strained family and neighbourhood relationships, with consequent deficits in the supportive networks that might have helped them with some of their difficulties. Of course, all these outstanding features are closely interlinked and amplify one another. Divorce rates, for example, are particularly high amongst manual workers;[9] low incomes, high unemployment and poor housing correlate with one another and with the unskilled working-class and one-parent families. Similarly, poor relationships damage support networks and can themselves be both the cause and the effect of family disruption.

The children

Against this background there were a number of characteristics of the children themselves which are worth noting. First, for example, there was a slight imbalance in the sexes: 56 per cent were boys and 44 per cent were girls, a ratio not very far removed from the proportions of children who come into care nationally, which in 1980 were 57 per cent boys to 43 per cent girls. On this evidence it seems that the somewhat greater susceptibility of boys to 'care' is manifest at an earlier stage than that of the final decision-taking. They are being pushed forward by parents and referral agents and are being considered by social workers rather more often than their sisters – a pattern which relates very clearly to their greater troublesomeness in terms of conduct disorders and delinquency, as subsequent data will show.

In terms of age, the children were naturally spread throughout the whole span of eligibility from babyhood to seventeen, but the two most heavily represented years were infants of under a year and 15 year olds, who each contributed 11 per cent to the total. Comparison with figures from our earlier research shows a considerable shift away from very young children towards those of school age and over. In the early sixties almost half (48 per cent) of those considered were under school age, compared with just over a third (36 per cent) in the present study – a change that is also reflected in admissions to care generally. (27,000, or 56 per cent of admissions in 1963 were children under school age, compared with 14,500, or 31 per cent in 1980.)

A disproportionate number of children were said to be illegitimate (one in five), at a time when the illegitimacy rate was around 12 per cent of all live births. It is possible that this is an underestimate, since it was something we did *not* ask parents to verify and social workers themselves may have regarded the birth status of many of the older children as irrelevant. However, adopted children featured very little in our sample and represented less than 2 per cent of the total, which, from the sparse evidence available, appears to resemble the proportion in the child population as a whole.[10]

We also looked at the children's experience of day care, schooling and work and found that less than a third (27 per cent) of the under-fives were attending some form of day care. The largest group (11 per cent) were with daily minders: the rest were spread fairly evenly between playgroups, day nurseries and nursery schools. Taken as a whole, the day-care proportion approaches that for provision nationally. (Places were available for 31 per cent of the under-fives according to the Central Policy Review Staff report of 1978, *Services for Young Children with Working Mothers*.) Given the priority that is accorded to children with special needs in statutory provision such as day nurseries, it is somewhat surprising that the figure in the sample is no higher.

So far as school-age children were concerned, 9 per cent were in special schools and a further 5 per cent had been excluded from school, with or without benefit of an alternative form of education such as a sanctuary unit. Not one of the 16-year-olds was in employment, though a couple were engaged in further education and another pair were on work-experience or job-creation schemes – a sad but perhaps predictable finding.

In terms of their health and handicaps, most of the children were unexceptional. Less than 4 per cent were thought to suffer from any form of mental disturbance. (Where they *were* so labelled by social workers there was usually some validation from other sources such as child-guidance clinics or psychiatric hospitals.) Rather more – approximately 10 per cent – were thought to be mentally handicapped, but a broad interpretation was used, including those regarded as very dull, whether or not they were receiving special education in consequence. Similarly, a little over 10 per cent were said to be physically handicapped.

In terms of their behaviour, however, the children presented a much higher profile. We should explain that we relied for estimates of the children's behaviour - as for those concerning relationships within and between the families and others - on the social workers, and we did not test the children, use objective measurement, or seek corroboration from any other source but the parents themselves. Thus all our behavioural data rests on the perceptions of some of the key adults in the situation - perceptions which might be expected to exert a powerful influence on eventual decisions.

Our questions were broad. Has the child any behaviour problems? If so, what is the nature of that behaviour; in what context does it occur, and who complains about it? The response was much greater than we had anticipated, and for over half the children in the sample (57 per cent) concern was expressed about at least one aspect of their behaviour. Frequently several aspects gave cause for concern.

In all, ten very rough categories of troubling behaviour were identified, with considerable degrees of overlap between some of them. Amongst the most commonly mentioned were the age-specific problems of *delinquency* (28 per cent) and *truancy* (22 per cent). The former heading covered all the children who had been subject to police referrals because of offences, whether or not they went to court, and it also included some who had established a pattern of stealing or other lawbreaking but were below the age of criminal responsibility. To be labelled a truant, complaints had to be about sustained non-attendance and not just odd days off school, and the schools were the most usual complaints for this group. Over half (56 per cent) of the 62 truants were also said to be delinquent.

Another distinct group were the *runaways* (15 per cent) - children who had disappeared from home for at least one night, without the knowledge or agreement of their parents, and who were often the subjects of police referrals. Some younger children who occasionally wandered off from home were *not* included. There was also a large, heterogeneous group of *aggressive* children (31 per cent), which embraced both the verbally and the physically aggressive, whose sins ranged from noisy defiance and a taste for slanging-matches to threats to and assaults on siblings, parents or others.

The largest group of all formed the catch-all category of the *unmanageable, disobedient or disruptive* (46 per cent). These children were all seen as being difficult to control and the behavioural label therefore related as much to the inadequacy of the parenting received as to the misdeeds of the child himself. Young children as well as adolescents were quite likely to be described in this way, and there was even a handful of babies and toddlers who were described as aggressive, unmanageable or both! These were the 'little devils' and 'right madams' of whom we heard vivid accounts when we came to interview the parents. The overlap between this broad category and some of the other 'acting-out' behaviours was obviously very large, and over half of the 'unmanageables' (55 per cent) were also labelled aggressive and 42 per cent were said to be delinquent.

Other problem behaviours were also mentioned, but with much less frequency, and none applied to more than 10 per cent of the children in the sample. *Lying* was occasionally the subject of parental complaints, when the child was seen as unusually devious and untrustworthy. *Sexual problems* applied to a few teenage boys who had committed indecent assaults, but more often concerned adolescent girls who were 'sleeping around' and placing themselves at risk. *Self-injury*, another small category, included children who had taken overdoses or mutilated themselves, as well as a few who had indulged in potentially harmful practices such as glue-sniffing. A few children (28 in all) were also described as *withdrawn*, though we sensed that this was a category that was underused because it was a form of behaviour that caused little trouble to adults unless it was linked (as it sometimes was) with self-injury as well. Finally there was a small number of children who were labelled *enuretic or encopretic*, because of wetting or soiling at an inappropriate age. Some, but not all, were receiving treatment at child-guidance clinics.

When we asked where all these behaviours were alleged to occur, the child's own home was, not surprisingly, the most usual locus, but the troublesome behaviour of about a third of the children (31 per cent) had spilled out into school, neighbourhood or the wider community, a point to be explored more fully later. The most frequent *complainants* were the parents themselves, followed by school authorities and the police, with social workers as a poor fourth. So the behaviours that were being recorded were more often the consequence of complaints *received* by social workers than of complaints initiated by them, and the resulting profile owes as much or more to *others*' judgements as it does to their own.[11]

Judgements of this kind about behaviour are not of course hard 'fact' in the sense that they have been objectively tested or verified. As such it is inappropriate to compare them with studies (such as those of Rutter[12]) which estimate the prevalence of behaviour disorders in whole child populations. But they give a vivid picture of how the adults concerned – parents, relatives, referral agents and the social workers themselves – saw the children in question and what was troubling about them. They also suggest the significance of children's behaviour in terms of decisions about admissions to care, a significance that is obscured by the published returns, which tend to concentrate on *parental* difficulties in their list of 'reasons' for admission. It was also notable that social workers were rarely unable to answer the questions about behaviour (whereas in several other areas of inquiry there was considerable uncertainty). They 'knew' what the child was like and what if any were the complaints about him or her, and only very occasionally said they did not.

Families, children and the social-services department

The rough outline of a profile of children being considered for care and of the families from which they come have now been described, but a further prominent feature that must be mentioned was their relationship with the social services departments. It was apparent that the vast majority of families were no strangers to the departments who were now considering the possibility of an admission to care. Only 16 per cent had been referred for the first time, within the last month, neither family nor child having previously been known. A much larger group (41 per cent) were *re*-referrals, where the family and/or child had been in contact before but where the cases had been closed or left dormant in the meantime. The largest group of all (43 per cent) concerned children who were already 'on the books' and had been so for more than a month previously. These were the so-called 'ongoing' cases, where the possibility of an admission to care had arisen in the process of work with the family and where we were alerted to the 'consideration' not by a formal referral to the department but by regular discussions with social workers and their seniors about the children on their caseloads.

Thus, in the vast majority of cases, children considered were already 'known' in so far as there were records and departmental contact, sometimes stretching back over several years. Indeed in no less than a third of the cases the child and/or his family had been known to the department for over five years. This did not necessarily mean that work had been continuous over that period: contacts may have been spasmodic and short-lived in many cases, but the records stretched back that far. There was even a smaller group (13 per cent) whose records predated the setting up of social-services departments in 1971!

There were other ways in which this association or entanglement with social services was demonstrated. Thus, 13 per cent of the children were currently on 'at risk' registers and 3 per cent had been so at some time in the past. More than one in five (22 per cent) had actually been in care before, 8 per cent on more than one occasion. For half of these 'old timers' their previous 'in care' experiences had not amounted to more than a couple of months, but the remainder had experienced lengthier spells away from home. Furthermore, 11 per cent of the children were already on supervision orders under Children and Young Persons, or Matrimonial legislation, and another 3 per cent had been supervised previously. Almost a third (31 per cent) had also come to the attention of the police in the past and had been subject to a previous referral to social services, either as offenders or as non-offenders causing concern. There was also evidence that other children in the households of the 'considered' children were themselves involved with social services. In 11 per cent of cases, siblings were already in care and in 18 per cent there was a record of previous admissions. A few were also on supervision orders.

The 'problem'

The picture drawn so far of the personal and family circumstances of children being considered for care indicates a whole range of often interacting factors which might be expected to generate concern about their welfare. But from within this complexity we wanted to know the *particular* focus of social workers' current concerns. Why was the child being referred or considered for care, and what were the main elements in that referral or consideration? What in fact was the 'problem' to which care might be an answer? These questions were posed at the beginning of our interview, before gathering the contextual details that have already been described. In some instances, therefore, the analysis of the problem was not necessarily that of the social workers themselves. If a referral had been made of a previously unknown case, the cause for concern was generally framed by the person who had made the referral. But we wanted to know how things looked at the beginning of the decision-making process, as well as at the end, when a decision was ultimately made.

The answers given were as varied, and often as complicated, as the circumstances of the families themselves, but it was possible to group them under eight main headings (plus a miscellaneous 'other' category, where the reasons given defied more precise classification). In many cases, more than one factor applied, and we recorded them all. In the event, three elements were dominant: parenting behaviour, the child's behaviour, and the child's health. By far the most common was what we termed *parenting-behaviour* - that is, the style and quality of care the parents were thought to be offering their children. For over half of the children (52 per cent) this was regarded as cause for concern and a major element in the consideration. Later questions, which sought social workers' evaluations of the parents' standards of child care and which asked about any special features which affected their capacity to be effective parents, made the grounds for their concern more explicit. For just over a quarter of the children the mother's standards of physical care were thought to be inconsistent (11 per cent) or poor (16 per cent) and her 'emotional' care was judged even more severely, with 44 per cent in all falling into the 'poor' or 'inconsistent' categories. Information about the fathers' standards was much harder to come by: partly because so many were absent, and partly because, even when present, the social workers rarely saw the fathers in action as parents, at least in the sense of physically caring for the children. We cannot be certain whether this was because most fathers in the sample rarely performed these tasks, or whether social workers generally visited at times when fathering could not be witnessed, but it is our strong impression that both factors had some bearing on the results. None the less, in the 98 cases where social workers *did* venture an opinion about fathers, concern was expressed about the poor or inconsistent physical care of

38 per cent of the children, and the emotional care of over half (58 per cent) of them.

Specific causes given for these perceived deficits in parenting ranged from drink, drugs and crime on the one hand to factors with less blame attached, such as ill health, low intelligence, the special demands made by a handicapped child in the family, and difficulties created by the hours or nature of a parent's employment. We only recorded these factors if social workers believed they had a direct bearing on the quality of parenting, and if they could point to difficulties which had arisen within the past three years. On this basis, none were given much prominence, but the most frequently mentioned was the father's employment problems (20 per cent – perhaps some reflection of the services element in our sample, with its tradition of long absences from home); and mother's ill health (17 per cent). Drink and crime were each allegedly a problem for 16 per cent of the fathers in residence, and for 12 per cent of the mothers as well. Otherwise, the remaining factors affected only a small minority of children, generally well below 10 per cent.

The *child's own behaviour* was regarded as the next most important constitutent of the 'problem' and was mentioned in over a third (35 per cent) of all cases. The particular forms of behaviour which gave rise to anxiety, and their relative importance within the whole sample, have already been discussed. There was almost equal concern with the *child's health* (31 per cent), but this usually reflected anxieties about the child's physical, mental or emotional wellbeing and development rather than a concern with childhood illnesses *per se*. Clearly, the presence of a child's name on an 'at risk' register (13 per cent) and the significant proportion of children who were said to have suffered neglect or abuse in the past (24 per cent) contributed to anxieties of this kind.

Obviously there is much interplay between all three of these major problem factors. Poor physical and emotional care on the part of parents gives rise to anxieties about the child's health and development; and a child's difficult behaviour may be seen as a response to inappropriate parenting, and vice versa. They are separated for the sake of clarity, but in practice seldom stand alone.

In contrast, the five other elements in the formulation of the 'problem' for consideration were much less in evidence. The parents' own poor health was regarded as a key element for 15 per cent of the children, and marital problems, the absence or loss of a parent, and financial and material difficulties each featured in 9 per cent of cases. Accommodation problems were recorded as a significant factor in only 6 per cent of the cases.

Thus, the crux of the 'problem' was defined most usually as being about faulty behaviour on the part of parents, children, or both; and about potential damage to the children's health and development. The circumstances in which such behaviours or risks occurred - the material and financial conditions of the family, its structure and marital relationships, its health problems and so on - were much less likely to be seen as major components. Rather, they were the relevant background, the fragile and often stressful context within which unacceptable behaviours and risks occurred. In this, the influence of the legislation of 1969 seems much more in evidence than that of 1948/1980. The priority given to establishing parental or child faults or failures has more in common with the 'grounds' for care-proceedings than it does with the more open-ended duties to receive children into care in a whole range of circumstances, which includes parental disease and misfortune. The significance of the statutes, and the social workers' attitudes to, and use of them, is a point to which we will return in subsequent chapters.

What the social workers knew

Finally, it is worth summarising which items of information gave the social workers least trouble, and which the most; where, in fact, our own line of questioning was in closest accord with their own investigations and where it appeared to diverge (Discussion of how it compared with the *families'* perspectives is postponed to a later chapter.)

Generally, they answered with most certainty questions concerning the 'here and now' facts about the child - age, school circumstances, handicaps, difficult behaviour (a high degree of certainty here), and about the immediate family situation - the structure of the household, facts about housing and neighbourhood, estimates of its financial position, and so on. They were also sensitive to the health problems of the mothers and were usually able to offer an evaluation of marital relationships and of the parenting-standards of the *mothers* of the children. They could also define the 'problem'.

There was less certainty when it came to questions about the extended family, and knowledge of wider kinship networks seemed to be confined largely to those stalwart supporters, the mothers' own parents. Beyond that it was shaky and faltering, as was their familiarity with the strengths and weaknesses of neighbourly relationships. Knowledge about the *fathers* of the children was also very patchy. To some extent this was inevitable; there were many one-parent families with a female head, and a father long since gone. But, even where a father *was* present, considerably less was known about him than about his partner, so he remained – at least in aggregated form – a rather shadowy figure.

Social workers were also on uncertain ground when asked about the past. If their department had long associations with a family, they were clearly helped by the records. But details of the child's early history and significant events in his or her development, such as separations and past trauma, were not necessarily known with any precision. The taking of a 'social history' that characterised an older style of child-care practice was not much in evidence. Not surprisingly, even less was volunteered about the backgrounds of the parents, and for a fuller picture of this we had to await the families' own account of their past.

There was, therefore, a tendency to focus on the immediate situation and to focus fairly narrowly on the child in the nuclear family, with particular emphasis on *mothers* as the significant parent figures. It is a focus which probably stems in part from the urgency and immediacy of the problems which are being presented for solution; in part from the fragmented family structures which characterise many of the children in question. It may also tell us something about the scope of the social workers' operational frames of reference; and, last but not least, it may say something about our own unconscious biases and uneven skills in eliciting the information.

We have described, in broadest outline, what the social workers knew and thought about the children who were being considered for care during the monitoring year. In the next chapter we shall turn to the decisions that were made about them and begin our attempt to understand why some were admitted and some were not.

4

The Decisions

At the first stage of our monitoring exercise we followed through all considerations until a decision had been reached to admit or not to admit the child to care. Deciding when a decision had been made was not of course as simple as the crispness of the word implies. Where admission was the plan, it was relatively straightforward. Where it was not, there was much greater uncertainty. Had a positive decision been taken to keep the child out, or was it really a non-decision, a *not* deciding to admit, rather than *deciding* not to admit? Were the options still open, the pros and cons still being balanced? We tried, in our questioning of social workers, to be sure that we did not record outcomes until minds had been made up, and for some cases this meant there was a protracted period between first consideration and the recorded decision. In approximately one in five cases it took more than a month, and for a small proportion over three months. In others the decision recorded was undoubtedly only an interim or tentative one, as the 'not admitted' children who subsequently came into care during our follow-up period testify. As the circumstances of the children and their families were developing and changing, so too were the social workers' assessments of their needs, so any cut-off point relating to outcomes is to some extent artificial and arbitrary. With this reservation in mind, we turn to the decisions made concerning the 361 children who had been considered for care.

Taking in and keeping out

Taken as a whole, and ignoring for the moment any differences between the two authorities, 161 children (44 per cent) were admitted and for

200 (56 per cent) the initial decision was that they should not come into care. We have already indicated that 45 of the latter group were subsequently admitted during the six-month follow-up period, but they are counted as 'not admitted' children in our analysis at this stage.

What then, if anything, distinguished the 'ins' from the 'outs'? This was clearly the first question to be asked, if we were to begin to understand the basis upon which the decisions had been made. We therefore examined the data that had been gathered from social workers at the time of consideration (and which was described in the preceding chapter) to see if the circumstances and characteristics of the two groups of children differed to any significant degree.

Our first impression was that they did not. Similarities far outnumbered differences, and in many ways the profiles of admitted and not admitted children and their families looked remarkably alike. Thus in terms of household size and structure, economic circumstances, accommodation, neighbourhood and degree of family mobility, there was little to choose between them. Details of parents were also broadly similar. There were no striking differences in their age, employment, occupation, social class, health or handicaps, and assessments of marital relationships were much the same for both groups. Similarly, the children were alike in age, birth-order, legitimacy, handicaps and in the (incomplete) accounts of their early histories of separation and trauma. Even social workers' evaluations of the quality of parenting did not clearly distinguish those admitted from those who were not. Indeed, poor and inconsistent levels of *physical* care were slightly (though not significantly) more prevalent in the *not admitted* group. In sum on most items of relatively 'hard' information the two groups were very alike: and in two crucial areas of 'softer' data, where social workers were evaluating relationships or behaviour, there was either similarity (as with the quality of marital relationships) or a slight difference (as with parenting-standards) which actually suggested that the admitted children were better off.

There were, however, a few small clusters of factors which did seem to discriminate between the admitted children and the rest. The first concerned the status of the referral. Admitted children were somewhat more likely to be 'new referrals', previously unknown to the social-services departments (nearly one in five, compared with one in ten of those not admitted). The police also figured more prominently as referrers of the admitted group (24 per cent compared with 10 per cent) and were also more likely to have made a previous referral to the department (39 per cent compared with 10 per cent). Though these differences were not statistically significant, this seemed to suggest that for some cases (perhaps where a crisis had blown up), unfamiliarity with the background made it harder for a department to avoid admission; that the police were particularly 'successful' referrers, in terms of securing admissions; and that these two factors might not be unconnected.

More striking were differences in the perceptions of the main elements of the 'problem' at the pre-decision-making stage, perceptions which for old or ongoing cases would be very much the social workers' own but which for new referrals would be framed by the referring person or agency. Two factors stood out (and were of statistical significance) for the children who were subsequently admitted: their parents' health was more often put forward as a feature of the consideration (21 per cent compared with 10 per cent),[1] and the children's behaviour was also more often seen as a key issue (44 per cent compared with 28 per cent).[2] This latter point was amplified when we looked at the specific behaviours which were causing concern. Though both groups were equally aggressive, disruptive and enuretic, admitted children were significantly more likely to be delinquents (28 per cent compared with 18 per cent);[3] truants (24 per cent compared with 12 per cent),[4] or runaways (20 per cent compared with 6 per cent),[5] to have sexual problems (9 per cent compared with 4 per cent), or to injure themselves (7 per cent compared with 2 per cent). In other words, behaviour that spilled outside the home or which attracted the attention or concern of people outside the family because of its extremity was apparently more likely to push the child towards the care system.

In contrast, concern over *parenting* behaviour was surprisingly more prominent for the group of *not admitted* children (61 per cent compared with 41 per cent),[6] which tied in with the slightly poorer quality of parental care already noted for this group. Clearly associated with this was a focus, at consideration, upon child 'health' problems – a rather neutral heading for what was often manifest as considerable anxiety over the health and development of children thought to be 'at risk'. This too was a factor which was more characteristic of children *not* admitted to care (37 per cent compared with 24 per cent) and seemed to link with the fact that more children not admitted were on child-abuse registers (23 per cent compared with 8 per cent),[7] and more had been subject to (or had siblings who had been subject to) neglect or abuse in the past (30 per cent compared with 17 per cent).[8] So our data seemed to suggest that, whereas troublesome children were more likely to be admitted than not, vulnerable children 'at risk' were more likely to be kept out of care.

Finally – and cutting across the finding of the slightly greater vulnerability of the 'new referrals' – there was a clear indication that children who had already been in care were more likely to be admitted again (32 per cent, compared with 16 per cent of those not admitted).[9] This in turn linked with the experiences of their brothers and sisters: twice as many of the admitted group had siblings who were previously in care (26 per cent compared with 12 per cent). It is as if resistance to admission diminishes once a child or members of his family have already crossed the threshold. Either the earlier admissions are used as evidence of neediness, or the 'worst' has already happened and is less to be feared.

Legal routes into care

One significant aspect of deciding to admit a child to care is the choice of legal route by which he or she may enter. Into what legislative framework does his or her particular situation fit most appropriately and, equally importantly, what are the likely consequences for the child's future welfare of using one legal provision rather than another? These were questions we asked of social workers and which were in our minds as we examined the data.

An immediate point to be made is that these proportions cannot properly be compared with national figures. Admissions to care in England in the twelve months up to 31 March 1980 comprised 68 per cent 'voluntary' and 32 per cent 'compulsory'. The discrepancy does not, however, mean that our sample authorities were therefore wildly atypical and prone to a much heavier use of compulsion: rather, it reflects the fact that we chose to include Place of Safety Orders as admissions, for the reasons already outlined. Although considerable concern has been expressed about the growth in the use of POSOs,[10] national figures are unsatisfactory and there appears to be considerable under-recording at that level.[11] So we were curious to see how often they were used in our sample authorities. In the event, we were surprised to find that no less than a *third* of all our admissions were via a POSO, and their domination of the compulsory route was even more marked, accounting for 60 per cent of the children admitted compulsorily,

This large number of POSOs – 54 in all – came as a shock to us and merits special attention. In fact, the significance of these emergency orders is even greater than such substantial figures indicate, because in virtually half of all the cases considered for care (49 per cent) such an order had been debated as an option before a decision was finally made. There were also cases where the *intention* to apply for a POSO was expressed in advance of any suitable circumstances in which it could be effected. Thus the 'emergency' was anticipated and the action planned to meet it when it arose – which raises the question of whether such an emergency might have been forestalled by arranging some other, less traumatic admission to care. It was also evident that, in Shiptown at least, the police were responsible for almost as many removals as the social workers: so the social-services departments were not always in control of such decisions.[12]

The circumstances from which children were removed in this precipitate way were varied. For example, the age-span was very wide: 30 per cent were under five year of age, but 46 per cent were teenagers and 6 per cent were 16-year-olds. Neglect or abuse, actual or suggested, was a prime factor in guiding the decision in a quarter of cases where a POSO was used (24 per cent); but it was the child's *behaviour* that prompted a removal in twice as many cases (52 per cent). The behaviours in question included delinquency (*not* a legal ground for any POSO[13]) and truancy (*not* a ground for which the police are entitled to use their powers[14]) and if those who acted were aware of this, we can only assume that such behaviours were being used to justify claims that the children were 'beyond control'. Alternatively some of the removals initiated by the police may actually have been made under their powers to detain certain offenders pending a court appearance,[15] and were not POSOs at all; in which case either they, the social workers, or both, were unaware of the distinction.

Whatever the explanation for such widespread and wide-ranging use of these powers, what was very clear was that POSOs are no longer primarily an emergency measure, used to rescue the (generally young) child from situations of extreme risk. Rather, they are also being used extensively to exert 'control' over unsatisfactory parents and over the unruly child - sometimes to protect *adults* in the process. Whilst this may be legal, by reference to the 'beyond control' ground in care-proceedings, it is in marked contrast to the situation before 1969, when (impressionistically at least - there is a dearth of data) POSOs were rarely used and then generally for children believed to be in physical danger. This calls into question the assumption that the increased use of POSOs throughout the 1970s is primarily related to greater sensitivity to child abuse. This must be part - but perhaps only a minor part - of the explanation. Our data also suggest that use of POSOs is by no means uniform and that wide discrepancies in inter-pretation and use may be occurring.[16]

Details of the legal mode of entry of our compulsorily admitted children are set out in table 4.1. Several points are made obvious in this table. Apart from the prominence of POSOs, and the considerable part played by the police in their initiation, there is the significance of remands in the total picture. Taken together, this means that four out

Table 4.1 Compulsory admissions to care by legal route

Route to care	%	(N = 90)
POSO - social-services department initiated	34	
POSO - police initiated[a]	26	
Remand	21	
Children and Young Persons Act 1969, care order (or interim care order)		
Section 1.2(a) - neglect, ill treatment, etc.	1	
Section 1.2(c) - moral danger	2	
Section 1.2(d) - beyond control	3	
Section 1.2(e) - not receiving education	2	
Section 7 (7) - criminal proceedings	2	
Matrimonial care order	6	
Other (e.g. Guardianship Act)	2	

NB: All percentages are rounded.

[a] Technically, Place of Safety *Orders* require a magistrate's signature, which the police, as well as social workers or any other interested person, can obtain. Alternatively, the police can use their own, more restricted, powers to detain in a 'place of safety', and many - perhaps most -of the recorded cases were probably of this latter type. For simplicity we refer to all as Place of Safety Orders.

of five of the compulsory group were initially removed from home under strictly time-limited orders, and any longer-term admission (or rehabilitation) plans were likely to depend on subsequent court decisions. In other words, for at least four out of five of the compulsory group, a provisional decision had been made pending further investigation. By contrast, the group for whom care orders were made without recourse to either remand or Place of Safety is small – in fact just 10 children under the Children and Young Persons Act (and even some of these were subject to interim, rather than full, care orders) and five more under matrimonial legislation. Here, perhaps, what is missing is as interesting as what is included. Thus throughout the whole year, not a single child from our sample teams was brought directly to court and committed under *care*-proceedings as the result of committing an offence (Section 1.2(f)), and only two offenders came in via prosecution. The fact that 'delinquents' nevertheless found their way in through the compulsory gateway is something to which we have already referred and to which we shall return.

When the characteristics of the voluntarily and compulsorily admitted children were compared, the patterns of difference were much more striking and consistent than those of the total admitted and not-admitted group, seen side by side. Distinguishing voluntary sheep from compulsory goats was, on the basis of our social-worker data, a much simpler process. It would be tedious to spell out all the many factors which differentiated the two groups of children, but the main outlines were clear.

So far as the children themselves were concerned, those received voluntarily were evenly divided between boys and girls and they were predominantly very young (54 per cent were under five years old and another 20 per cent were between five and nine). Nearly a third (13 per cent) were known to be illegitimate, but hardly any (1 per cent) were on 'at risk' registers. 30 per cent had been in care before, all of them on a voluntary basis and usually for only short periods of time. Few (3 per cent) were on supervision orders, but 17 per cent had been the subject of previous police referrals to the departments. Their behaviour was not problem-free (30 per cent were said to be 'disruptive', for example), but it was much less complained about than that of the other group.

In contrast, the compulsorily admitted group of children contained rather more boys (59 per cent) than girls (41 per cent) and over half (56 per cent) were teenagers, though one in five were under five years old. Fewer of them were said to be illegitimate (17 per cent), but, unlike the voluntary group, there were a few adopted children (4 per cent) amongst their number. Considerably more (13 per cent) were on an 'at risk' register and 30 per cent (the same proportion as the voluntary group) had been in care before. However, half of these had been *compulsory* admissions, so many had trodden this particular path before. Their most outstanding characteristic was however, their behaviour. Complaints were at a consistently higher rate, whatever the behaviour, but most particularly for the age-related, 'anti-social' sort, such as 'delinquency' (47 per cent), truancy (38 per cent) and running away from home (30 per cent). The spillover effect of these behaviours was evident in the patterns of complainants and referrers. School authorities were complaining about as many as half the children, and police complaints were almost as numerous. Similarly, schools, police and the probation services between them accounted for 55 per cent of the major referral agents for this group, and 56 per cent of the children had also been the subjects of previous police referrals. Their past and present visibility as 'troublesome' to powerful agencies outside the social-services departments was very clear.

So far as their *family* situations were concerned, the patterns were also distinct. Almost half of the voluntary group (48 per cent) were from one-parent families. Three quarters of them were in financial difficulty; more fathers in this group were unemployed and, of those in work, more were in unskilled, manual occupations. More maternal illness was recorded (38 per cent had been ill recently) and they were more often faced with the problem of having a handicapped child in the family (14 per cent, compared with 2 per cent in the compulsory group). In general, standards of physical care were not unlike those in the compulsory group, but there was rather less criticism of the quality of emotional care.

The compulsory group looked rather different. Families were more frequently 'intact' (54 per cent were headed by a married pair and only 28 per cent were one-parent families) and consequently fathers were much more in evidence. However, these were not necessarily the *natural* fathers of the children concerned. Indeed, although 41 per cent of the compulsory group lived with their own fathers, another one in four (26 per cent) lived with a stepfather, in addition to the small proportion with adoptive fathers. In contrast, only 13 per cent of the voluntary group were with non-natural fathers. Current family 'intactness' did not therefore mean the marital situation had always been secure. On the contrary, no less than 64 per cent of these children had suffered from a previous marriage breakdown (the figure for the voluntary group was 44 per cent); over a quarter (27 per cent) had lived through marital violence, and nearly one in five (19 per cent) had suffered neglect or abuse. Nor was their present family situation necessarily stable, for social workers rated exactly half the marriage relationships as 'fragile' or 'poor'. Given the background of severe adult-relationship problems, it was not perhaps surprising that the *emotional* care of the children was especially criticised, most particularly with regard to fathers. Nearly half the fathers (49 per cent) were rated as giving inconsistent or poor care. Judgements about key factors which hampered good parenting were also harsher for the compulsory group. One in five of the mothers were said to drink to the detriment of their parenting-capacity, and both mothers and fathers were more often said to be engaged in criminal activity which was thought to affect their standards of child care. (In comparison, the parenting-problems of the voluntary group were more likely to be put down to ill health, low intelligence, or the demands of a handicapped sibling.) On the other hand, the compulsory group were materially better off – more often in employment, having more family wage-earners and more fathers in skilled occupations. But they were also more likely to find the nature of their employment a problem in carrying out parental roles – some reflection, perhaps, of the 'service' element in our sample population.

Given these two rather different profiles for voluntary and compulsory admissions, as well as the different legislation that was being invoked in each case, it was no surprise to find that problem definition at the outset of the consideration was very different too. Thus in the voluntary group the parents' or child's health was to the fore (45 and 27 per cent, respectively) and material problems were also of some significance (17 per cent); whereas for the compulsory group it was child and parental *behaviour* that predominated (63 and 53 per cent), quite obviously often in interaction with one another. And, linked with these patterns, the families themselves and the health services were the major referrers of the voluntary cases (49 and 23 per cent), whilst, as we have seen, it was the police and the schools which stood out as referrers of the compulsory children.

Comparison of the admitted children in terms of their legal route of entry proved useful for at least three reasons. It started to demonstrate the differences of circumstance and problem which were concealed within the broad-brush profile of 'considered' children with which we had begun our analysis. It suggested that there was at least a rudimentary 'fit' between cases and the legislation used to deal with them. It also began to make somewhat clearer the bases on which decisions to admit children were made, and indicated that they were not quite as random as at first appeared. By looking at *all* the 'ins' and 'outs' we had been superimposing at least two distinct profiles one upon another, and the resulting blur doubtless concealed some of the differences that separate analysis would reveal. These were all themes that we were to pursue further, but for the moment we turn to look at the two sample authorities and at how their decisions compared with one another.

The sample authorities

We had deliberately chosen Shiptown and Clayport for their basic similarities in terms of social indicators, but also for their past and present differences so far numbers and categories of children in care were concerned. We were therefore anticipating (to be honest, *hoping*) that some difference in the patterns of their decision-making would emerge in our monitoring year. We were not disappointed. Shiptown admitted a higher proportion of its considered children to care than Clayport - 51 per cent, compared with 37 per cent - and when we noted the number of 'not admitted' children who had subsequently come into care during the follow-up period the gap was wider still. Shiptown's *ultimate* admission rate was 60 per cent of all considered children; Clayport's was 42 per cent. The majority of Shiptown's admitted children also entered care by a compulsory route: 65 per cent, compared with 35 per cent received voluntarily. In contrast, Clayport's proportions were the other way round - 41 per cent compulsory admissions to 59 per cent voluntary. So there were at least two major differences to be investigated and explained.

The details of the compulsorily admitted children also seemed to merit attention. The proportionate use of POSOs (as well as their actual number) was greater in Shiptown, but this was largely because of *police* activity in this sphere. They were responsible for almost as many POSOs as the social-services department in that authority, in contrast to Clayport, where the police made a much smaller contribution. Remands were also much more common in Shiptown and, though numbers were very small, there were more matrimonial care orders as well. But in neither authority, in the monitoring year, were more than a handful of care orders made under the 1969 Act without a previous removal from via a POSO or a remand. Table 4.2 summarises the decisions made in the two authorities and highlights the differences that were apparent.

Table 4.2 Summary of decisions made

	Clayport		Shiptown	
	(No.)	(%)	(No.)	(%)
Admitted at first decision	61	37	100	51
Not admitted at first decision	105	63	95	49
Legal route of admissions				
Voluntary (Child Care Act 1980, section 2)	36	59	35	35
POSO – social-service department initiated	11	18	20	20
POSO – police initiated	5	8	18	18
Remand	4	6	15	15
Children and Young Persons Act 1969, care orders and interim care orders	4	6	6	6
Matrimonial care orders (and others)	1	2	6	6
All compulsory admissions	25	41	65	65

Villains, victims and the volunteered

The simple separation of the admitted children into those received voluntarily and those taken in by a compulsory route had produced two clearly distinguishable groups of children, and had revealed variations in practice between the two authorities in the process, but a further breakdown of the compulsorily admitted group was the next step. Children and Young Persons legislation covers both children in need of care because of parental faults and failings, and children whose *own* behaviour has led to their removal from home. It seemed important to separate these out and to compare them with one another and with the group of children admitted voluntarily. The exercise was illuminating from several points of view, and in the process, as a convenient shorthand, we came to call them the 'villains', the 'victims' and the 'volunteered'.

The villains

A majority of children admitted compulsorily (52 out of 90) were said to have been removed from home primarily because of their own behaviour. These were the 'villains', and they occupied a distinctive place at one end of the spectrum of family circumstance and personal characteristics that our monitoring data had revealed. Their families were amongst the better-off of our generally deprived, working-class sample. They had, for example, more family wage-earners, were less likely to be unemployed, and had fewer financial and accommodation problems; more fathers were in skilled, manual occupations and more were owner-occupiers. They were also more likely to be intact families with a married pair in charge (65 per cent), though this did not necessarily mean that marital relationships were harmonious (over a third were said to be fragile or poor). Only one in five of the committed villains came from a one-parent family.

The children themselves were, not surprisingly, mostly teenagers. Four out of five were 12 and over, and boys outnumbered girls by two to one. By definition, their behaviour was the subject of many complaints, and it was not only its seriousness that gave concern, but the fact that it often occurred in a public arena and was highly 'visible'. Besides being described as 'unmanageable' at home, the villains produced the highest proportions of offenders, truants and runaways, and were more likely to have been referred more than once by the police, to be excluded from school and to have experienced statutory supervision and substantial periods in care.

By comparison, their *parents'* behaviour was seen as relatively unproblematic on many dimensions. There were very low scores for crime and drinking, for example (it was the parents of *victims* who were judged most harshly in this respect), and their physical care of the children was generally rated as satisfactory. But it was in their *emotional* care and in their ability to *control* their children that the parents of villains were most frequently found wanting. Next to the child's own behaviour these were the two outstanding factors that were said to have 'caused' the admission. Thus, by definition, 100 per cent of the villains had been admitted because of their behaviour but 75 per cent also came in because 'poor control' was exercised over them, and 38 per cent because of 'poor emotional care'.

The victims

The compulsorily admitted children whose behaviour was *not* considered to be a factor in their admission formed an equally distinctive group at the opposite end of the spectrum. These were the 'victims', and for them levels of material and emotional deprivation and family disruption were high. Three out of five lived either in a one-parent family or in a household where the parents were not married to each other. They were often poorly housed and in severe financial difficulty. To these difficulties were added serious relationship problems with partners, neighbours and kin. For example, although relatives were accessible and in contact to an average degree, relationships with them were markedly worse than for the villains, and for the sample as a whole.

Most child victims were young – nearly half were under school age and only a quarter were 12 or over. By the same token their parents also tended to be young – many of them mothers in their teens or twenties, living alone. Slightly more of the children were girls (53 per cent) and a third were illegitimate. Their past and present vulnerability was evident in several ways. A quarter were on 'at risk' registers and over a third had experienced neglect or abuse in the past. Even more (39 per cent) had lived with marital violence, and we found a close correlation between these two factors (nearly a third of the children who had suffered neglect or abuse had also had experience of marital violence). Not surprisingly, the *parents'* behaviour and their parenting-capacities were often criticised. There were high scores for parental drinking and crime (for example, 46 per cent of mothers were said to drink and a quarter to be engaged in criminal activity, to an extent that adversely affected their parenting). In addition, the parents of approximately one in six of the victims were said to be hampered by illness or low intelligence, or both. The children's physical care was as much at issue as their emotional wellbeing, but, when it came to summarising the reasons for admitting victims, social workers stressed both parental *and* environmental factors. Thus nearly half were admitted because of poor physical and/or emotional care, and one in five were said to suffer from a poor moral climate at home. But financial and material reasons were also given for a quarter of the admissions, and parental absence or loss contributed to nearly a third. These young children were therefore seen not only as victims of parental faults and failures, but also as victims of circumstance. To this extent, their parents – though failing badly in many ways – were perhaps seen as victims too; and this may be one reason why, despite their vulnerability, children with many of the characteristics of victims were less likely to be admitted to care than villains.

The volunteered

Occupying the middle ground between villains and victims were the more diffuse group of children voluntarily admitted to care – a group whose profile has already been outlined. They shared many of the characteristics of both victims and villains. Like the victims, they were predominantly young, many were from one-parent families, and they too frequently suffered financial and material hardship. Like the villains, the children's behaviour was sometimes criticised, but it was much less likely to have spread outside the home or to have caught the attention of neighbours and officials. 'Unmanageability', 'aggression' and 'withdrawn' behaviour were the chief sins of the volunteered, and it was generally the parents who were the prime complainants.

The parents of the volunteered were not all seen as blameless. Standards of physical and emotional care were often criticised – as they were for both victims and villains – and a minority (15 per cent) had suffered from neglect or abuse in the past, though hardly any were currently on an 'at risk' register. But for this group it was *situational* difficulties rather than child or parent behaviours that were given most emphasis in accounting for the admission. The parents' health problems, the lack of a parent, and marital difficulties were all given some prominence, while elements of 'risk' or troublesomeness, though present, tended to take second place.

Tables 4.3–4.5 outline some of the main features of the three groups we have identified and demonstrate not only their distinctiveness, but also the degree to which they overlap. Villains, victims and volun-

Table 4.3   Villains, victims and the volunteered,[a] selected features: the children

	Villains (N = 52) %	Volunteered (N = 71) %	Victims (N = 38) %
Characteristics			
Boys	69	49	45
Girls	31	51	53
Under five years	2	54	47
Teenagers	81	17	21
Illegitimate	4	31	34
On risk register	4	1	26
Delinquent	73	4	10
Truant	42	7	16
Runaway	42	7	13
Unmanageable	71	30	13
Self-injury	21	-	-
Withdrawn	11	10	8
Past trauma			
Neglect/abuse	8	15	34
Marital violence	17	18	39
Marriage breakdown	60	44	71
Previously in care	33	30	33

NB: All percentages are rounded.

[a] These profiles (and those in the following two tables) are drawn from the data on children *admitted* to care only, and figures relate to the proportions of each group falling into the selected categories.

teered were *not* clearly demarcated groups, but occupied different but overlapping places along a spectrum, or family life-span of deprivation and disruption. At one end were the young victims – members of fragmented or never fully constituted families, suffering extremes of material or emotional deprivation; relative 'unknowns' to the social-services departments (a third of them were 'new referrals'), raising high levels of anxiety in all agencies. In the middle were the volunteered – also, on average, young, deprived and subject to disruption, but better known to the departments, and their own behaviour and parents' standards of care causing somewhat less concern than *external*

Table 4.4   Villains, victims and the volunteered, selected features: their families

	Villains (N = 52) %	Volunteered (N = 71) %	Victims (N = 38) %
Circumstances			
One-parent family	21	48	37
Step-/adoptive father	42	13	27
Owner-occupied accommodation	36	27	13
Five years or more in neighbourhood	48	25	21
Father unemployed	12	21	42
No family wage-earners	21	51	50
Financial difficulties	19	75	58
Mother recently ill	29	38	30
Poor/fragile marital relationship	35	20	62
The parenting			
Mother drinks	4	7	46
Mother criminal	2	10	24
Mother's physical care inconsistent/poor	12	18	36
Mother's emotional care inconsistent/poor	62	42	42
Father's physical care inconsistent/poor	9	10	21
Father's emotional care inconsistent/poor	53	14	42

factors such as parental health, finance or housing. Finally, at the other end were the villains – much older (most were in their teens), well known to controlling agencies such as the police and education services, members of rather better-off, more settled families where past disruptions had been 'mended' by new marriages or liaisons. For them, anxiety was focused on their wayward or anti-social behaviour and on their parents' failure to control or to offer appropriate emotional care.

We are aware that there is more than a hint of the 'deprived' and the 'depraved' in our analysis, with a large hybrid category in between.

Table 4.5 Villains, victims and the volunteered, selected features: the referral, the problem, and the reason for admission

	Villains (N = 52) %	Volunteered (N = 71) %	Victims (N = 38) %
Referral			
New referral	17	16	32
Self-referred	19	49	5
Health-service referral	2	23	21
Education-service referral	21	1	5
Police/penal-services referral	50	3	34
Main elements of the problem (multiple answers)			
Parental health	2	45	3
Child health	4	27	47
Child's behaviour	98	21	16
Material difficulties	4	17	24
Main reasons for admission (multiple answers)			
Lack of parent	10	28	29
Parental health	4	49	21
Marital problems	8	18	24
Material prolems	6	8	24
Parents' physical care	8	11	45
Parents' emotional care	38	28	47
Parents' control over child	75	14	8
Child's behaviour	100	15	–

But we would emphasise the many areas of overlap and the different life-stages that each may represent. Some villains were undoubtedly victims or volunteered grown older. They too had suffered material deprivation, marital breakdown, violence and neglect in the past, and their present *relatively* affluent and stable homes were none the less often fragile and strained, as our follow-up material was later to underline.

All we have said so far relates to *groups* of considered children and to their features in aggregate. It might be useful to conclude this section with some brief examples of particular children who fall into the three categories we have identified. This may help to bring the generalisation to life, but should also remind us of the unique features of each case and of the rough justice that is done to individual idiosyncrasies by any such generalisations.

A victim

Jane G. was eight months old when she was referred by another social-services department which needed information for the preparation of a custody report. Her mother had recently left the natural father, and Jane, and moved alone to Clayport. She was living in a privately rented, one-roomed flat and there were acute financial difficulties. Jane had already suffered several changes of caretaker through a sequence of marital rows, and she was on the 'at risk' register. A half-sister was previously in care. Both parents had had troubled childhoods. Mrs G's mother had died when she was a child and she herself went into care. Mr G. was an adopted child. Mrs G. had more than once attempted suicide.

A crisis arose one weekend when Mr G. arrived in Clayport seeking his wife, and when he failed he left Jane at a local police station and disappeared. When the baby was examined she was found to have a fractured skull. The police promptly took a Place of Safety Order.

The volunteered

Lionel, Sally and Theresa B. were aged seven, four and two years respectively. The Bs were natural parents to Sally and Theresa, but Mr B. was Lionel's stepfather. They lived in council accommodation on a very low income (qualifying for Family Income Supplement) and had been in contact with the social-services department several times in the past because of debts. Mr B. was said to be of low intelligence and had a poorly paid, unskilled manual job. His wife had had difficult pregnancies and each baby had been born by Caesarian section. She had been a victim of incest in her childhood. Lionel was something of a problem; he was enuretic and encopretic and had been referred to child guidance.

The parents requested admission to care while Mrs B. went into hospital to have her fourth child. A family aide was considered as an alternative to admission, but it was decided that, even with this form of help, Mr B. would not be able to cope adequately. All three children were therefore received into care under section 2 of the Child Care Act 1980.

A villain

Andrew C., aged 16, had a long history of referrals to the social-services department. Over a four-year period he had been accused of stealing, lighting fires, receiving, taking and driving away, and actual bodily harm, and he had already spent time in a detention centre. But complaints about his behaviour stretched back to his primary-school years. A police referral during the monitoring year came after he had indecently assaulted a young girl.

Andrew's mother and father had split up a few months before this last incident, but there had been difficulties for Andrew earlier in the marriage, when he was small. He had seen little of his father, who was then serving in the Army. Mr C. was said to have been a rigid disciplinarian, and had himself been committed to an approved school for delinquency as a juvenile.

Andrew was remanded to a secure unit following his court appearance for the latest offence, and a care order was one of the options to be considered.

Another villain

Barry S. was an unlikely villain in one respect – he was only eight years old. Under the age of criminal responsibility, he was nevertheless well known to the police and his school for trespass, stealing, arson, criminal damage and truancy, amongst other misdemeanours. Over a period of three years he had been the subject of more than twenty referrals to the social-services department. He lived with his natural parents and sister in a very comfortable, well-furnished council house which his parents hoped to buy. His father operated in business on his own account, apparently with some success. Standards of physical care were said to be excellent, but the parents' emotional care of Barry was judged to be cold, and quite inappropriate to the child's needs.

A few months before the beginning of the monitoring year, care-proceedings were instituted on the grounds that Barry was beyond control. A supervision order was imposed, and he became involved in an intermediate-treatment scheme. However, his delinquencies continued unabated and he was brought back to court under section 15 of the Children and Young Persons Act 1969 with a request to substitute a care order for the original supervision order. The request was granted.

There were at least two advantages in looking at our data within this tripartite framework. The first was that it made more sense of the differences between considered children who were admitted to care and those who were not, and thus it began to make more sense of the decision-making itself. By looking at villains, victims and the volunteered separately, more consistent patterns of difference began to emerge between those who came in and those who stayed out. The villains serve as a good example.

Despite the fact that admitted villains were very like all other children in the sample whose behaviour was a key element in the original consideration for care, there were some crucial - and related - areas of difference. One was the degree and nature of the troublesome behaviour itself. Those who came into care were more likely to be difficult in several directions at once, their difficulties causing wide ripples and exciting a range of complainants. They were also more likely to be involved in anti-social activities which challenged the outside world as well as their own families. Thus almost three quarters (73 per cent) of the admitted villains were said to be delinquent and over 40 per cent were accused of truancy. Inevitably, it followed that admitted villains were also distinguishable by their age. Four out of five were teenagers, though, of the badly behaved children of all ages who were actually considered for care, nearly half were under 12. The nature of their behaviour also means that the police and schools played a significant role as referral agents, between them accounting for nearly three quarters of the referrals of villains who entered care. Finally, considerably more admitted villains were already enmeshed in the care system. A quarter were on supervision orders; a third had been in care before; and three quarters had been the subject of previous police referrals. They had already come some way along the path to compulsory care.

The crucial elements distinguishing the 'ins' from the 'outs' were different again for the victims and the volunteered. Victims, for example, were rather more at risk of admission if they were worryingly unknown to the departments, the subjects of a new referral. Identifiable faults in their parents, such as too much drinking and crime, also weighed heavily in favour of their admission. Nevertheless, for any or all children considered, the differences between those admitted and those kept out were differences of degree rather than kind. Decision-making in child care is clearly no easy matter of sorting out apples from oranges or sheep from goats, and, however the data is shuffled and rearranged, the complexity of the social workers' task is very evident.

The second advantage arising from our rather laborious analysis was that it enabled us to pinpoint more precisely the ways in which practice in our two sample authorities actually differed. We were able to see that it was in their response to the *villains* that Shiptown and Clayport differed most. Where a child's behaviour was *not* at issue, the two authorities appeared to respond in remarkably similar fashion. Both admitted less than half of such children (43 per cent in Shiptown and 42 per cent in Clayport) and, of those, both admitted two thirds (67 per cent) by the voluntary route, and the remainder compulsorily. However, when the child's behaviour *was* at issue their response was quite different. Shiptown admitted 55 per cent of its villains to care; Clayport admitted 30 per cent. Furthermore, Shiptown used the voluntary route for only one in five of them (22 per cent) but Clayport received nearly half (45 per cent) of its villains on a voluntary basis. The picture was further complicated by the fact that it was Clayport which appeared the more likely to admit *victims* to care. Although both authorities were more inclined to keep abused or neglected children out of care than to take them in, the tendency was less marked in Clayport and its use of POSOs for children at risk was striking (69 per cent of Clayport's POSOs were taken primarily for reasons of neglect or abuse - the comparable figure for Shiptown was 5 per cent).

A picture was therefore beginning to emerge of two authorities which, despite much common ground, had different and distinctive biases in their child-care work. One leaned towards the teenage troublemaker - its focus child-centred, its concern rebellious adolescent behaviour, its solutions often framed in terms of compulsory removal from home. The other appeared to place more emphasis on the child at risk, and, where this was identified, was liable to act swiftly and decisively. But for the most part its work was concerned with *family* difficulties and situational problems, for which *non*-admission, or, as a last resort, voluntary care, was the preferred solution. Exploration of these different emphases, and a search for explanations form important themes in the chapters which follow.

5

The Decision-Making Process

Referrals

Social-services departments are typically at the 'receiving end' of requests and complaints – asking, urging or insisting that they 'do something' about the problems of a great range of people in need or difficulty. Quite often it is the needy people who refer themselves, but in the majority of cases others do so on their behalf; or on behalf of their own agencies, neighbourhoods or society at large, to whom their neediness has become worrying, uncomfortable, troublesome or disruptive. Who refers children for consideration and what pressures are exerted on departments in the process are important components of decision-making about admissions.

By a 'referral' we mean a communication from an outside person or agency, drawing a child to the attention of the social-services department. In our study such referrals were not always requests for an admission; often they simply alerted the department to problems, and consideration of care sometimes came a good deal later in response to fresh information, or as the work with the case developed and assessments crystallised. If more than one agency or individual had made an approach, all were recorded, but in the text which follows we concentrate on the 'original referral' – that is, the contact made by the *first* person or agency to alert the department, leading to its most recent period of continuous contact with the case.

In both our authorities the majority of considerations for care had thus begun with a referral from outside the department (although, for a small minority, the family was already so well-known that the identity of the original referral agent was forgotten or no longer appeared relevant to the present situation). In a quarter of cases referrals came from more than one source, and sometimes as many as four or five had been involved. Yet sheer *numbers* of referrers made no discernible difference to the eventual outcome, for children were admitted or refused at much the same rate however many people were agitating on their behalf.

The largest single source of original referrals was the families themselves, who brought a third of our 361 children to the attention of the departments. Usually this meant the parents, but occasionally relatives were instrumental in contacting the authorities, and in a few cases (12 in all) the children themselves had asked for help. The police ranked next in importance and, together with the related services of probation and the courts, they accounted for 18 per cent of referrals. Close behind, the health services (including general practitioners, health visitors and hospitals) were responsible for 15 per cent. Education services in the broadest sense (schools, education welfare, child guidance, the school psychological service, and organised pre-school facilities) together accounted for little more than one in ten of all referrals – a surprisingly low figure, considering their responsibility for children in general, and for vulnerable children in particular. The remainder (15 per cent) were spread thinly over a wide range of statutory and voluntary agencies (of which other social-services departments were the most prominent) as well as concerned individuals such as neighbours and clergy.

Table 5.1 summarises this data and makes comparisons between referral patterns for all considerations, and those for the children admitted or not admitted to care. There is very little here to suggest that admission decisions are linked in any consistent way with the identity of the referrer. Only the police stand out as being more successful at steering children into care, for their share of referrals in the admitted group is more than twice as large as for the not-admitted children – though it is a difference which fails to reach statistical significance.

The 'success' of the police as referrers is doubtless due in part to the urgency and extremity of many of the cases which come their way. Their involvement almost presupposes some kind of domestic or delinquent crisis, and this is powerfully reinforced by their ability to *act*. Barring the courts, no other external agency (apart from the NSPCC, which featured very little in our sample) is able to effect the

Table 5.1   Referral agents (original referrals)[a]

	All children (N = 361)	Admitted (N = 161)	Not admitted (N = 200)
	%	%	%
Parent(s), child, relative(s)	31	29	33
Police, probation, courts	18	26	12
Health services	15	16	14
Education services	11	9	13
The rest	15	16	15
No referral agent	8	4	12

NB: All percentages are rounded.

[a] If multiple referrals and subsequent referrals are considered, they do not alter the overall pattern in any significant way.

removal of a child and therefore to be both referrer and decider at one and the same time. As we have seen, 23 children in the year were actually admitted by the police on Place of Safety Orders and, although consultation occurred with the social-services departments over where to place the children, the *initiative* in these decisions was usually with the police. Where they did not exercise this power many cases were nevertheless referred on to a court, where again the decision about admission was taken out of the social-services department's hands. It is therefore not surprising that the police emerge as the most influential of referral agents, in terms of securing admissions.

Families were also rather more influential than table 5.1 suggests. Asking for help is not necessarily framed in terms of asking for the child's *admission*, as our family interviews showed very clearly. On the contrary, when parents were asked what form of help they wanted when they contacted the departments in the first place, only one in five singled out admission of the child to care. But this was nevertheless a discriminating factor in terms of eventual outcome, as parents had specifically asked for admission for a third of the admitted children, but for less than one in ten of the children who were not admitted. So what the families actually *want* appears to have some effect in terms of outcome. In the same way, what other referrers actually expected of the social-services departments may have been equally persuasive, but we were not able to ask them and we failed to code our social-worker data in a way that would shed light on this aspect of the referrals. We can therefore only speculate, but our impression is that how *any* referral is framed and with what clarity and insistence admission to care is posed as the preferred solution certainly exerts some influence on the eventual outcome.

The identity of referral agents also has a bearing on the choice of legal route into care, and hence on the contrasting referral patterns in our two authorities, as table 5.2 shows. The families themselves, the health services and a range of other agencies and individuals were the major sources of referral for children who were subsequently *received* into care on a voluntary basis. In contrast, the police and education services played a very peripheral role. On the other hand, those removed compulsorily were most often referred by the police and related services, and to a lesser extent by education services. For them, it was the health services, other agencies and the families themselves who played a relatively minor part.

Table 5.2 Referral agents (original referrals)

	Voluntary admissions (N = 71) %	Compulsory admissions (N = 90) %	Clayport, all cases (N = 166) %	Shiptown, all cases (N = 195) %
Parent(s), child, relative(s)	49	12	37	25
Police, probation, courts	3	43	10	26
Health services	23	10	20	11
Education services	3	14	9	13
The rest	21	12	18	11
No referral agent	1	8	6	10

NB: All percentages are rounded.

Such differences are largely unsurprising and logical. The 1980 (previously 1948) legislation outlines the misfortunes and adverse circumstances in which parents may be 'prevented' from caring adequately for their children and places a duty on the local authority to receive them into care. Few will know better than the families themselves what difficulties they are facing in this regard, and under the law they are free to make application on their own account. Further, parental ill health is a major creator of short- and long-term difficulties in child-rearing, and it is no surprise that the health services played a key role in passing on cases to the social-services departments.

In contrast, the Children and Young Persons Act 1969 is primarily concerned with faulty behaviour - on the part of parents in the upbringing of their children, and/or on the part of children accused of criminal or civil disobedience. Furthermore, in order to bring such behaviour to the courts for a hearing (or to the magistrate's attention, in the case of POSOs), it is *officials* who act - the police, NSPCC or local authorities - and not the families themselves. Indeed, a right once held by parents to bring their own children before the courts as being 'beyond control' was taken away from them in 1963 and passed to the local authorities.

Police and schools are clearly crucial in drawing acts of delinquency and truancy to the attention of the social-services departments, and their role as referral agents is therefore not surprising. On the other hand, the comparatively small part played by the health services in compulsory admissions is worthy of comment. Recent research[1] has stressed the vital part played by the medical and para-medical profes-sions in identifying cases of child abuse and neglect and in referring them to social-services departments for action. Yet only one in ten of our compulsory cases was referred in this way, and this clearly reflects the overwhelming predominance of 'villains' over 'victims' in our sample of compulsorily admitted children. The table also reminds us that compulsory removal of parental rights and of the child into care can sometimes follow on from a family's *own* request for help - 12 per cent of compulsory cases were in fact referred by the families them-selves. When we come to examine the families' perspective in more detail, we shall see what their reactions were to this apparent paradox.

Table 5.2 also shows that the sample authorities' differential use of child-care legislation was faithfully anticipated in their patterns of referral. Clayport, with its emphasis on voluntary admissions, received most of its referrals from families, the health services and other agencies. Shiptown, with its compulsory bias, was at the receiving end of a far greater weight of referrals from the police and education services.

By the same token, *what* was referred – the nature and extent of the 'problems' as presented by referrers and formulated by social workers – showed marked differences of emphasis in the two authorities, despite broad similarities in most of the characteristics of the families and children concerned. Shiptown apparently faced more problem behaviour in both children and parents: there were, for instance, many more complaints made about children's behaviour of every kind (and for all ages) in Shiptown, but especially those behaviours which involved and irritated people and agencies beyond the family. Thus a quarter of Shiptown's considered children were said to be truants, compared with 7 per cent in Clayport;[2] 18 per cent, compared with 5 per cent, were labelled runaways;[3] and half of Shiptown's children were deemed 'unmanageable', compared with a quarter in Clayport:[4] all differences of statistical significance. Shiptown children also had more-disrupted histories: more were said to have suffered separation through parental imprisonment and through the nature of their parents' employment. They were also more likely to have changed schools and accommodation during their lifetime and to have undergone the stress of adapting to new step-parents, as well as living through episodes of marital violence.

Judgements about the parents were also harsher in Shiptown than in Clayport. Significantly more mothers were said to have been involved in crime and heavy drinking, and their standards of emotional and, more especially, *physical* care of their children were more frequently judged as inconsistent or poor.[5]

For their part, Clayport's children were clearly more materially deprived. They were significantly more likely to have a father who was unemployed[6] or who was in an unskilled manual job[7] and this obviously contributed to the larger proportion who were said to exist on a very low income and to be in financial difficulties on that account.

Thus, pressures upon the two departments to admit children to care were different, in terms both of the balance of problems presented and of the sources from which the referrals came; and the decisions taken reflected this fact. So Shiptown's greater numbers of troublesome children and problematic parents were more frequently steered in the direction of social services by the police and education authorities, and more often ended up in compulsory care in consequence. Clayport's larger proportions of deprived children, from families who frequently referred themselves or whose doctors or health visitors interceded on their behalf, were more easily turned away from care; or, if admitted, were often received in a voluntary capacity. In effect, rough pathways into or away from care were already sketched out at the referral stage.

Typically, referrals – whether made in person, on the telephone, or by letter – would be directed to the district offices from which the teams of social workers operated. Occasionally a referral would be passed down from on high – perhaps a councillor had complained to the director about the plight of one of his constituents – but, in the main, the route taken was direct to the social workers' operational base. There it would be allocated to an individual social worker, and methods of allocation – by team-leader or group-meeting, democratic or dictatorial, swift or slow – varied from team to team irrespective of the local authority they served. But in terms of the decisions made we could find no measurable differences in outcome which related to these variations in style. Even the structural contrast between the intake and long-term teams in Shiptown was reflected in only one sharp difference in our monitoring data. In the course of the year the former considered two and half times as many children for care as did its long-term partner (44 compared with 17), so its role as a buffer was clearly demonstrated. But both teams admitted similar proportions of children, and both sets of admissions were heavily weighted towards compulsion.

Reaching a decision

Once admission to care was, so to speak, 'on the agenda' for serious consideration, the processes which ensued followed no one pattern. There was considerable variation in who became involved, how place-ments were secured, who appeared to carry most weight in making the decisions, and how long such processes took. Differences were apparent according to the legal route chosen if an admission was to be made, and between practices in the two authorities, but also between indi-vidual cases of the same type.

The time taken to reach decisions provides one example. Over half the decisions were made within a week, and more than a third within 24 hours of first consideration. For the rest, deliberations took longer, and roughly one in five took a matter of months. But this was so whether the decision was for or against admission to care. Predictably, however, when admitted children were distinguished by their legal route of entry, differences emerged. Over half of the compulsory cases were decided within 24 hours – a reflection of the urgent response to crises of the many POSOs and remands in this category. In contrast, snap decisions affected just over one in four of voluntary admissions. Time taken to reach decisions is important for at least two reasons: to make space for adequate assessment and a weighing of alternatives; and to enable plans to be made on how to effect the child's admission in the least damaging way, including preparing him or her and the placement for each other. In the majority of voluntary cases there was at least *some* scope for reflection and planning – albeit a matter of days only, in some instances. But this was something that was possible for only a minority of the compulsory cases.

How much consultation occurred, and with whom, was another important but variable aspect of the decision-making process. It was clear that there were very few cases in which social workers acted entirely alone, without some discussion with others, even in times of emergency (see table 5.3). Their most usual reference point within the departments was their senior social worker (team-leader) and in seven out of ten cases he or she was drawn into deliberations before decisions were reached. Other departmental personnel played a less prominent

Table 5.3 Persons with whom social workers discussed the case

	Admitted (N = 161) %	Not admitted (N = 200) %	Voluntary admissions (N = 71) %	Compulsory admissions (N = 90) %
Senior social worker	61	79	62	60
Other social workers	14	19	8	18
Manager	37	37	41	36
Adviser/advisory body	14	12	15	13
Outside officials	41	43	20	58
Parents	47	37	76	24
Child	9	7	7	12

part. Managers - usually a director or his assistant at district level - became involved in over a third of all cases, but specialist advisers or advisory bodies were contacted fairly infrequently (13 per cent of cases). Furthermore, despite the impression we gained of much 'shop talk' and sympathetic support available within teams, social workers claimed to have had serious discussions with their peers in a relatively low proportion of cases (17 per cent).

Consultation was not confined to social-services personnel, however, and officials from other agencies were involved in two out of five cases, playing a part second only in significance to the senior social workers. Parents were consulted to much the same degree, so, although almost all were obviously party to discussions about their *problems*, according to their social workers only two out of five were actually consulted about the *decision* itself. Finally, the children in question - the ultimate consumers of the service on offer - were the group least likely to be consulted, and there was discussion with less than one in ten before adult minds were made up. In this regard, practice apparently did little to counteract the legal anomaly whereby the duty to ascertain a child's wishes and feelings in decisions which affect him or her applies once the child is *in* care, but not beforehand.[8]

The nature of the decisions taken clearly affected (or was affected by) these patterns of consultation, and differences in practice were also apparent between the two authorities. The role played by outside agencies, for example, was greatest where a compulsory admission occurred, and least where voluntary reception was chosen. By contrast, discussions with *parents* were uppermost in voluntary cases (though even here a quarter were apparently not consulted beforehand about the decision to admit). In other words, decisions of a compulsory nature were normally preceded by discussions *between* officials *about* the families, whereas admissions to admit voluntarily usually (but not invariably) explicitly involved the parents as parties to the decision. More surprising was the fact that decisions *not* to admit to care were preceded by rather more internal, departmental discussions, and by less attention to parental viewpoints, than decisions to admit - a finding of some significance which became apparent when the parents themselves were interviewed.

Predictably, patterns of consultation in the two authorities followed somewhat different paths (see table 5.4). Shiptown's bias towards compulsion was reflected in a much heavier involvement with outside

Table 5.4 *Persons with whom social workers discussed the case*

	Admitted		Not admitted		Voluntary admissions		Compulsory admissions	
	C(N=60) %	S(N=100) %	C(N=106) %	S(N=95) %	C(N=36) %	S(N=35) %	C(N=25) %	S(N=65) %
Senior social worker	73	53	81	77	75	49	72	55
Other social workers	15	13	10	28	11	6	20	17
Manager	10	54	16	60	11	71	12	45
Adviser/advisory body	22	9	16	7	28	3	16	12
Outside officials	22	52	29	58	17	23	32	68
Parents	55	43	34	40	75	77	28	23
Child	12	8	7	7	11	3	16	11

C = Clayport; S = Shiptown.

agencies, whether or not the child was actually admitted to care. There was also evidence that the 'official' versions of procedures for decision-making, described in chapter 2, were not mere figments of departmental imagination. In Clayport, all levels of staff had agreed that – apart from some cases where non-accidental injury was at issue, or where care-proceedings were being contemplated – admission decisions were for social workers to make, in consultation with their team-leaders (senior social workers). In Shiptown, policy was different, and besides consulting with a senior, social workers were expected to refer all admission decisions upwards to the managerial level above that of their team-leader for 'endorsement of the need for admission'. It was a policy that had been applied expressly because of departmental concern about high rates of children in care, and it was assumed that managerial oversight might reduce 'unnecessary' admissions to care, especially those under the 1948 (1980) legislation where 'too loose an interpretation' had been suspected in the past.

There was partial compliance on the part of social workers with these official models of decision-making. In Clayport, roughly three quarters of all decisions were indeed discussed with senior social workers, and in Shiptown rather more than half of all cases were referred to a manager (rising to over 70 per cent of those where voluntary admission was the outcome). But there were substantial numbers of exceptions in both authorities and, in this area of decision-making at least, social workers appeared to be guided rather than bound by the rule book. In other words, the social workers had some power and space (and perhaps an overriding need as well, in cases of urgency) to bypass the formal channels of communication and consultation, to find alternative sources of support, or to reach their own conclusions with little or no discussion with others.

But it was also apparent that social workers were more inclined to follow the procedures laid down when the reasons for them were explicit and departmental anxieties were high. Shiptown had expressed considerable concern about receptions into care and the dangers of too readily admitting children in this way, and its procedures sprang directly out of this concern; it was in relation to voluntarily admitted cases that its social workers 'toed the line' most frequently. To a lesser extent, *both* authorities also stressed that 'care' of any kind should be a 'last resort', and social workers in both tended to consult their superiors more often in cases where the ultimate decision was *against* admission than otherwise. However, whether this meant that senior members of the departments were better able to stand back, take risks and resist 'unnecessary care' remains an open question.

There were some indications that departmental structures and procedures for deciding on the *placement* of admitted children were another potential source of influence on the admission decision itself. In Clayport a Children's Panel of managers and advisers had been set up to oversee admissions to residential care. It met weekly; social workers attended to present and petition for their cases, and its aim was to bring some overall planning and order into the use of residential facilities. It was hoped by this means to match placements to children's needs in a more effective way and to put a stop to direct approaches by social workers to the residential establishments of their choice. So far as foster-placements were concerned, there was an equivalent, multidisciplinary Family Placement Panel in existence throughout the monitoring period (though it came to an end soon afterwards), but this was concerned with long-term placements only. For short-term placements, social workers relied on their own knowledge of local foster-parents or on the updated lists kept in their district offices. It was our strong impression – though we have no quantifiable data to support this – that, if social workers wanted space and freedom to act with a minimum of oversight, they inclined towards a voluntary admission (when there was no necessity for a formal 'vetting meeting', as there was for all cases that might involve care-proceedings), and towards the use of temporary foster-care, thus circumventing the formal structures to which they would surrender some of their personal control.

In Shiptown there was a somewhat similar division between procedures for obtaining a residental placement and those for securing a foster home. The latter depended on the advice of a district specialist; but, for the former, social workers had to refer to the Admissions Section at area level, which was staffed by administrative officers with professional advisers in attendance. Apparently, however, the result was rather different from that in Clayport. It was claimed that residential resources were only guaranteed if the child came into care 'on an order' – partly because the law then obliged the authority to make provision, and partly because it was averred that at least one of the assessment centres would refuse beds to any but the compulsorily admitted over whom it would have some legal 'control'. On the other hand, social workers complained that, if a voluntary admission to residential care was proposed, there was likely to be delay and prevarication in offering a placement because there was not the legal evidence of 'urgency'. It was also possible for the Admissions Section (guided by the professional adviser) to refer cases back to a social worker, expressing doubts about the wisdom or legality of the admission decision itself. In the social workers' eyes (and in our own), therefore, placement procedures in Shiptown could sometimes have a direct influence on the decision to admit and were also likely to encourage compulsory admissions at the expense of voluntary care. The special structures and procedures for securing placements in both authorities may therefore have skewed decision-making in contrasting and unintended ways.

Finally, we asked the social workers who, in their eyes, carried the most weight in terms of the ultimate decision. Given the many parties to most negotiations, both inside and outside the social-services departments, who seemed to have been most influential in shaping the final outcome? For roughly a third of cases they believed that the weight of responsibility was evenly shared between two or more of the people concerned. For the rest, they were prepared to attribute to an individual or an agency the lion's share of the responsibility. Their answers are summarised in table 5.5.

Their perceptions were interesting in a number of ways: first, the social workers saw themselves at the centre of decision-making – either individually or in collaboration with their immediate managers – more often than anyone else. This applied most strongly in the case of voluntary admissions, where they claimed some responsibility in 59 per cent of cases, and when children were not admitted to care at all, where it applied to exactly half of the group. In contrast, social workers reckoned they carried significant weight for only a minority (36 per cent) of the decisions to admit compulsorily. It was also evident that discussions with superiors were generally understood in terms of advice, guidance, assistance or rubber-stamping, rather than the giving and receiving of orders, for seniors and managers were rarely credited with having taken prime responsibility for a decision in their own right – and the advisers hardly at all: this, despite the social workers' frequently expressed feelings of powerlessness within their organisations.

In the majority of situations, the locus of child-care decision-making was seen to be firmly within the social-services department itself or (by

Table 5.5   Persons carrying the most weight in decision-making

	Admitted (N = 161) %	Not admitted (N = 200) %	Voluntary admissions (N = 71) %	Compulsory admissions (N = 90) %
Intra-/interdepartmental				
NON-SHARED				
Social worker	25	32	34	18
Senior social worker	6	11	1	9
Manager	3	3	4	2
Adviser/advisory body	1	–	–	1
SHARED				
Social worker/senior social worker	7	16	8	7
Social worker/manager	8	2	17	1
Case conference/other shared	17	16	11	21
Total intra-/inter-departmental	67	80	75	59
Extra-departmental				
Outside agency/official	22	6	4	36
Family (parents/relative/child)	11	9	16	4
Not known	1	5	3	1
Total extra-departmental	33	15	20	40

means of interdisciplinary case conferences) at the boundaries, where its interests and responsibilities were shared with other agencies. For the minority it rested elsewhere: in the hands of officials from other agencies (over a third of compulsory admissions were laid at someone else's door in this way); or, more rarely, with the families themselves, who were said to have played the major part in 16 per cent of decisions leading to voluntary care.

Within this framework there were the usual differences of emphasis in the two sample authorities. The greater degree of managerial oversight operating in Shiptown meant that its social workers were rather less likely than their Clayport counterparts to claim major responsibility for decisions taken, and more often conveyed a picture of *shared* decision-making. The two authorities also diverged in ways which reflected their legal bias. Shiptown attributed three times the proportion of its decisions to other agencies (18 per cent, compared with 6 per cent), reflecting its high rate of compulsion. Conversely, Clayport social workers were more likely to perceive families as playing a key role (12 per cent, compared with 7 per cent), albeit a very minor one.

Summary

In summary, the jigsaw fragments of data that have been outlined tell us something about the pressures that are exerted on social-services departments to admit children to care, and about the procedures by which they reach their decisions. They also provide clues - but no conclusions - about how such pressures and processes may shape the decisions themselves.

First, we have seen that the scale, nature and source of referrals were rather different in our two sample authorities and that such differences could be related to the balance struck between voluntary and compulsory admissions to care and, more speculatively, to their overall admission rates. Thus Shiptown's greater use of the compulsory gateway could be seen as a response to the presentation at its door of large numbers of teenage 'villains' by such powerful referral agents as the police; whereas Clayport's situationally biased referrals, which came more frequently from the health services and from the families themselves, generally pointed in the direction of voluntary care.

The procedures for reaching decisions also differed, both according to the legal route used and as between the two sample authorities. We have explored the former in only the very simplest way, by comparing receptions under the Child Care Act 1980 with all other 'compulsory' admissions. There are of course a whole variety of compulsory routes into care: Place of Safety Orders, remands, care orders following criminal, care or matrimonial proceedings, and each of these is likely to follow on from a rather different set of procedures, involving a different mix of agencies and individuals who carry varying degrees of authority and 'weight'. Others have investigated small sub-categories of compulsory admissions in more detail than we have been able to manage,[9] but our simple distinction nevertheless makes sense.

Predictably, consideration of an admission via a court or magistrate's order often results from the initiative of other agencies and usually involves consultation with extra-departmental personnel. Other agencies are also, more often than not, credited with a share in making the decision, and, in a substantial minority of cases, social workers attribute the decision entirely to these other agents. What is interesting is not that this should be the case - for technically, *all* compulsory admission decisions are made extra-departmentally - but that initiative, influence and responsibility are nevertheless seen to lie *within* social services in relation to so many compulsory cases. Comparisons with the processes leading to voluntary admissions are therefore ones of degree rather than of kind. For the latter, the locus of decision-making rests more firmly within the social-services department itself, and the 'outsiders' with whom decisions are most often negotiated are the consumers themselves - the parents of the children in question, rather than other agencies. But the overlap between the two systems is considerable, and there is no suggestion that social-services departments are all-powerful in relation to voluntary care, or that they are the passive recipients of the decision-making of others, in relation to all compulsory cases.

We have seen, too, that procedures for consultation and decision-making within the two local authorities differed, not only as a reflection of their differential use of compulsion, but because managerial oversight was built into the Shiptown system in a way that was foreign to the Clayport philosophy. It also emerged that social workers in both authorities usually - but by no means invariably - followed the official procedures as laid down, so deviation was possible within either system. What remains unclear is whether these different procedures affected the outcome of decisions. We have no unequivocal evidence which links the mechanics of *how* decisions are reached with *what* is decided. Whether this is because no such connection exists, or because we have failed to pin it down and measure it, must remain an open question.

Finally, both the pressures and the processes that we have examined are, of course, aspects of policy. The number and type of cases that an outside agency or individual chooses to refer to a social-services department, and the manner in which referrals are framed and expressed, must be determined in part by expectations concerning the response they will receive. This in turn depends upon previous experience and upon the social-services department's own definition of its role and function. Negotiations concerning the boundaries between agencies and the appropriateness of 'care' as a response to referrals are the responsibility of the receiving social-services departments at least as much as, if not more than, that of the agencies which refer. Consequently, such definitions are (or should be) key features of departmental policy: they will take shape willy-nilly and by default if they are not hammered out by design; and we have seen that they matter in terms of admissions to care. The choice of procedures for arriving at decisions is similarly a matter of policy, though its significance in relation to what is decided about admissions is less obvious. In the next chapter we shall therefore attempt to examine more closely the part played by departmental policy in shaping child-care decisions.

6

In Search of Policy

Policies, as expressed in departmental structures and procedures, have already been discussed in the previous chapters. But what of other local policies which impinge directly or indirectly upon the decisions about admitting children to care? Our search led us in a variety of directions and to many different levels of the social-services departments. In trying to draw together our findings, our difficulties have been twofold. First, we have had to be selective, choosing to look at some issues of policy and ignoring others; and in doing so we may have missed some vitally important clues as well as doing violence to the complex and 'seamless web' of decision-making.[1] Secondly, we have found great difficulty in tracing the links between policy and practice, or, in the words of Webb and Wistow, in 'bridging the gaps between broad statements of policy and the detailed guidance of production processes and the work of practitioners'.[2] It is a difficulty that many of our respondents shared, and our data on this remain generally equivocal and inconclusive. Nevertheless, the search was instructive and illuminating and helped to round out our view of processes and relationships within social-services departments as a whole, as well as underlining the complexities of child-care decision-making in particular.

Our discussion touches on two broad categories of policy – 'service, or output policies and resource policies'.[3] It is with the latter that this chapter begins.

Resources

The resources which a department has at its disposal are certainly a manifestation of policy and must surely affect the outcome of child-care decisions. Indeed, the social workers whom we interviewed sometimes felt their hands were tied by lack of appropriate placements:

> Departmental policy is to avoid bringing kids of sixteen plus into care because of lack of resources . . .

and,

> We should be making provision within the law, but in reality we have nothing to offer within social-service provision.

Two examples may suffice to highlight the potential significance of resources and to make some comparisons between the two sample authorities: day-care provision for the under-fives, and residential care (in particular for teenagers).[4]

In Shiptown, with an under-fives population of something over 14,000, the social-services department ran four day nurseries, with places for nearly 300 and with an additional 38 places for handicapped children. More than 200 child-minders were registered with the department, with places for over 900 children. There was also an under-fives project providing support for mothers with young children in one of the Shiptown districts, jointly funded by the social-services, education and health departments of the local authority. In addition there were over 50 playgroups and another 50 or more mother and toddler groups running in the city, and an unknown (to us) quantity in neighbouring Plainfields.

In Clayport, with its larger population of children under school age (approximately 17,000), a survey of day-care provision was undertaken in 1980. At the time there was only one small local-authority day nursery for a dozen children, which was closed during our monitoring year and reopened as a family centre – part of a deliberate preventive strategy which laid emphasis upon parental participation. This provision was boosted somewhat by two private nurseries catering for 80 children in all. All these three nurseries were situated in only one of the city's two administrative districts. In addition (and in the same half of the city) there were two community projects run by voluntary bodies, which offered some day care, but one of these was under threat of imminent closure. For handicapped children there was a mixture of special schools and hospital units, which in all offered places for about

60 children. Direct provision by the social-services department was therefore minimal, but over 150 child-minders were registered with the department and playgroups were fairly numerous (130 in 1980). There were also over 50 groups for mothers and toddlers.

It is difficult to make exact comparisons of provision in the two authorities because we do not have precisely the same figures for each one. It is clear, however, that Shiptown was vastly better provided with local-authority nursery places (300 compared with a dozen), despite its somewhat smaller population of young children. Nor did private nurseries and other forms of day care in Clayport compensate for this discrepancy. Total day-nursery places amounted to less than a third of those in Shiptown; there were rather fewer registered child-minders and roughly the same number of mother and toddler groups. It was only Clayport's playgroups that were more numerous than those in Shiptown - and of all day-care resources they are the least likely to be able to offer the sustained sessions of care that might be a real alternative to admission.

There were hints, in our monitoring data, of the significance of day care in averting admissions, and of the effects of differential provision in the two authorities. 27 per cent of 130 under-fives were in some kind of day care at the time they were being considered (28 per cent in Shiptown and 25 per cent in Clayport). But for children subsequently admitted the proportion was only 12 per cent, whereas it was three times as large (38 per cent) for the children who were *not* admitted to care. It seems obvious that day care can weight the scales against admission, and that for a number of young children it provides a useful alternative to full-time substitute care. Furthermore, Clayport did in fact consider a larger number of pre-school children than Shiptown and subsequently admitted a higher proportion of them to care; and, although the differences were not statistically significant, it can be assumed that its markedly thinner network of day-care facilities played some part in this.[5]

Residential facilities for children in care in the two authorities were also in marked contrast to one another. Again, it was Shiptown which had by far the larger number of places, spread over a much wider range of establishments. In 1981 the Shiptown area of Shire had 279 beds distributed over two observation and assessment centres, one hostel, ten family-group homes for no more than a dozen children apiece, five larger children's homes, and a secure unit. In addition to this social-services provision there were a number of hospital-authority psychiatric in-patient units for disturbed children and adolescents, in or around Shiptown, and these catered for over 50 children in all. There was also a children's home, run by the naval welfare authority. Within the department, adolescents were especially likely to be accommodated in the observation and assessment centres or the working-boys' hostel, and together these facilities housed just over 80 children. It was noticeable that it was these establishments which were overfull, with occupancy rates as high as 135 per cent in some weeks of our study period. In fact, Shiptown's many residential homes were usually full, with an average occupancy rate of 97 per cent – the highest in Shire.

In contrast, at the beginning of our monitoring year, Clayport social-services department provided a maximum of 85 beds. These were spread over one observation and assessment centre (which also contained a nursery and longer-term family-group facilities), two homes for adolescents, designed for a maximum of 30 youngsters but offering fewer places because of a change of use; and a small family-group home for younger children which was underoccupied and which eventually closed. In addition there were five voluntary children's homes – though two of these were being run down, and had in fact closed by the time our research came to an end. Finally there was one small psychiatric in-patient unit and a hospital unit for handicapped children. Taken together, these extra-departmental facilities offered about 100 beds. At the beginning of 1982, the average occupancy rate of residential facilities in Clayport was 84 per cent.

In sum, within the Shiptown area there were nearly twice as many residential places available for children and adolescents in care as there were in the Clayport area; and, whereas over 80 per cent of Shiptown's resources were provided by the social-services department, less than half (46 per cent) of Clayport's stock was its own. Furthermore, Clayport's residential facilities were shrinking and were somewhat underoccupied, while in Shiptown, by contrast, many establishments seemed to be bursting at the seams. What the authorities did have in common was an explicit policy discouraging out-county placements; this had been introduced as an economy measure at a time of financial cutbacks.

Of course, the contrasts have to be set against the size of the 'in care' population which each authority had to accommodate. Over the period 1980–2, the Shiptown area was carrying approximately 770 children in care at any one time and the figure was fairly static. In the same period, numbers in care in the Clayport area were on the decline – the mean figure amounted to approximately 600 children. In other words, for roughly 20 per cent more children, Shiptown possessed more than twice as much residential accommodation.

To attempt a full explanation of such a discrepancy we should need to examine each authority's complementary policies for foster care, and the origins and history of each of the residential units concerned, neither of whch was possible in the time available. We can therefore only report the differences and speculate about their effect on admission decisions. Plainly the two are linked and the links go both ways. Pressures of need beget resources, and resources may stimulate pressures of need.

It seems plausible to suggest, therefore, that the contrasting amounts of residential care available in the two authorities have made some contribution to their different patterns of decision-making at the point of entry. Shiptown's relatively generous provision may well have enabled social workers to admit children (and especially teenagers, who are disproportionately heavy users of residential care) more readily. On the other hand, Clayport's comparatively sparse provision could have had the opposite effect. Either way, departmental policies appear to have played a significant part.

Admissions policies

But what of policies which relate directly to whether or not certain sorts of children in certain sorts of circumstances should be admitted to care; and whether one legal route is to be preferred to another? In each of the sample authorities we looked for written statements which might throw further light on their differences in practice, and we asked managers and advisers at a variety of levels for their opinion. There was apparently no shortage of such policies, and we were struck by many similarities between statements in the two authorities as well as some obvious differences. But what was also apparent was their level of generality, and the degree of confusion, ambiguity and contradiction in terms of their status and their acceptability.

Departmental handbooks and codes of practice for social workers are one potential source of policy statements, though their necessary preoccupation with procedural details and form-filling makes them an awkward vehicle for this. As one Shiptown manager put it,

> We're concerned that there ought to be concise and comprehensive guidelines . . . but it's difficult to know how to pitch it. . . . You can't [set out policies] in a manual - vignettes of circumstances which are applicable . . . only when a decision has been made should the manual come into play. . . . professional guidance and instruction is the arena so badly neglected. . . .

Nevertheless, handbooks in the two authorities provide some clues.

Shiptown, for example, had updated parts of its fieldwork manual in 1979 (a year before we began monitoring decisions) and had divided entries under the headings 'policy' and 'procedures'. Its policy on receptions into care was simply stated. Social workers were told that, 'in considering the application, the need for care must be clearly established and satisfy the conditions of the Children Act, 1948', and the relevant section of that Act was quoted. Emphasis was also placed on a local authority's duty to *prevent* admissions, and social workers were reminded that they must discuss 'alternative ways in which the family could be helped, other than reception into care'. Relatives and neighbours must be investigated as potential sources of help.

Admission via care-proceedings was dealt with in similar fashion. Section 1 of the Children and Young Persons Act 1969 was quoted in full, and attention was drawn to the implications of the care or control test. 'This "care or control" test implies that community resources, including social work, have been considered and/or tried but are not effective in helping the particular child.' So, again, *prevention* was emphasised. The need to think about 'the benefits and disadvantages which could flow from such action' (i.e. care-proceedings) was also stressed. Social workers were urged to *plan*, and to encourage parents 'to feel they have an ongoing part to play', assuring them they would 'continue to have social work help although the child may be in care'. There was also considerable emphasis on consultation with extra-departmental officials, and 'No care proceedings should be taken unless a full case discussion has taken place' - an emphasis that was clearly reflected in our data.

Significantly, the section on Place of Safety Orders followed the one on care-proceedings and in no way suggested (as our monitoring data did) that such orders were considered the main, or 'normal', route to a care order. POSOs should be applied for 'if the child seems at severe risk and the situation cannot hold while care proceedings are initiated'. Once more, attention was drawn to the law and to the need to relate to at least one of the conditions set out in section 1 of the Children and Young Persons Act 1969 – though the manual failed to point out that the 'offence' condition is *not* a ground for a POSO. Yet again, 'alternative ways of ensuring that the child receives adequate care' should be fully investigated first.

In sum, therefore, policy guidance in the Shiptown manual was brief, rather general, and low-key. There was some emphasis on prevention of admissions of all kinds, and a definite requirement to explore alternatives. But there was no attempt to elaborate on different types of admission or to offer detailed guidance to social workers. Significantly, there was no hint that 'villains' loomed large in the department's thinking, or that special policies needed to be spelled out to deal with them. Furthermore, the law itself was seen as the main reference point for decision-making – so much so, in the eyes of one of the Shire managers we interviewed, that the scope for any admission policy at all was questioned:

> You can't have a policy . . . for the application of the law, because if you understand the law properly . . . you will inevitably find children coming in by certain routes because these are appropriate. . . . There is no policy which *interprets* the law [emphasis added].

This was an especially intriguing opinion in the light of an earlier, controversial Shiptown policy document which was still talked of in the department. The document in question, entitled 'Admission of Children to Care', had been written by a senior adviser in the mid-seventies and submitted to the director for the area. It was a strongly worded, detailed and urgent attack on social-work practice over admissions to care. It was alleged that social workers were *mis*interpreting the law, and were receiving children into care voluntarily (under the 1948 Children Act) in an unnecessary and illegal fashion. It was believed that some such admissions should more properly have been effected through care-proceedings and that others need not have occurred at all if proper preventive strategies had been attempted. Social workers were accused of misunderstanding not only the 1948 Children Act, but also the Children and Young Persons Act 1963, which refers to the need to avoid not only admissions to care but appearances of children before the juvenile court as well. The adviser believed that, in consequence, appropriate care-proceedings cases were being diverted along voluntary channels and that this was wrong. Furthermore, a strict interpretation was placed on the 'grounds' for voluntary admission, and many of the reasons given for such admissions by social workers were declared illegal. The document recommended a clearer statement of departmental policy, clarification of guidelines, and closer monitoring of admission decisions.

Though allegedly 'out of date', it was of interest to us for several reasons. One was the reaction it had provoked from Shire's legal department, to which it had been rapidly referred for comment. The adviser's interpretation of the legislation was itself declared erroneous – so the law, far from being self-evident and out of reach of any policy, was clearly open to a variety of interpretations by even experienced and senior local-authority personnel. The thrust of the document also lay very much in the directions that practice had actually taken in our monitoring year, with its stress on court action in preference to voluntary admissions. Moreover, the institution of managerial oversight of decisions, with its aim of eliminating 'unnecessary admissions' and 'too loose an interpretation of the 1948 Children Act', dated from the same period, and was certainly believed by some to be directly attributable to the disputed document.

It was also the only written statement we came across which actually referred in particular to troublesome children and adolescents with reference to admission to care and to policies for dealing with them:

One of the most difficult cases concerns teenagers who refuse to return to their homes and parents who refuse to have their children back and are only too ready to agree to reception into care. . . . all . . . recalcitrant teenagers should be given the option, in no uncertain terms, of going home (and receiving our support there in the difficulties experienced) or face a court appearance as being beyond control. . . . the deterrent effect of a court appearance is a valuable brake on all concerned. . . . the great value of dealing with these cases under the appropriate Act (1969) is that we have adequate control over a child with a court order if admission has to take place. . . . Children of whatever age, however young, should be dealt with under the 1969 Act if they are 'beyond the control of their parents'. . . .

Given the congruence between many parts of the document and some of the practice we observed, it was interesting to find that social-services department personnel (if they knew of its existence at all) were sharply divided in their opinions about its status, its relevance and its significance. We were told by an adviser, for example, that 'in its day it had been influential and very much so in some quarters', though it was suggested that those days were now over. A senior manager, on the other hand, rejected it as 'highly biased . . . punitive and moralistic', and it was implied that the speedy counterblast from the legal department had effectively killed it off. In the eyes of several people it had never *been* policy and had had no official status as far as they were concerned. Yet in one of the district offices in our sample a manager produced a copy from his drawer, expressed general agreement with it and thought it represented policy, at least in his area; and, in another, the manager expressed considerable suspicion about the whole notion of voluntary admissions to care. Only in the third were we told, 'We don't do things like that here.'

Whether or not a preference for court action rather than voluntary admission was, or ever had been, official departmental 'policy', the comments of managers and advisers in Shiptown (and indeed of the social workers themselves) revealed a wide range of opinion about what caused such an emphasis in practice and whether the evident trends towards compulsion were to be welcomed or deplored. At Shire Hall, for example, an assistant director equated the growth of Place of Safety Orders with poor work. 'If we have a shortage of social workers or the work isn't of the standard it should be, you'd expect the numbers of admissions to go up and drastic action to go up.' A senior adviser's comments followed on from this. It was 'better to work with parents by agreement if at all possible . . . but this demanded more skills. . . . voluntary admissions could be appropriate for cooling off after a bust-up, rather than doing a POSO and setting the court in motion.' Another argument against admissions in general, and compulsory admissions in particular, was that of cost. More than one Shire Hall official referred to the financial constraints. 'One must continually reinforce the resource implications of the decision to admit a young child to care.' Further, 'It is *expensive* to put children in care on care orders because they can last until 18, committing the local authority to between £90 and £400 per week. You can't divorce child care from finance.'

At the area level, managers saw this pressure towards compulsion coming from *outside* the department. 'Society's norms and standards have changed; we're not as tolerant as we were and we have to reflect society's social norms.' Or, as someone else put it, 'People fight authority much more, so local authorities must therefore become more authoritarian.' The *benefits* of taking an authoritarian line were expressed most fully by an area specialist. 'A care order can provide flexibility of approach . . . guarantee of access to the child without difficulty, ease of removal, a controlling element over the rest of the family to galvanise them into trying.' Care orders also 'gave children, foster-parents, natural parents and social workers some security and prevented impulsive action on the part of parents, enabling planning for the child's future . . . aggressive, definite planning'. The familiar arguments against 'drift' and a passive, reactive style of social work, which have gained national credibility and momentum since the early seventies, were thus explicitly rehearsed.

If we were to attempt to characterise specific admissions policies in Shiptown, therefore, we should have to stress the absence of any comprehensive or coherent statement on child care that was universally accepted. Certain themes had undoubtedly emerged and recurred over time: the issue of control and oversight over admission decisions; costs and their policy implications; compulsion versus voluntarism; prevention and community care versus admission and institutional solutions. But there was no real consensus, even amongst senior personnel in the department, about what the policy was, or should be, on these issues.

To be fair, the department itself was well aware of this. At the end of our monitoring year a massive reorganisation occurred with the department, in which the middle tier of management was abolished and new structures were created at Shire Hall. One was the Programme Development Section, where an early task was said to be 'producing under each of the broad client categories, documents which clarify policies'. As the new head of the section commented,

We're now at the stage of agreeing the need to produce programme-headings and a position statement - i.e. saying clearly what policies

have been pursued, how they've evolved and how much progress has
been made, what the constraints are if any, and addressing the question
of whether the policy objectives are still valid.

Unfortunately for us, this promised review came too late to illuminate
our monitoring data.

In Clayport the situation was rather different from that in Shiptown.
Its 'Code of Practice' for fieldworkers was, like Shiptown's manual,
rather low-key and careful, with a similar reliance on the law as a
framework for decision-making. It too stressed the importance of seeking out alternatives to admission, and drew attention to the legal limits
to receptions into care. 'It is not, for example, sufficient for a parent to
say they no longer wish to care for the child' - a sentiment with which
the author of the ubiquitous Shiptown document would have agreed
wholeheartedly! Interestingly, however, in view of Clayport's lesser
use of compulsion, the Clayport guidelines on court work were a good
deal more comprehensive than those in Shiptown. The code tended to
emphasise the gravity of court proceedings by giving detailed guidance
on court reports, court procedures, and available sentences and disposals, and also by its stress on prior consultation and co-operation.
Social workers were reminded that the 1969 Act places 'emphasis on
consultation between local authorities and the police *and the parents* of
young people before considering action at law' (original emphasis).
The code acknowledged that many social workers might feel 'that
there is conflict between their caring role and the requirement to
exercise authority, particularly within a Court setting'. However, they
were assured that 'reasonable control is regarded by eminent child care
specialists as being essential to the proper development of young
people'. 'Villains' seem to have been in mind at this point, but compulsion appears to be presented as an unfortunate necessity rather
than a first option. There was no hint, otherwise, that voluntary care
was to be *preferred*. Indeed, the reverse was the case: in the special
guidelines for cases of child abuse, it was stated that reception into
care, 'like all voluntary action, should be used with extreme caution as
the parents may change their minds and ask for the child's discharge'.

The same point, expressed more broadly, was a recurrent theme in
Clayport's Area Management Committee minutes. A cautious approach
to voluntary admissions was in fact a feature of both our sample authorities, and in Clayport it had a long history. Before local-government
reorganisation, the city of Clayport had had a reputation for high

admission rates under the Children Act, of which the neighbouring County strongly disapproved. After amalgamation it became a priority to bring that rate down, closer to the County average. It was felt that too many voluntary admissions were ill conceived and loosely planned and that a sharper focus and shorter spells in care were necessary to counteract 'drift'. The voluntary route was to be used for only the most clear-cut and brief admissions. It is perhaps significant, therefore, that our data suggest that, despite their divergent practice in the use of compulsion, the two authorities decided in much the same way when faced with the 'volunteered' (see chapter 4).

By far the clearest and most comprehensive expression of child-care policy in Clayport, however, came from its area director - newly appointed in the year before our monitoring began. Together with the area specialists and an officer from County Hall, he set about preparing papers on each of the client groups, and began with children. In April 1980 a 'Policy Review on Child Care Services' was circulated, in which three main themes were to be developed over the next three years. These were: increased availability and effectiveness of preven-tive services; residential care as 'intervention' (i.e. treatment) and *not* long-term substitution for family life; and - a complementary theme - *family* placement for children in care. As part of the preventive package, there were specific plans to foster and develop fieldwork skills, day-care resources, intermediate-treatment and self-help and voluntary schemes in the community. Further, targets were actually set for reducing the number of admissions - for example, by 20 per cent in 1980-1 (our monitoring year), and by smaller percentages in the years which followed.

We shall discuss the success of these initiatives later in the chapter, but the clarity and coherence of the policy statement did not mean that it was automatically accepted without question by all the Clayport staff. Consensus was no more apparent here than in Shiptown. There were cynics who saw it merely as a respectable cloak for unacceptable financial cutbacks; and others who mistrusted, or were wearied by, the enthusiastic sweepings of a 'new broom'.

The social workers' view

We have spent some time identifying policies which were directly related to the admission of children to care in our sample authorities, and have relied, so far, on written statements and the words of senior personnel in the two departments. But what of the social workers, who played a key role in influencing and implementing admission decisions? What was *their* understanding of departmental policies, and how did they link with the child-care cases they were handling during the monitoring year? Even more crucially, did departmental policies actually influence their actions in any consistent or measurable way?

In our interviews with social workers we asked if they were aware of any departmental policy which was relevant to the case in question, in terms of whether or not it ought to result in an admission; and whether or not a particular legal route would be preferred. Because we were also interested in any other common reference points the social workers might use (from training, research literature, professional associations and so on), we asked in addition if any general rules or principles applied to the case. We also queried where and how they had learned of any such principles or policies.

In the event, we experienced the asking of such questions as an awkward and uncomfortable point in what were generally absorbing, long and free-flowing interviews. Linking the particular case to any general rules, whether of policy or principle, was apparently not easy; and perhaps our questions were clumsy and simplistic in their assumption that such links existed, or were readily identifiable. With some thought, and a good deal of embarrassment on both sides, social workers could see some connections in a fair proportion of cases. But in a great many instances they could not.

Broadly, the Clayport social workers were more likely to be aware of departmental policies in relation to compulsory admissions; both authorities seemed equally alive to departmental attitudes regarding voluntary care; and Shiptown social workers appeared specially sensitive to departmental dictates where admission was averted. In both authorities, social workers were on somewhat firmer ground when they were considering principles rather than policy - but this was much more marked in Clayport than in Shiptown.

Particular comments are a lot more revealing, however, than our own crude generalisations, and they indicate large areas of overlap between the two authorities as well as highlighting some important points of difference. In both authorities, for example, there was fairly frequent denial of the existence of policies of any relevance:

Policy - what's that? (Clayport)

There isn't any. The SSD [social-service department] is about to make a policy about deliberate homelessness - it's being discussed. (Shiptown)

The trouble is, knowing exactly what it [policy] is. (Clayport)

It's difficult to know what *is* department policy. There are things which are part of the old Shiptown city policy, and have been carried over to Shire - so it's difficult to known if it's Shire policy, or just practice. . . . (Shiptown)

You tell *me* what the department's policy is and I'll tell you if it fits. (Clayport)

Some social workers approved of this perceived absence of policy as allowing them the discretion necessary to respond to the unique circumstances of each case:

I don't see it as departmental policy, but as individual children. (Clayport)

No - and there shouldn't be, either! It's a professional, on the spot decision, and in the end it's down to the ground worker. . . . (Shiptown)

This last comment was an interesting one, and reflected a fairly widespread view among social workers and to some extent their superiors as well. It was the Director of County who had written, in his preamble to the 'Code of Practice', 'This kind of service organisation relies upon the flexibility of judgement at field level'; and, in the words of a Shire Hall official, 'You can't have a policy for professional judgement.' The dilemma for social workers and their managers is put in a nutshell - and so, incidentally, is our difficulty in asking social workers to make connections between policy and practice. Policy presupposes that people, or the situations they are in, can be categorised and that general statements can be made about how to deal with this or that sort of case or set of circumstances. Yet a basic tenet of social work is that help must be tailored to meet individual need, that each person is indeed unique, and that it is to this uniqueness that a truly personal service must respond. But, against this, the strain of judging each case on its merits and 'from scratch', with no guiding framework, can be considerable. So, while practitioners may resist the notion of policies, they may nevertheless construct their own categories and concepts in order to simplify and make sense of their decision-making. The tension between these perspectives is obvious, is not peculiar to social work, and is one to which we shall return. '

Nevertheless, there *were* policies to which social workers referred, and none more frequently than 'prevention'. In both departments the theme of trying to keep children *out* of local-authority care was strong.

> Policy is to provide maximum support to prevent reception into care. (Clayport)
>
> I think the Department's policy is to do everything we can to avoid admission. I don't think we're slap happy about it. (Shiptown)
>
> Prevention must be the first resort. Care may be appropriate further down the line. (Clayport)
>
> Departmental policy is that you should keep children out of care at any cost. (Shiptown)

Awareness of this aspect of policy did not necessarily mean that social workers agreed with it, however; and, for a Clayport social worker who had argued for an admission but was blocked by management, it seemed that 'we have abdicated responsibility'.

Departmental caution about the voluntary route into care had also got through to many social workers in both authorities.

> Departmental policy is to err on the side of caution. If in doubt, put it before the court, to safeguard the child. It's not a persecution but a protection thing. (Shiptown)
>
> I'm very aware of the Department's preference for court. (Clayport)

On this particular issue we picked up a number of cases where social workers had *resisted* policy, some of them successfully and some not. In a Shiptown case, for example, where a father was mentally disturbed, a social worker argued for reception into care:

> I must admit, I'd assumed I'd be advised to take a Place of Safety Order. I assumed this was agency policy.

In the event, and to his surprise, his view prevailed.

> I think in the situation the father was acting very co-operatively . . . the law clearly says in this situation take section 2, 1980 [Child Care Act].

It seems the law, departmental policy and my own views coincided slightly unexpectedly.

In Clayport, a social worker had similar success when arguing for reception of two teenage boys whose father had committed suicide and whose mother was not coping with their care. The long-term, open-ended nature of the admission effectively ruled out the voluntary route so far as departmental policy was concerned, and the chairman of the area Children's Panel said as much. But the social worker argued that compulsion was inappropriate and unnecessary, and won. In both cases, 'policy' proved to be more flexible and more responsive to the circumstances of particular cases - and to their own powers of persuasion - than the social workers had assumed.

Two more identifiable themes emerged from our discussions with social workers, though these were expressed mainly in Shiptown. The first and most important was the requirement to follow procedures and *consult* - with seniors, managers and others, if necessary, through the medium of case conferences *before* decisions were made:

> You need a round-table discussion of the possibility of reception into care.
>
> [Policy is] to consult with senior and manager and go through to the adviser or admissions to get confirmation from them.
>
> . . . always corporate consultation before reception into care, even if it's a straightforward case.

Shiptown's particular stress on this style of cross-referencing and shared decision-making certainly appeared to have been absorbed by a substantial proportion of its fieldworkers. Some social workers also assumed that the law and policy were really indivisible - rather as one of their senior managers had done:

> Shire policy is to uphold the law re child care. In terms of the legislation . . . the law is quite clear and I don't see a department *has* a policy independent of that.

This was a view that we could not share, not least because we had so much evidence that interpretations did in fact vary, from person to person, place to place, and over time. Child-care legislation, quite properly in our view, uses vital concepts such as 'neglect', 'moral danger', 'proper development', and so on, which are not precisely defined in law and whose meaning must be a matter for debate and able to develop and change with changing knowledge and standards. Phrases such as 'any other circumstances' in the Child Care Act 1980 also indicate that no legal code, however exhaustive could encompass or anticipate the wide variety of situations in which parents might be prevented from caring for their children. To us, interpretation of the law seems the very stuff of policy, and in Titmuss's words, 'all legislation is experimental . . . in spite of its literally "black and white" appearance in the statute book, legislation is in essence part of the dynamic process which is social policy'.[6] It was interesting, therefore, that a number of our respondents did not see it that way.

Where and how social workers had absorbed such policies as they acknowledged was even harder to pin down than the policies themselves. Codes of practice were referred to occasionally – most usually when a worker was new to the department, or when an unfamiliar situation first arose. But, although copies were said to be 'about' in each team, they were not much in evidence, and there was no impression of well-thumbed works of reference always to hand. There was also the problem of keeping them up to date. Clayport's manual had not been comprehensively overhauled for several years, due partly to the complications of the staggered implementation of the 1975 Children Act, and partly to 'waiting for new technology' which hadn't yet arrived.

Other written policy statements that circulated in the departments were known about with varying degrees of interest and precision, but the most usual source of information and influence seemed to be colleagues and superiors – particularly team-leaders and (in Shiptown) the managers to whom decisions were referred. Indeed the special significance of the team-leader as an upholder (and perhaps creator) of departmental policy was well illustrated in Clayport. One social worker commented, 'Policy? – my team-leader has not told me what that is!' Another managed to effect a voluntary admission in her team-leader's absence, knowing she would have recommended a Place of Safety Order (incidentally, in this the social worker received support from the leader of another team, who took a 'softer' line). Ironically, the absent team-leader was *herself* responsible for a similarly 'deviant' voluntary admission during the monitoring year, and remarked ruefully, 'What *I* needed was a team-leader to keep me in line!'

For some social workers, however, the sources of policy were as obscure as the policies themselves: 'There's no policy - other than, as far as I know, we're trying to cut down the need for care . . . [but I] don't know where I heard this from!' (Shiptown). If the role of policy in shaping their thinking or actions was not always apparent to the social workers themselves, what of any general rules or principles that they applied? As we have indicated, they were somewhat clearer about the existence of such principles, at least in Clayport, but were not necessarily in agreement about what they were, or from where they had originated. Experience, colleagues, senior staff, legislation, common-sense, manuals, training-sessions, courses and 'in the course of working in the office' were all mentioned, but, as one social worker put it, 'These things grow into you - you don't necessarily know where you pick them up from.'

The greatest degree of consensus seemed to exist on the priority to be given to 'the welfare of the child', which was sometimes seen as an aspect of policy and sometimes as a vital counterpoint to it.

> The welfare of the child is the social worker's key criterion. (Clayport)
>
> The welfare principle. I think these decisions should be made at agency/grass-roots level. We are aware of all the facts and are in a position to judge. (Shiptown)
>
> [This case] highlights the foolishness of policy re preventing a child coming into care. The need of the child is the paramount consideration. (Clayport)

Aspects of the welfare principle were sometimes spelled out. The importance of stability for the child and the significance to the child of his or her family were often quoted.

> Keeping children within the family is a basic principle. (Clayport)
>
> A principle that the child should be with parents *if parents are able and willing to cope.* (Shiptown; emphasis added)

But putting the child's welfare first could also lead to opposite conclusions:

> Protection of the child - his interests are paramount. (Clayport)
>
> You cannot leave a 15 year old in that situation - the immediate task was to remove the daughter, once the assault was made. (Shiptown)

Concern for the welfare of the family as a whole was also expressed by several social workers in both authorities. A Clayport social worker, for example, saw 'danger in making children clients at the expense of the family unit'. The importance of holding families together was not always expressed in terms of 'welfare', however. Some social workers stressed that parents were, and should be, *responsible* for their children, and it was not the job of social workers to take those responsibilities from them:

> Families should take responsibility for their members. (Clayport)
>
> No, I didn't press unduly for care. Parents had to take the major responsibility. (Shiptown)

Respect for parents was another, more positive theme:

> A basic principle was respect for the values of parents, however questionable in the eyes of others *provided that* the care of the baby was OK [original emphasis].

Fairly frequent reference was also made to the damaging consequences of 'care', which had to be borne in mind when reaching decisions. There were anxieties about institutionalisation, the alienation of children from their families and the tendency for them to languish in care for long periods:

> The worry that when you get children in care they tend to stay there. (Shiptown)
>
> I think for me it's this business of space closing up – it's so easy once a person is out of a situation or family for the space to close. (Shiptown)

In other words, every rule or principle had its opposite, and within each rule or principle there was an inbuilt proviso – an 'if' or 'but' to modify its force. Just as 'many hands make light work', but 'too many cooks spoil the broth', so children need their families, but also need protection *from* their families; and families should be responsible, but social services must also be responsible when families fail.

The complications and contradictions are not the product of social workers' woolly-mindedness, but are a feature of the difficult balancing-act between the rights and needs of individuals, and between the relative risks and harms of pursuing one course of action rather than another, that must precede child-care decisions. Small wonder, therefore, that different people in different situations placed different degrees of emphasis upon the principles which guided them. The picture was not entirely idiosyncratic and without pattern. Sometimes a team of social workers appeared to share a set of attitudes that produced a measure of coherence. One Clayport team argued strongly for early and decisive action (including severing parental links) in order to pursue the goal of stability and 'permanence' for children in care. Another seemed to set more store by voluntarism and parental participation. In Shiptown, where the influence of district managers was stronger, both teams in one district leaned more heavily in the direction of 'planning for permanence' than those in either of the other two districts. The potential for developing shared values and a group ethos seemed considerable, especially where the leadership of a senior or manager was strong and decisive. But it did not always happen, and in some we could discern no common theme.

Summary

How, then, can our observations on policy and its relationship to child care decision-making be summarised? First, and most obviously, there is no neat and simple relationship, because policy is no neat and simple matter. It embraces structures, procedures, resources, intra- and interdepartmental relationships, as well as setting specific objectives in relation to the admission of children to care. Even if we narrow our perspective to the last of these (as we have done in the second half of this chapter) and look only at the policies which bear directly and specifically upon admission decisions, the picture is still complicated.

Looking from the top downwards in our sample departments, official policy statements were generally fragmented, partial and sometimes elusive and of uncertain status – and other research suggests that this is not atypical.[7] The Clayport Area Director's policy document was the most up-to-date and comprehensive statement that we found – but even this did not address the issue of legal pathways into care and, like most others, was pitched at a very broad and general level. This is not to say that it should or could be otherwise. Managers and workers alike agree that there must be room for professional judgement in social work, and the decisions involved require a balancing of too many factors and a variety of sometimes conflicting needs and interests, which would defeat any clear-cut or detailed directives sent down from above. A plurality of goals invites a plethora of policies. In any case, the greater the distance from the operational level, the more general and abstract statements of policy are bound to be.

Looking from the bottom up, the sense of confusion and ambiguity is intensified. In the social workers' eyes, policy is not always acknowledged or recognised, and its links with practice on a case-by-case basis are frequently obscure. Some of their uncertainties and denials are doubtless due to the slippery elusiveness of the policies themselves. Some maybe wilful obtuseness - the kind of professional bloody-mindedness which refuses to acknowledge the relevance, or even the existence, of the policies that 'they' have devised. Some of their apparent lack of awareness may also be because departmental policies have been so well absorbed that they are no longer recognised as such - a case of talking prose without realising it. Certainly, some of the principles to which social workers alluded were very like some of the policies that their department espoused; and, as they were often unclear about their origins, a degree of unacknowledged socialisation into departmental norms may well have been going on.

Confusion is compounded by the fact that social workers - in our eyes, if not their own - are also makers of policy. There were plenty of instances of them circumventing or challenging official policy, and here their general principles were often brought into play. There were also examples of new developments, which stemmed directly from the initiatives of fieldworkers and were only later taken up as official policy. A special fostering scheme in Clayport was one example of this movement upwards and outwards from the grass roots.

All our evidence suggests in fact, that social-services departments are far from being well-oiled bureaucratic machines, where the operatives do the bidding of their superiors according to the rule book. Departmental guidelines appear to be just that, and are not strait-jackets, however much they may seem so at times to the workers concerned. For all the constraints upon them - and there are many, not least of resources - those working at the gateway to the department do have some room for manoeuvre.

This leads us, finally, to the crucial question of whether the effects of admission policies on practice can be measured or demonstrated in any unequivocal way, and, given the complexities we have described, it is perhaps not surprising that they cannot! Two illustrations make the point.

Conveniently for us, Clayport's Area Director produced his review of child-care policy just a few months before our monitoring year began, and in it set targets for considerably reducing admission rates in the area. A 20 per cent reduction was the goal for 1980-1, with an easing-off to a 15 per cent and then 10 per cent reduction in the two following years. His boldness was no doubt strengthened by the fact that admissions were already falling dramatically throughout 1979-80, while his document was being prepared – the figure for that year being 23 per cent less than for the previous 12 months. He was also frank about the unscientific nature of his targets, which were seen as direction-markers rather than precise goals to be achieved.

In the event, area admissions *did* continue to decline in 1980-1, by 12 per cent. For that year at least, it seemed that a newly stated policy might have prolonged or reinforced an existing trend. But by 1981-2 the pattern was broken and the admission rate shot up again, by 29 per cent. Other factors were apparently at work, overriding any temporary grip that policy might have established over admission practice.

In Shiptown we encountered paradoxes of a different kind. In our discussions on policy we received a very strong impression that management and the teams in one of the districts that we covered were more suspicious of voluntary care and more sympathetic to the use of court action than were their counterparts in either of the other two districts studied. From what those working there said of themselves, and from what others said about them, this to our minds was the district still somewhat influenced or in tune with the style of child care that had been advocated in the famous and disputed policy document of the mid seventies. Indeed, it was here alone that we were able to run a copy of the document to earth. Yet the district's admission rate in the monitoring year was considerably higher than elsewhere in our Shiptown sample (64 per cent of all considered children, compared with 40 and 41 per cent in the other districts); and, more intriguing still, its proportion of voluntary cases was also much higher (59 per cent, compared with 16 and 26 per cent).

The apparent perversity of practice in response to policy in both these illustrations merely emphasises the complexities of the relationship between them. It seems plausible, for instance, that there is considerable circularity in that relationship; that policy is quite likely to evolve in reaction to practice trends - seeking to reinforce or reverse them - and that practice, in its turn, may sometimes react *against* policies which are perceived as too extreme or insistent.

It is also evident that there are many other reasons why the direct effects of policy upon practice seem so elusive and equivocal. Policy itself is not necessarily clearly articulated or disseminated; in fact there are likely to be many policies at large within a department, and some may conflict with others. Except when stated in the broadest and most abstract terms, child-care policies do not command a consensus of support - and this is hardly surprising, since the professional literature is also divided on what a child's best interests are likely to be and how to set about securing them. Furthermore, degrees of compliance vary at all levels of the departments and there is space for the independent exercise of professional judgement; thus there is considerable room for manoeuvre and deviation. This is particularly crucial at the operational level, where social workers and their immediate superiors are key actors in the decision-making process. Finally, and most obviously, policy is only one among many influences at work in shaping child-care decisions. We have looked at some of them in previous chapters, and in the next we shall turn to another - that of the families themselves.

7

The Family Perspective

We sought a family perspective at two stages of the monitoring exercise: first, around the time that decisions were made, or as soon after as was feasible; and, again, approximately six months after the decision. This chapter is concerned with the first set of interviews, which covered similar ground to those conducted with the social workers at a comparable stage of the study. The methods of reaching the families have already been described in chapter 2. Permission to approach the families was asked of social workers. In a very few cases they refused outright; in some they advised considerable delay, judging the situation too delicate or the families too vulnerable to cope with the intrusion of a questioning stranger. More usually they acted as intermediaries on our behalf, seeking the consent of families and conveying their answers to us. Some families were inevitably lost to us in the process. Sometimes we were advised to make a direct approach, and this was done in person rather than by letter. A few more families were lost by this means, but doorstep refusals were surprisingly rare.

Taken as a whole, most of our failures to reach families were the result of decisions taken on their behalf by social workers or, occasionally, by the researchers themselves. There was, for example, a reluctance to interview parents who had given up their children for adoption, because of the fear of imposing additional strain at a time of acute stress and because they would in any case be subjected to interviews by guardians *ad litem*. By comparison, only a very small proportion of families *themselves* refused an interview. Comparative figures in Shiptown, for example, were a loss of 18 per cent of families through a social worker's or researcher's decision but only 5 per cent loss through their own refusal. We cannot be sure whether the professionals were protecting families who would have refused anyway, or whether direct access to all families would have produced a higher participation rate. Certainly it was apparent that a few individual social workers denied access to a far higher proportion of their cases than the rest of their colleagues, which suggests that part of their protectiveness may have been of themselves.

Nevertheless, interviews at the first stage of the inquiry were achieved with the families of 270 out of the 361 children in the cohort – a rate of 75 per cent. Bearing in mind the sensitive nature of the decisions being made, and the considerable degree of conflict involved in some of them, this seems an encouraging proportion. It also reflects credit upon the social workers, who were of key importance in enabling the interviews to take place. Since they were aware that their own work would be open to scrutiny, without the compensatory satisfaction of actually hearing what their clients had to say (except anonymously and in aggregate), they demonstrated a high degree of professionalism and commitment to the research project.

The characteristics of the 25 per cent of families we failed to interview were examined by means of the social-worker schedules to see whether they were distinguishable from the cohort as a whole. Differences were generally modest. More of the missing group had avoided an admission to care – 68 per cent, compared with 56 per cent in the total cohort – and more had actually been unaware that the department was considering care for their children, which may have been one good reason why social workers were reluctant to allow a researcher to interview them. More were new cases, never before known to the departments (25 per cent, compared with 16 per cent in the total group) and lower proportions of the children had been in care before, or were on 'at risk' registers. Their family circumstances and standards of child care were judged rather more favourably than those of the group as a whole. More parents were said to be in work and in satisfactory accommodation, fewer histories of marital breakdown or child neglect were recorded, and the physical and emotional care of their children was criticised less frequently.

In sum, there was certainly no suggestion that the most difficult or contentious cases had slipped through the net. On the contrary, if our family perspective lacked anything, it was a balanced representation of the views of those whose lives are only lightly touched by social services and who manage to cope – at least in the short term – without much intervention. This is a pity, because we were particularly interested in this significant but unresearched group. Nevertheless, as our data will show, a fair number of the families interviewed fell into this category, and their answers provide some useful insights.

The 'families' who *were* interviewed were, in effect, one or both of the 'parents' (caretakers) of the children being considered for care. We did not attempt to interview the children, partly because of the complications of the enormous age-range involved; partly because it was evident that (aside from some notable exceptions, usually involving teenagers) admission decisions are made by adults and not the children themselves; and to some extent because time and resources did not allow the inclusion of this complex extra dimension to the study. Sometimes, and especially where admission to care had been avoided, the children in question were in fact present for all or part of the interview, but their observations did not form an aspect of our recorded material. Occasionally they presented the researchers with awkward dilemmas – as when they were found at home when they should have been in care! However, unless it was estimated that serious risk was involved, information of this kind was not relayed to the social workers and it was understood that confidentiality would be observed. Sometimes the children's behaviour underlined or refuted what their parents were saying. One of us has vivid recollections of the absurdity of an interview in which a mother was boldly asserting that relationships between brothers and sisters were harmonious to the accompaniment of a loud and alarming battle that raged between them in the hall!

In approximately a quarter of interviews, both parents were seen together; in two thirds it was the mother alone who was seen; and in the rest (about 6 per cent) the father alone, or occasionally someone else (usually a relative) acting as caretaker, was the respondent. Overall therefore, the view presented is a predominantly female one, with mothers outnumbering fathers by three to one. This reflects in exaggerated form the family composition of our sample. The bias to a female viewpoint is also the result of considerable difficulties in arranging interviews at times when male breadwinners were likely to be present, and may also be some measure of their reluctance to be involved in such matters. It therefore also mirrors the bias towards working mainly with mothers which social workers demonstrated. In this respect, the researchers were no more successful in tipping the balance than they were.

First let us compare the families' account of their circumstances, problems and the subsequent decisions and interventions that were made, with that given by the social workers. It should be noted that comparisons were made between the two sets of data, each taken in aggregate. They were not linked together on a child-by-child basis for this analysis, so agreements or discrepancies between individual social workers and the families on their caseloads are inevitably concealed within the broad, general patterns which emerged. The comparison is thus between the *composite* views of families and social workers concerned.

Families' circumstances, problems and need for help

On a sizable number of issues the two views were in reasonably close accord, and occasionally the high degree of consensus came as a surprise to us. The accounts that the families gave of their living-situations – the basic facts of family size and structure, their employment situation and occupation, accommodation, the number and whereabouts of children living away from home, how often they had moved and where they originally came from – were all much as the social workers had described them. In other words, and to their credit, the professionals had generally got their facts right.

But it was not just in respect of 'hard' data of this kind that the two accounts tallied. Some retrospective views were also shared. Although there was little evidence that social workers took a traditional social history in respect of each considered child, their accounts of previous separations experienced were echoed by the parents. Death, desertion, imprisonment, boarding education and being in care featured in both stories to a similar degree. Some more subjective views of their present circumstances were also similar. The state of family finances, for example, was not something we attempted to ascertain with any precision, in terms of income or expenditure levels, but we did ask both social workers and families whether there were any financial difficulties. Again there was close agreement and, as in the social worker account, it was Clayport families who more frequently reported financial difficulties. There was in fact no suggestion that social workers were blind or insentive to family hardships of this very basic kind and this too we found encouraging. Table 7.1 makes comparisons between the two views for a few selected items on the circumstances of families.

Table 7.1   Proportions of children living in selected circumstances: family and social-worker versions compared

Family circumstances	Social worker (N = 361) %	Family (N = 270) %
One-parent family	40	39
One-child family	20	17
Four or more children in family	20	17
Owner occupiers	25	29
Council tenants	58	56
Private tenants	6	5
Mother employed	20	20
Father *not* employed	32	35
Financial problems	47	49

NB: All percentages are rounded.

Equally striking - and rather to our surprise - were the shared perceptions of the behaviour of the children. At a stage when only the social-worker schedules had been analysed, we wondered whether the concern being expressed about the behaviour of well over half of the children considered was shared by their families. Although we were told that parents were in fact amongst the main complainants, the role of the police, schools, social services and other agencies also loomed large and it seemed plausible that children's behaviour was being measured according to official standards which parents might not accept. The differences between the two authorities were of special interest here. We were inclined to doubt that Shiptown's children were 'really' so much more troublesome than Clayport's youngsters, as the official version implied, and expected to discover that family views in the two areas had more in common with each other than with those of their social workers. We were wrong. Parents and social workers across the two authorities, and within each one separately, presented an almost identical picture of the extent and nature of behaviour problems, as table 7.2 shows.

What sense can be made of such a convergence of lay and practitioner views? Clearly it brings us no closer to an objective picture of what the children in each authority were 'really' like, because no independent measures or assessments were used. Nevertheless, it must be of

Table 7.2 Proportion of children exhibiting difficult behaviour: family and social-worker versions compared

	All		Clayport		Shiptown	
	Social worker (N = 361) %	Family (N = 210) %	Social worker (N = 166) %	Family (N = 116) %	Social worker (N = 195) %	Family (N = 154) %
Aggressive	27	25	21	21	32	29
Delinquent	22	22	16	16	28	26
Truant	17	15	7	6	26	21
Runaway	12	9	5	5	18	12
Unmanageable	39	41	26	29	51	49

NB: All percentages are rounded.

significance that two important sets of actors in the decision-making process - parents and social workers - shared a view of reality on such a crucial issue as child behaviour, around which so many admission decisions turned. Parents apparently contributed as much to the recognition and definition of problems of 'villainy' as the social workers, and therefore played their part in the different emphases accorded to such problems in the two authorities. The bias towards admission of troublesome teenagers in Shiptown (and the different pattern in Clayport) was evidently not all of the social workers' making. But a distinction has to be made between what parents complained about - the child behaviours (where there was consensus) - and what they hoped would be 'done about' the children (where agreement often broke down) - a point to which we shall return.

It seemed therefore that parents were generally at least as troubled by their children's behaviour as social workers, and it was only in a minority of cases that they denied or challenged official versions of their misdeeds. Furthermore it was they who suffered most directly from its effects. Unlike the social workers, who usually saw themselves as the recipients of complaints from others - the persons to whom bad behaviour was referred - the parents complained loud and long on their own behalf, and often with apparent good reason. The strain of living with disruptive behaviour that they could not explain or control was vividly expressed by numbers of families in both authorities. In Clayport, Sam was said to have 'turned the family into a battleground'.

Richard had been running away, threatening to 'do away with himself', stealing, climbing roofs and bedwetting. Penny was 'having sex, going out at night and running wild'. In fact, 'Penny is bolshy about everything.'

In Shiptown, Terry's mother said,

> My husband ran him up to the police station a couple of times to try and frighten him that way . . . he was aggressive, and I was thinking he was at school, but then we found out he wasn't going and when he *did* go he was a problem.

Paul's mother also talked at length:

> He always seems to attract the wrong type – all the villains [*sic*]. . . . If he watches TV and sees someone being hurt he's really into it. He's vicious . . . he might hit someone out of the blue. . . . He's always been a problem since he was a baby. At two and a half or three he'd go wandering off to look at the trains. He stole milk bottles off doorsteps at ten. . . . He set fire to a yard. . . . He needs 24 hours a day supervision. There's no set pattern to it other than villainy.

Predictably, perhaps, Paul's parents felt some relief when he was admitted to care:

> We realised, without him, how different life could be and realised how disruptive he was. . . . we'd resisted care for a long time and then found how quiet and peaceful it was without him.

On other issues there were disparities in the accounts of families and social workers. Sometimes this was because parents could answer questions and fill in details about past or present circumstances or events where the social workers' knowledge was rather shaky. Information about the extended family and its whereabouts was one such topic. Parents were able to give a more comprehensive picture, and in the process some differences between the two authorities emerged. More parents in Shiptown had kin living nearby and they were in more frequent contact with them: networks seemed tighter-knit. Unhappily this did not necessarily mean better relationships. Shiptown parents also reported being on somewhat worse terms with their relatives, and more than half said relationships were mixed or poor, or at best neutral, whereas the equivalent figure for Clayport was 38 per cent. Perhaps this was a case of familiarity breeding contempt! Where parents and social workers *did* agree was in the significance accorded to different branches of the family. Information about mothers' kin was much more forthcoming than for fathers' relatives – an unsurprising finding, given the absence of so many fathers – and maternal grandparents headed the list of relatives who were nearby and in touch.

The parents' accounts of their own childhoods were also much more revealing than those given by social workers – again with good reason, because it was their *children* who were the main focus of the practitioners' concern. Sadly such accounts were often distressing and even harrowing. Half of the mothers (49 per cent) said they had been separated from their own parents, through death, divorce or other reasons (social workers had thought 20 per cent); a quarter (26 per cent) had had contact with a child-care agency, and nearly one in five (18 per cent) had lived away from home, 'in care', or under some other voluntary or private arrangement. Equivalent figures for fathers were much lower, but too many were not known about to give an accurate picture.

Given such records of disruption, it is not surprising that many parents recalled their childhoods as being unhappy. Indeed, only two out of five mothers (41 per cent) were prepared to say they had been mainly happy, and we were obliged to code some of their most negative answers into two distinct categories – the 'merely' sad and the truly dreadful. On this basis, almost a quarter of mothers (23 per cent) felt they had had sad or dreadful childhoods. Their own words convey this much more adequately than any categories or percentages.

> I went into a children's home in London for two years when my parents split up. Church of England – my Mum couldn't afford to keep us and it wasn't heard of to go to social services then; only nowadays everyone does it – before, it was charity. I hated it in the home. As soon as Mum got a job she got us out and married someone she didn't like to give us a home.

One father, who had been in foster homes, observation and assessment centres, detention centre, Borstal and prison, said,

> Dad beat up my old lady and used to drink a lot. . . . I was close to me Mum, but used to thieve from an early age. . . . I'd never put my kids through what I went through.

A mother described her childhood as

> miserable - because mother was always walking out, there were rows and she said we were no good. *He* was leaving, then *she* was. Me and my sisters always had to do all the housework - she never did any. My sister got married to get out - the other has a baby and is leaving to get out of it. My Dad used to have a go at us because he was unhappy, but now I think he understands how I feel. When I took the overdose my mother said 'why didn't you do it properly?' - if I had a chance I'd do something really horrible to her!

Another mother responded,

> I can always remember our Dad hitting me . . . my Dad tried to interfere with me when my Mum was in hospital [psychiatric] - I was about eleven, and I threw a metal candlestick. . . . I had a dreadful childhood. Mum was always in and out of hospital.

Given such data, it would be tempting to speculate about 'cycles of deprivation' and to assume that childhood separations and trauma beget separations and trauma in the following generation; or that the experience of poor relationships with parents, as a child, makes it difficult to establish good relationships with spouse, kin or own children in adult life. But, despite the very strong impression that our families contained a disproportionate number of parents who had suffered in their own childhoods, evidence of any more precise linkages between past and present difficulties was sometimes contradictory. The parents of children in the cohort who were admitted to care, for example, were no more likely to have been separated from their own parents, or to have been in care themselves, than the parents of children who avoided admission. Indeed, the tendency was rather the other way round, for 23 per cent of mothers of children not admitted had themselves been in care, whereas only 14 per cent of mothers of admitted children had had experience. On the other hand, the intensity of *unhappiness* experienced by parents *did* seem to correlate with an admission to care of their own children for twice as many parents (mothers *and* fathers) of the admitted children described their own childhoods in unhappy terms, and every 'dreadful' description belonged to a parent of an admitted child. Perhaps some of the bitterness and despair which these parents expressed about their own youth had been reawakened and amplified by the recent loss of their own children into care.

In the same way, an attempt to link the parents' accounts of their own childhood with their evaluation of present relationships produced some interesting and contradictory patterns. There was, for instance, no evidence that those who recalled unhappy times were more likely than the rest to complain of a difficult relationship with their child. The percentage of mothers (we have too little data on fathers to be usefully included) who confessed to having a difficult relationship with the child being considered for care was much the same, whether their own childhood had been happy or not.

However, there *were* indications that those who had suffered in childhood were more likely to have difficult relationships with their marital partner and with their kin. A quarter of those with unhappy childhood memories were on poor terms with their relatives (compared with only 7 per cent of the 'happy' group); and half of them were experiencing poor or fragile marital relationships, compared with one in five of those whose childhoods had been good. Benign or vicious circles in terms of relationships did seem to be occurring in the lives of a substantial number of these parents.

Another small piece of history that we sought from parents (though not from social workers) was the circumstances of each considered child's birth. Was it a difficult birth and had any such difficulties involved the separation of child from mother - into a special-care baby unit, for example? 74 out of 259 mothers (28 per cent) said it had been a difficult birth, and for 28 (11 per cent) it had involved early separation. But such difficulties were apparently not reflected in subsequent problems in mother–child relationships - at least according to the mothers' own account. Perversely, mothers who had given birth without difficulty were apparently more likely to be locked in difficult relationships with their offspring than those who had had such difficulties - and twice as likely as those who had been separated from their child at, or soon after, birth. Numbers are very small and we had no independent verification of either kind of difficulty, so no great weight can be placed on such findings. But they do fly in the face of the accepted wisdom, and, if nothing else, suggest that the parents themselves are unacquainted with expert literature on the subject!

The parents' descriptions of their current relationships - with kin, neighbours or spouses, for example - were also somewhat at odds with what the social workers had conveyed. It was not that they denied difficulties altogether: sometimes their descriptions of fraught and wretched relationships were vivid in the extreme. One mother said,

> I got sacked for having black eyes from my husband. . . . Just before the year ended I told Joe I just realised I was pregnant and he kicked me and I think I had a miscarriage - I weren't pregnant any more. In the same year I went to hospital with a cup sticking out of my arm, where he'd thrown it at me.

But, to balance this, they were more likely to mention the good or helpful aspects as well, especially in relation to their spouses. The ups and downs of many relationships, the good sides as well as the bad, were often mentioned. In the words of one couple, 'We're all good mates together - we insult each other right, left and centre!' And, as another put it, 'We get on very well - sometimes!'

Putting the two accounts side by side, the parents' version was less gloomy than that of the social workers, who seemed to stress problems or were quite frequently unable to describe the qualities of some relationships at all. Sometimes it may have been that, for the benefit of the researchers, or to avoid recriminations later, the parents were painting a rosier picture than was warranted. There were certainly occasions, usually when both partners were being interviewed together, when we sensed that the rather favourable account given of their relationship did not match the reality. But, on their side, the social workers' vision seemed too narrowly restricted to the negatives - to what was weak or wrong in the family situation, without acknowledgement of compensating strengths. Thus they reckoned that, of the neighbourly relationships they knew about, a third were poor (the parents said one in ten). Similarly, a quarter of families were thought to be on poor terms with maternal kin, compared wtih the parents' estimate of 10 per cent; and social workers reckoned over half the marital relationships were fragile or poor - double the proportion indicated by the parents.

Although relationships were presented in a rather more favourable light by parents than by social workers, other aspects of their lives looked considerably blacker. On the whole, for example, the families were much more critical of housing and neighbourhood. Nearly a quarter (23 per cent) of those interviewed were unhappy with their accommodation (social workers had been critical of the housing of approximately one in seven families), and more than a quarter (28 per cent) disliked the neighbourhoods in which they lived. There were frequent complaints of damp or decrepit dwellings and of the problems of too little space and shared facilities. One family, amongst many, had 'tried to do everything to get out'; another had 'been asking for a transfer for the last eleven years', without success. One not atypical city couple with a baby had one room and shared bathroom and toilet facilities with ten other people. Another inhabited a cramped, poorly decorated flat which leaked when it rained. At the other extreme, some country-dwellers spoke of their 'idyllic setting' that was nevertheless massively expensive to run and was 'devouring resources'.

Some urban neighbourhoods were specially disliked. They were (accurately) perceived as the dumping-grounds for 'problem' families, or as notorious areas of neglect, decay and vice. Parents despaired of thefts and break-ins – even the washing on the line was said to be unsafe – of blocked drains, rubbish in the streets, prostitutes and drunks, and noisy, nosy or hostile neighbours:

> The area's terrible. My health has deteriorated since being here.
>
> This is a rough area. Neighbours throw things at the dog.
>
> We've never liked the area. People poke their nose.
>
> The neighbours are not trustworthy here.

But, as always, there were those who appreciated the selfsame districts: 'People in the block are really great.'

For its part, 'idyllic' rural living created special difficulties for numbers of families. There were complaints of isolation, transport difficulties, lack of support, or intrusive attention:

> There's no regular bus service.
>
> We're very cut off here and feel bad at having had to ask for lifts for four years.
>
> This is a very cliquey village. You've got to fit in.
>
> It's a bit like living in a goldfish bowl.

Where people lived clearly affected all aspects of their lives and assumed an importance to the families themselves that was not always acknowledged by their social workers. Perhaps this apparent insensitivity was not through lack of imagination, but because it was something they had little power to improve or change. They may well have shared implicitly some of the helpless, hopeless feelings about altering their environment that many families actually expressed.

Poor health was another factor which the families emphasised a good deal more than the social workers. More than a third of the mothers (35 per cent) reckoned they were in poor health at the time their children were being considered for care (the social workers had thought this applied to one in ten); and one in five fathers (20 per cent) made a similar complaint (social workers estimated only 4 per cent). 'Health', whether good or poor, was not measured objectively in either case; it was subjective perceptions that were being recorded. But there is little doubt that the daily demands of raising children on low incomes, in poor surroundings and often without an adult partner to share the task taxed the physical and mental health of many of the parents we interviewed. A number were understandably worn down and apathetic, retaining little energy or resilience with which to face the inevitable crises of their lives.

Similarly, although social workers had alerted us to the high levels of unemployment amongst families and to the number of fathers who, though in work, worked away from home for long stretches of time, the parents gave greater emphasis to its effects. The stress upon marital and parental relationships of long-term unemployment (over half of the out-of-work fathers had been so for over a year, and this was especially marked in Clayport) and of working away or at unsocial hours were frequently described.

Given the different emphases and interpretations that families gave to some aspects of their lives, it was predictable that their perceptions of the nature and extent of their problems did not match exactly that of the social workers. At the extreme, there was an often-vociferous minority of parents (13 per cent) who denied having any 'problem' at all - something that social workers were prepared to acknowledge in only a handful of cases.

There are no problems. The only problem was that social services thought there *was* a problem!

We were not *asking* for help.

There are no major problems that the family cannot deal with.

More equivocally, one parent said,

> I didn't need any help - I can help myself. The only help I need is for my drinking.

For others, their difficulties were described in much simpler or more moderate terms than a social worker would have used. One woman reckoned her problem as 'not keeping the place tidy' - 'a slight understatement', as the researcher himself observed, in brackets, on the interview schedule!

Even where parents gave a more comprehensive account, they were in general (and not surprisingly) rather less likely than social workers to see difficulties in terms of their child's health and development and their own shortcomings as parents, and more inclined to put things the other way round: to emphasise their own poor health and to blame their *child's* behaviour. For example, parents saw the child's development as a central issue in only 8 per cent of cases, compared with the social workers' 31 per cent, and mentioned their own problems of physical and emotional care or control of their children in 37 per cent of cases, compared with the social workers' 52 per cent. So, for one mother her problem lay in her children's wilful refusal to accept her control, but the social worker's definition was one of suspected non-accidental injury.

But the mismatch was by no means universal, and there was evidence that many parents shared the social workers' perceptions, to a degree if not in their entirety. Indeed, many parents were very self-critical:

> I was starting to hit Michael - just tapping him, but beginning to feel I could wring his neck.

> Emotionally and physically I wasn't coping with Helen. There was no physical violence, but I did hit rock bottom because of the divorce and worries over accommodation.

> There was no one to help. My Mum had her own problems at the time and there were no friends I could call on. I was really desperate - I ended up down my sister's beating Cliff up something rotten.

Even one very embittered mother, who was highly critical of her social worker and of the department as a whole, admitted,

> They want Mickey in care because they say I'm not a fit mother. Well I'm *not* a fit mother, not compared to other mothers. I think it's because I'm still young and still want my freedom.

The parents' accounts of how they and their problems came to the attention of the social-services departments – and what they felt about it – were also revealing. A third (34 per cent) had referred themselves, and another 20 per cent, though referred by others, were aware that this was going to happen and were generally happy about it. So a little over half of the parents had actually sought help from the social-services department or had consented to others' doing so on their behalf. In contrast, over a third (36 per cent) resented the fact that others had engineered the intervention, sometimes without their knowledge. There were also a few cases (7 per cent) where it was the child who had asked for help, and the parents felt threatened and aggrieved by this. An even smaller, though none the less disturbing, number (2 per cent) seemed quite unaware that they were known to the social-services department at all. They had apparently been the subjects of distant or anonymous surveillance rather than identifiable contact or help.

The wide range of feelings engendered by the referral process is captured in a few of the answers that we elicited:

> I didn't know anything about it until the social worker came and said they were putting Teresa into care. I was very upset.

> It was the school that contacted them. I was blooming sick, annoyed –all the feelings going!

> I don't know how the social-services department came to hear – I thought it was shoddy.

> The police referred. We didn't like it, but when you go to court you have to have someone to speak up for them [the children].

> The police referred. It was a necessity – Kevin was getting out of control.

> The health visitor put me in touch. I'd no objection – I was clutching at any straw.

Two 'abusing' parents reacted quite differently. Mrs P. was angry and humiliated when Olive went to the department, alleging her mother had hit her, since she felt she was being put in the wrong when she was only trying to bring her daughter under control. Mr B., on the other hand, was glad that the school had contacted the department when they spotted handmarks on Simon. He admitted he had 'lost control' and regretted what he had done. 'I'm not angry with the school – not at all. I'm glad they contacted social services.' In his case, intervention was apparently a relief.

Some other referrals, however, seem to have been made on more dubious grounds. Mrs G., for example, was referred by the DHSS, according to her because she 'needed a rest, and to get rid of her TV'! No doubt her expectations of the help she would receive were somewhat unrealistic in consequence.

We were also anxious to learn what other sources of help had been tried, before contact with social-services departments had been made. A number of statutory services might be expected to offer relevant help with family problems, and, in addition, present national policies stress the advantages of informal and non-statutory networks of support. It was interesting to see to what extent these other networks had already come into play and whether they had proved useful, or insufficient. Apart from the health service, in all its many guises, which had been contacted by roughly one in five, no other service or set of individuals had been approached by more than a small minority of the parents interviewed. Even relatives were rarely contacted, for only 12 per cent of families claimed to have asked their kin for help, and even fewer – 7 per cent – had looked to friends and neighbours for support. Even where help *had* been requested, it was, as like as not, seen as inadequate or not forthcoming. The highest proportion of 'successful' contacts with other helpers had been to health services and to the penal services (mainly police and probation officers). For the rest, the negatives equalled or outweighed the positives.

> My ex-husband was no help. He said 'put him in a home'!
>
> I went to the Housing Department originally, and got nowhere.
>
> We tried the school, GP, Educational Psychologist and Probation Officer. There were termly interviews with the Educational Psychologist and lots of hand-wringing in between.
>
> Both grandmothers helped a lot – but it was not enough.

For some, alternative sources of help were seen as inappropriate, or inferior to what the social-services department could offer: 'I don't believe in others knowing my business'; 'Friends could have looked after the children, but I couldn't have paid them, and the kids would have been split up.'

For others, there was simply no alternative: 'I automatically thought of my social worker. When you are a single parent they are the natural people to talk to.' Or, more bleakly: 'There isn't anyone.'

In sum, a rich reservoir of alternative means of support was certainly not evident to most of the families we interviewed, and the usefulness and benevolence of kin and neighbours cannot be taken for granted.

Social workers' help

The kind of help parents anticipated or wanted from the *social workers* gives some idea of how their role and the resources they can call upon appear in the families' eyes. We were struck by the wide range of responses to our question. There was a substantial minority (17 per cent) who wanted nothing – either because they reckoned they had no problems, or because social workers and their departments were seen as inappropriate, intrusive or worse: 'Nothing. The best thing they can do is keep away.'

An equally sizable group *wanted* help, but were very confused and unclear about what form it might take, or what indeed might prove helpful to them: 'I don't know what I was looking for'; 'I've very little idea. I don't want to be a burden to the social worker.'

For the majority, however, there were hopes or expectations that the social workers might tackle problems in a variety of ways. Some saw them as influential go-betweens who could put pressure on other agencies or individuals. They wanted 'the social worker's backing for a council house'; 'help to put pressure on the doctor to get Terry's medication right.'

They also looked for legal and financial advice. Indeed, 'advice' was frequently mentioned, sometimes coupled with notions of support and the value of someone to talk to:

> I was looking for advice.
>
> I wanted someone to talk to. Someone older to advise.
>
> Support in terms of someone I can talk to regularly.
>
> Regular social-work contact. . . . I laid it on thick about the problems, in case the social-service department took no notice.

This emphasis on *regularity* of contact was in fact further reinforced when we came to the follow-up stage and found many parents disappointed and let down by the infrequency and unpredictability of social workers' visit – a point to which we shall return.

For other parents, it was mediation in difficult personal relationships that was wanted. A few parents, for example, were quite clear about seeking help with their marriage. More often, however, social workers were expected to 'sort out' the unacceptable behaviour of others - most usually the child: 'We wanted something to straighten her out'; 'I just more or less thought he [the social worker] would be able to *do* something with Andy.'

The different parental views on what it was that social workers might in fact 'do' illustrates the variety of roles they may be expected or persuaded to play. Some parents were seeking to understand the behaviour and sought the social worker's help in this: 'We couldn't make it out. . . . I wanted social services mainly to talk to Karl and get to the reason for his non-school attendance.' - and she added, showing that social workers' efforts do not always have to be 'successful' to be appreciated, 'They didn't get to the bottom of it, but did their best.'

Some wanted advice on how to handle the behaviour itself:

> We were just way out of our depth. They said using a belt wasn't the answer to the problem. When I was brought up, our Dad had a camel whip - so we hadn't thought it wrong to use it. They said, 'There are other ways. This hasn't worked, so try *our* way', which I thought very logical.

Others, again, were clearly wanting to use the social worker as disciplinarian and threat: 'We wanted to frighten Sam into thinking that he might go away if he didn't stop stealing. We wanted the social worker to come and give him a good talking to.'

Sometimes it was actually removal of the child which was wanted:

> I was asking them to put Sally somewhere.

> I want Robin in boarding school but they just don't want to know because of the financial reasons. Doctor said it would cost £50,000. . . . If he broke in and stole something, they'd soon find him somewhere then.

Even removal meant different things to different families. Some wanted 'help - not punishment. Training and treatment.' Others felt the opposite: 'You've got to frighten her into acting properly. The place is an open house. I was expecting a bit of discipline.'

Admission to care was, in fact, the principal form of help wanted by one in five parents, and many others included it as one amongst several measures which they hoped would be available. By no means all these were parents of troublesome children. Many simply wanted admission because of circumstances such as their own poor health, or housing-problems. Others desperately sought it for their own peace of mind and the safety of their children.

> I wanted William taken into care because I couldn't cope. I thought I was going to kill him.
>
> They should be put away from here. I'm frightened of what I might do to them. My mind goes blank when I hit them.

Social workers as gatekeepers to the care system were obviously of crucial importance to many parents in our sample.

It remains to explore how far what the social workers offered measured up to parental expectations. What, for instance, did they think of the decisions that were made and of how they were reached? The majority - approaching two-thirds - expressed at least some measure of satisfaction. They reckoned that the social workers had shared their own perceptions of the 'problem', at least in part, and they had responded to some, if not all of what the parents wanted. A rather smaller majority of parents (58 per cent) felt they themselves had had some influence on the decisions reached. In contrast, approximately a third were conspicuously dissatisfied - feeling their problems had been wholly misunderstood, that decisions had been taken right out of their hands, and that the action that had (or had not) been taken was against their wishes. There was also a small but nevertheless disturbing group who were quite unaware that their children had been considered for care and were ignorant of any decisions that had been taken about them.

The qualities and attitudes of the social workers, which were part and parcel of these feelings of satisfaction or dissatisfaction, were often made very clear. The ability to *listen* was rated very highly: 'She guided me all the way through, and was a very good listener'; 'He was a nice man to talk to.'

Informality and a natural, 'human' approach that included real sharing of feeling was also often appreciated.

> She is interested in me. We've become quite good friends - more than just a social worker.

> She's almost part of the family. She came to the baby's funeral and I told her off for crying, because she was trained not to.
>
> She'd say 'bloody' and smoke like anyone else. She'd say - look, I'm being my real self - you can be yours - and this made her easy to talk to.

But friendly informality without the necessary help was *not* appreciated! 'She's a complete and utter waste of time . . . though quite a nice person. But she doesn't seem to be doing anything practical. She just has a coffee and a fag and goes!'

Practical help was in fact highly valued, but so too was the more intangible support described in some of the quotations above, and put more succinctly by one mother: 'It's the social worker herself who is the help.'

Honesty and directness was also important: parents liked to know where they stood, even when what they were told was unpalatable. The mother in a case of incest said, 'She's given me full information and has been very honest and has answered me very fully, everything I've asked: very much moral and emotional support.'

Parental dissatisfactions clustered around some of the opposite qualities or attitudes: failure to listen to their point of view, 'taking over', and what was seen as evasiveness or deceitfulness:

> They were too pushy, and tried to tell me what to do.
>
> If you call people in to help, you expect them to help. But they've just taken full control.
>
> I'm very wary of her . . . when she visits I wonder what she's got up her sleeve.

One mother of a violent teenager was specially eloquent about the dissonance between her own perceptions and those of the social worker:

> When he came, I really felt they'd waded in in wellington boots. My mother died four weeks before. He says I'm very unfeeling because he thought I looked very blank when the boy left. But I'd watched my mother die and then had the problems with Derek - I was under an awful lot of pressure. I feel he [the social worker] overworks himself and gets very wrapped up in what he's feeling and is less concerned about what *you're* feeling. At one time I seriously felt like asking for

another social worker – he seemed to be playing people off against each other . . . saying something to Derek and that would stir *him* up. And then saying something else to me or my husband – it's difficult to explain. He wasn't entirely straight . . . though obviously it might be his way. I'd never go to social services again.

The main issues raised

So far we have compared parental and social-worker perspectives on the whole cohort of considered children. It remains to look at some of the main issues that are raised when the family data is broken down into some of our major sub-categories: the admitted children and those not admitted to care; the voluntarily received and those removed compulsorily; the 'villains' and the 'victims'; and the two sample authorities.

First, do the parental accounts shed any fresh light on why some children were admitted and others not? Like the views of the social workers, most differences between the two groups tend to be faint and of no statistical significance, though they nevertheless make sense. For example, problems of relationships and behaviour were rather more prominent for the admitted children, whereas practical, financial and environmental difficulties – low incomes, unemployment, poor housing, for example – loomed larger in the not-admitted group. It appears logical that the former problems should be the more likely precipitators of an admission; the latter, the background factors to which other solutions are sometimes available, or to which admission is really no answer. Similarly, parents of children who were not admitted claimed to have slightly closer and better contacts with kin and neighbours and to have been marginally more successful in rallying help from such sources. Presumably, such help was sometimes enough to avert an admission.

More striking was the fact that parents confirmed that admitted children were twice as likely to have been in care previously, and to this they added information about their own backgrounds. As we have seen, the parents of admitted children were twice as likely to remember their own childhoods with sadness or despair. We can only speculate about the meaning of the connection. Was their own childhood impoverishment a factor in their failure to hold on to their own children? Or did the recent loss of a child bring these sad memories to the surface?

More unequivocally, the parents *did* reveal some important differences in their definition of problems, their attitudes to the referral process and in their hopes and expectations of the social workers. For example, no less than one in five of the not-admitted group claimed they had no problems at all, compared with only 6 per cent where the child was subsequently admitted. To some extent, therefore, social workers seem to have taken them at their word! In tune with this denial of difficulties, a third of the 'not admitted' parents expressed considerable anger at having been referred to social services in the first place, whereas the predominant feeling amongst parents of admitted children was one of relief. Contrasting patterns of response were also evident when parents were asked to specify the help they required. Not surprisingly, parents of the not-admitted group were twice as likely to say they wanted no help at all – but they were *also* twice as likely to be unclear about what they needed or could expect. Nearly half of this group of parents responded in one or other of these two ways. In other words, they could contribute only a negative, or very unclear, sense of direction to their negotiations with the social workers. In contrast, a third of parents of the admitted group said it was, first and foremost, *admission to care* that they wanted, whereas less than one in ten of the other parents identified admission as the form of help they required.

There is evidence, therefore, that parental wishes and feelings can have an influence on child-care decisions and that their own definition of problems and hoped-for solutions can play a part in shaping eventual outcomes. That this is only part of the story, and that many parents feel powerless and resentful, has already been demonstrated, but becomes more pointed when we compare those who were admitted by the voluntary route with those who were propelled into care by courts, magistrates or the police.

The experience and responses of the parents of these two groups of admitted children do, in fact, throw up some sharp and consistent contrasts, in addition to the rather different range of problems and family circumstances which were also evident in the social workers' accounts. It was clear that the parents of the volunteered were more likely to have played an active part in seeking social-work help and were happier to have been referred by others where this was not the case. They were also more inclined to feel that social workers shared their own view of what their problems were, and that they themselves had considerable influence over the decisions that were made. The majority, after all, had wanted their children to be admitted to care. In fact, the participation in the decision-making which the legal provision for reception into care presupposes was a reality for the majority of these parents.

For their part, the parents of the children who had been removed compulsorily were a far more disgruntled group, and table 7.3 illustrates this point. Half of them had been referred to social services by others, without their consent or approval; some denied that they had a problem, and only a minority believed that the social worker shared their own view of what their problems were. The majority also felt that they had little or no influence on the decisions that had been made. A minority said they had wanted their child to be admitted - though it is worth nothing that one in five *did* want admission, which raises the question of whether compulsion was really necessary in every case.

The aggravation caused by unwanted or, as they saw it, inappropriate intervention was further compounded for the compulsory group by

Table 7.3 *Referrals, problems and decisions: some comparisons between the views of parents of voluntarily and compulsorily admitted children*

	Voluntary admissions (N = 56) %	Compulsory admissions (N = 75) %
Self-referred	39⎫	23⎫
Referred by others with parental	⎬62	⎬34
approval	23⎭	11⎭
Positively *no* help wanted	5	17
Admission to care wanted	61	19
Social worker shares family's perception of problems (at least in part)	70	29
Social worker disagrees with family's perception of problems	4	39
Parents claim much influence over eventual decision	58	19
Parents claim little or no influence over eventual decision	18	55

NB: All percentages are rounded.

the way in which the admission of the child was actually effected (see table 7.4) Half of the parents of the volunteered said they had accompanied their children to their first placement – not perhaps a very satisfactory proportion, given the importance of supporting children through change by maintaining links with familiar adults. This was, however, considerably better than the compulsories, and there were

Table 7.4 Experience of the admission process: comparison of voluntary and compulsory admissions

	Voluntary admissions (N = 56) %	Compulsory admissions (N = 75) %
Parent accompanied child to placement	48	15
Pre-placement visit made	21	5
Access banned or restricted	18	56
Circumstantial (inadvertent) restrictions on access	45	12
Visiting achieved	48	63

NB: All percentages are rounded.

similar contrasts in the number who actually managed a pre-placement visit or who had at least prior knowledge of their child's destination. (For the compulsories this was normally residential care; for the volunteered it was more often a foster home.)

Indignation about the removal itself was keenest for the group whose children had been take into care under a Place of Safety Order. In nine out of ten cases there was no discussion with parents about the child's destination, and hardly any parents accompanied their children into care. Inevitably, some children were not even escorted by an adult whom they knew, but were taken to an unknown placement by a strange duty social worker or by an unfamiliar police officer. Hence the terms 'Gestapo', 'SS' and even '1984' were used by a few parents to describe such interventions, and at least one family spoke bitterly of the removal of their son in handcuffs.

Restrictions – or even a total ban on access – were imposed on many more parents of the compulsory group (one in ten claimed they were banned from seeing their children), which in turn gave rise to more discontent with access arrangements. But the voluntary group had their own difficulties in keeping in touch, though these were largely circumstantial and inadvertent and arose out of parental illness, poverty, and travelling-problems associated with distant placements. Paradoxically, it was therefore the parents of the compulsory group, chafing under social-services restrictions, who were nevertheless more likely to visit their children. The volunteered needed more than an absence of explicit restrictions to help them maintain contact; they needed positive help, which was rarely forthcoming – a point to which we shall return at the follow-up stage.

Within the compulsory group there were also 'victims' and 'villains'. The parental perspectives associated with these two groups differed in similar ways to those of their social workers, though we gained some fresh insights as well. The attitudes of victims' parents tended to cluster at one of two extremes. Either they denied problems, resented interference (a quarter wanted no help at all) and were fiercely defensive; or they were desperate for help and actually sought admission for their children, and examples of this have already been quoted. The villains' parents were more ambivalent. They were usually concerned about their children's behaviour and were anxious for help, but were frequently unclear what form it should take and often had mixed or angry feelings about what had in fact occurred. For some the intervention had been too harsh – for others, too soft – and, again, examples had been quoted. The figures bear out the strong impression that their words made: parents of troublesome children are generally insistent that 'something should be done' but are often unhappy with the consequences of official intervention.

In sum, therefore, the parents of children who tread the compulsory path into care are often at odds with social workers from the start, and this is obviously one reason why the law is used against them, thus increasing the confrontation and the conflict. But by no means all of them deny their difficulties or are averse to intervention or even to admission to care, and the compulsory process itself involves much more potential trauma for the child than most voluntary admissions. The choice of legal route is therefore crucial to both the child and his parents and to their future relationship with social workers and their departments.

Finally, what did the parents think of the two departments with which they had become involved? Given the different patterns of practice in the two authorities, how did the families concerned react? In general their responses reflect quite faithfully the biases towards compulsion and voluntarism in Shiptown and Clayport respectively. Thus Shiptown's parents were the more disaffected and the more inclined to talk of a 'take-over', whereas a larger proportion of parents in Clayport felt they had participated in problem-sharing and the decision-making that had occurred. Table 7.5 shows that more Clayport parents had referred themselves or had approved of others doing so on their behalf. Slightly more believed the social worker shared their own view of their problems, and only half as many thought they had no influence whatsoever on the decisions that had been made. Their experiences of the admission procedures were also in sharp contrast to

Table 7.5   Parental responses in the two authorities
(a) *Problems and decisions*

	Clayport (N = 116) %	Shiptown (N = 154) %
Self-referred	40	30
Referred by others with parental approval	24	18
Social worker disagreed with family view of problem	23	32
Parents had *no* influence on eventual decision	19	38

(b) *Admission experience*

	Clayport (N = 43) %	Shiptown (N = 88) %
Parent accompanied child into care	45 ⎫	24 ⎫
Familiar social worker accompanied child into care	39 ⎭ 84	24 ⎭ 48
Parent knew child's destination	79	51
Pre-placement visit made	32	3
Restrictions on access imposed	21	52
Visiting achieved	47	62

NB: All percentages are rounded.

those of Shiptown parents. Many more Clayport children were accompanied into care by their parents, or at the very least by a social worker they already knew. More knew where they were going, and ten times the proportion had actually made a pre-placement visit. Restrictions on access were only half as likely to be imposed as they were in Shiptown, but – the paradox again – visiting by parents to children (or vice versa) was actually more likely to happen in Shiptown than in Clayport. The unwitting restrictions that hampered access to children in voluntary care dominated the visiting-pattern in Clayport, and neither authority apparently did much to overcome these, for only two sets of parents – one in each authority – said their social workers had actually *helped* them over visiting.

In Shiptown, therefore, the stage seemed set for considerable conflict between parents and the social-services departments; in Clayport something closer to a consensus model prevailed. How this worked out in practice, over a longer time-span, is the subject of our follow-up material. For the present we shall attempt, in the following chapter, to summarise and make some sense of the complicated patterns of decision-making and practice that have emerged.

8

Weaving Threads or Tying Knots?

In the previous five chapters, child-care decisions in the two sample authorities have been looked at in a number of different ways. We have examined the circumstances and characteristics of the children who were considered for care; the decisions that were made about them; the processes by which they came to be considered, and decisions were reached; and the policies and principles which played some part in shaping those decisions. We have also attempted to incorporate the perspectives of both the service-providers (and in particular, the social workers at field level) and the parents (usually the mothers) of the children in question. On the way, we have tried to understand why practice is not apparently uniform, but varies from place to place. It now remains to conclude this section by drawing together the many threads and trying to make sense of the pattern as a whole.

First, there is the question of 'needs' and how far their quality and quantity determine the outcome of decisions: a deceptively simple question about a far from simple concept! If we begin with our choice of sample authorities, our assumption was that, because of their similarity on a whole range of social indicators, their child-care needs might be much the same. The differences between them – at least in so far as the cities at their heart were concerned – were generally slight and their particular stress points seemed to balance up and complement each other. Needs, as they were presented to and perceived by the sample teams showed that the social indicators which had guided our choice were of some relevance. It was clear that the children who were referred shared certain characteristic features. They were more likely than not to come from disrupted families at the bottom end of the social-class spectrum, where relationships within and beyond the family were strained or fractured and where economic hardship was common. But, within this framework, at least three rough categories of children in need of care could be identified. There were those whose behaviour was troublesome and for whom 'control' was both a private (i.e. family) and a public issue - the 'villains'. There were those whose care was judged so inadequate or damaging that they were believed to need protection and rescue - the 'victims'. And there were those whose parents faced circumstances or misfortunes which prevented them from caring for their children on a temporary or permanent basis - the 'volunteered'. On the basis of even this very rough-and-ready classification, the 'need for care' was plainly not unidimensional, but in reality a complex tangle of different kinds of (overlapping) need for different kinds of (overlapping) care.

When the monitoring data for our sample authorities were compared, considerable differences of emphasis were apparent in relation to these various aspects of need. Villains were predominant in Shiptown; the victims and the volunteered showed up more prominently in Clayport. To a limited extent, therefore, what the social workers were faced with in terms of children referred and considered for care was a reflection of the indicators of need in the areas they served. Thus, victims and volunteered were particularly liable to suffer economic hardship - the Clayport bias; and villains were more likely to enjoy *relative* prosperity, but to have histories of family disruption - the Shiptown bias. Quite evidently there is some relationship between the stress and risk-producing features of an area and the character and extent of referrals that a social-services department receives, and it would be odd if it were otherwise.

Nevertheless, the particular prominence of villains in Shiptown's cohort of considered children seemed to warrant further explanation. The contrast with Clayport was striking. The behaviour of nearly two thirds of its considered group was complained about, compared with less than half of Clayport's children; and delinquents, truants, runaways and the disruptives were all apparently at least twice as numerous. We looked at some 'independent' measures of juvenile delinquency in the two cities, to make comparisons. In the year 1980 the rate of children identified as offenders (i.e. those prosecuted plus those who were cautioned) was somewhat higher in Shiptown than in Clayport - about 40 per 1,000 10–17 year olds, compared with 34 per 1,000. Prosecution rates also followed this pattern - 18 per 1,000

10-17 year olds, compared with 13 per 1,000.[1] To this extent Shiptown appeared the more villainous city, and this impression was amplified by folklore and the comments of some residential workers who received delinquents from both authorities. Shiptown youths were perceived as tougher and more street-wise than their Clayport counterparts, and the hooliganism of the Shiptown football fans was legendary.

Such established indicators and anecdotal evidence are not, of course, any firmer measures of the 'real' extent of villainy than the accounts of the social-services departments themselves. Delinquency rates depend upon reporting and detection rates, and the police exercise wide discretion over decisions to prosecute. This last point was illustrated in our two authorities. Cautioning-rates were higher in Clayport than in Shiptown (60 per cent compared with something over 50 per cent) and analysis of a year's cases coming before each court showed that the more serious offences (of burglary, assault, criminal damage, and taking and driving away) formed half of the total in Clayport but only a third in Shiptown.[2] More vigorous diversion can plainly mean that the courts deal with proportionately more cases at the heavier end of juvenile delinquency. This may account for their disposals in the same year, as Clayport's courts sent almost twice as many youths into the penal system (to detention centres and Borstals) as Shiptown's. Paradoxically, therefore, to the *courts*, villainy may have appeared a more serious problem in Clayport than in Shiptown.

How then can our analysis of the influence of 'needs' on decisions be carried forward? If we stay with juvenile villainy as the aspect of child care which distinguishes our authorities most sharply from one another, we are persuaded by all the evidence that the youth of Shiptown may indeed be rather more troublesome than their Clayport counterparts, and that the activities of the social-services departments are some reflection of this. Nevertheless, the *degree* to which they are more problematic defies precise measurement and seems in any case to be relatively modest. Established social indicators had certainly not alerted us to the striking differences which emerged.

Needs or social problems are not, of course, immutable but are social constructs which vary in dimension and character according to who is defining them. Thus in the field of juvenile offending and general troublesomeness, the police are important and powerful definers of problems. It was no surprise to find, therefore, that the constabularies in the two authorities operated in rather different ways. Clayport's Chief Constable had established a clear policy of 'community policing' which laid stress on preventive strategies and on consultation and collaboration with other services, as well as with the communities themselves. The Shiptown police, in contrast, adopted a more traditional approach. In the juvenile sphere this meant that Clayport's social workers were drawn into consultation *before* decisions about cautioning or a court appearance had been made, whereas Shiptown social workers received their police referrals at a later stage, when the police had already made a preliminary decision in the matter.

Such differences undoubtedly had an effect on which young people, and how many, were perceived as villains in need of the attention of social services and were consequently pointed in their direction. But this is not to say that social-services departments are simply the passive recipients of needs, as defined by others. Quite clearly they play a part in establishing the boundaries between themselves and other agencies and in defining their own role in relation to social problems. Although we found no evidence of an established and explicit *policy* about villains in the Shiptown department, the expectation that it was there to deal with them in large numbers (as expressed for example by the extent of its residential resources) must have owed something to its own attitudes and actions, as well as those of the individuals and agencies who referred. Had it wished to change or challenge the pattern, there was at least a possibility of doing so.

The families themselves are also important definers of need and their perceptions were equally fascinating. We saw that there was a very close correlation between their own views about the troublesomeness of their children and those of the officials. Definitions were not apparently imposed from without, but shared – though what was *done* about the behaviour was not so readily agreed. It was also our impression that Shiptown parents not only grumbled more about their wayward teenagers, but also more often displayed a preference for calling in the police to deal with them, sometimes setting in train drastic action which they may not have anticipated or wanted. We were told many times of the beneficial effects of a 'nasty fright'. A good 'telling-off' by the police fell into this category, and several parents regularly resorted to the local police station with their erring offspring in tow. The families' perceptions were no doubt shared by others in their neighbourhoods and may have been representative of widespread community attitudes. In this sense, lay definitions of need put considerable pressure upon concerned agencies.

From the evidence of only two local authorities our tentative conclusions would therefore be the following. Children who 'need' admission to local-authority care are of many different, though related, kinds. Because they tend to come from an identifiable section of the population and have certain material and family disadvantages in common, social indicators derived from the Census and the Office of Population Studies can give a very crude idea of where needy children are likely to be concentrated and which local authorities are therefore liable to be under the most pressure. Sophisticated statistical calculations could doubtless also allow for the fact that not all child-care needs are associated with the same social factors, so that a formula which allowed for villains, victims and the volunteered, or, ideally, more elaborate and subtle manifestations of child-care need, could be developed.

What cannot be easily measured or predicted is the *local* definition of need that operates in an authority – or, more accurately, within particular *communities* within that authority. Such definitions seem to us to derive from the interaction between the perceptions of laymen – both potential consumers and concerned or complaining 'others' – and a whole range of officials and their agencies. Between them, and over time, a local pattern of needs and service responses tends to set in. We suspect that such culturally defined needs can be hard to shift and change, because so many actors are parties to their definition and this may account for some of the historical continuities in child-care figures that can be observed.

Thus, the pressures exerted on social-services departments (referral rates) and those that they impose on themselves (numbers of children seriously considered for care) may be the nearest we can get to meaningful measures of local needs. On this basis, we can see that there was in fact some relationship between such pressures and the decisions that were eventually made, but that it was not the whole story. The *responses* of the social services were also important, and it is to these that we now turn.

How the two social-services departments responded to the differential pressures placed upon them in the monitoring year was looked at in several ways. First, there was the organisational response: how the departments were structured and where decisions were made, in theory and in practice. We saw that, superficially, the departments were very alike, being organised on a three-tier basis with considerable managerial autonomy at the second (area) tier, which owed something to the previously independent status of the two one-time county boroughs. There was a similar mixture of specialist posts at county, area and district levels, the same difficulties over the ambiguous role of advisers, and a shared structure of small teams of social workers, led by seniors, at the operational level. The three major differences were the way the workloads of teams were organised; arrangements for duty in out-of-office hours; and the level at which decisions on child-care admissions were meant to be made.

So far as the teams were concerned, Clayport's geographically based system, with each team serving a separately defined area, contrasted with Shiptown's mixed model, in which several teams served the same geographical area but work was divided between them, either by a rotating duty system, or functionally by means of intake and long-term teams. Could such differences account for differences in the decisions made? Our evidence on this, as on so many issues, is inconclusive. Clayport's pattern *may* have made some contribution to its lower rate of admissions. Arguments for patch-based systems do, after all, emphasise their preventive potential, based on strong community links.[3] But only one of the Clayport teams we studied could be said to serve anything approaching a single, identifiable 'community' and, tantalisingly, its proportion of considered children admitted in the monitoring year was not the lowest in the sample. For the rest, their patch was large, heterogeneous, and nothing like the community models in the literature. We saw, too, that patterns of decision-making in Shiptown's intake and long-term teams looked very similar, so we had no evidence there that organisational structure had any overriding effect on outcomes. The caveat – as with all our team-based material – is that numbers of cases were generally small, so apparent similarities or differences must be treated with caution.

For out-of-office hours, Clayport had no social-worker cover during the study period, though one or two area managers were 'on call' for other agencies to contact in emergencies. Shiptown, in contrast, had a special Emergency Duty Team. Predictably, perhaps, more admissions to care were effected out of office hours in Shiptown than in Clayport (17 per cent, compared with 10 per cent) – a hint that if a service is provided it will be used! But, perversely, it was also in

Shiptown that *extra*-departmental decisions were made much more frequently. The number of Place of Safety Orders initiated by the police, for example, far outstripped those in Clayport, though it might have been anticipated that the reverse would be the case. In this, police policies and practice seem to have been more powerful determinants of outcome than the organisational niceties of the departments themselves.

The third, and perhaps the most interesting, difference between the two departments was the organisational level at which most decisions about admissions were supposed to be taken. In Clayport this was set firmly within the team and involved the social worker in consultation with his senior. In Shiptown, team decisions had to be referred upwards to the district manager for endorsement – and this was conceived as more than mere rubber-stamping, for the explicit intention was thereby to cut down on unnecessary admissions to care. In practice, we saw that in both authorities there was only partial compliance with the official version of decision-making. Team-leaders were not always consulted in Clayport, and managers in Shiptown were quite often bypassed. This in itself tells us something about the relative strengths of the front-line professionals and those who manage them – a point to which we shall return.

The effects of these different procedures upon the decisions taken are hard to interpret. There was a tendency for patterns of admission (i.e. the proportion admitted and the legal routes of entry) to be similar in teams within the same *districts* of Shiptown, whereas there was no such consistency within the Clayport districts. Here teams varied, and varied independently of where they were situated. This suggests that Shiptown's managerial oversight does indeed have some standardising effect, though differences *between* districts are still considerable. In other words, the unit of variability is shifted upwards in the system, but does not disappear.

More crucially, did Shiptown's system succeed in reducing admissions to care, as it was meant to do? Once again, the answer must be equivocal. Admissions rates had apparently not declined since 1978, and Shiptown's numbers in care remained at the high level they had occupied since the early seventies. What we could not know was whether they had actually been checked and would have gone on rising, but for the system that had been introduced. Ironically it was Clayport, with its greater degree of social-worker autonomy, that had succeeded in pulling down its admission rate, albeit fitfully, since the mid seventies. It was, however, the case in *both* authorities that social-worker consultation with superiors - whether team-leaders or managers - was most likely to occur in cases where children were kept *out* of care. So some kind of check on social workers' decisions may act as a brake, and marginally reduce admissions, though whether the particular form of oversight chosen is related in any direct way to outcomes remains an open question.

A second major area of departmental response that we explored was the decisions themselves. Here again, there were local-authority and team differences, both in the proportion of considered children admitted and in the legal gateways that were used. What sense could be made of such differences, and how far could the social-services departments be held accountable for them?

As we have indicated already, variations at the team level - though intriguing - have to be treated with caution because of the small numbers involved and the restricted timescale of one year. The busiest team considered 48 children during that period, but two others had fewer than 20 cases each. The *degree* of difference in the proportion of considered cases admitted, even at the local-authority level, also needs to be handled with care. What was meant by a 'serious consideration' was carefully worked out, and social workers were regularly reminded of the definition, but interpretations may still have varied. A serious consideration for some may have been regarded as too trivial to be included by others, and the resulting ratio of admissions to considerations could be affected. But individual idiosyncracies should have cancelled each other out, and we have no evidence to suggest that one authority applied a consistently narrower (or broader) interpretation than the other. So, though we place no great weight on the precise extent of the differences that were revealed between Clayport and Shiptown in this regard, we are confident that their general direction was 'real': that is, that Shiptown tended to admit children somewhat more readily than Clayport.

There could be no dispute about their differential use of legal routes into care, however, nor of their contrasting responses to 'villains', and to some extent to 'victims' as well. But to what extent were the social-services departments themselves responsible for this? Compulsory admissions depend upon court (or magistrates') orders, so technically the decisions are made within the judicial system and quite outside the departments. Nevertheless, some decisions are more extra-departmental than others and can usefully be separated out.

The admission of 'villains' to care provides an example. It may be remembered that of all the children whose behaviour was identified as problematic (205 in all), 93 - or 45 per cent - were admitted to care. However, in Clayport only 30 per cent were admitted, whereas in Shiptown 55 per cent came into care. Furthermore, nearly half of Clayport's admitted villains entered voluntary care, but only one in five of Shiptown's villains were admitted voluntarily. Clearly the police, with their powers of removal and prosecution, and education departments, who refer cases to courts, contribute to these differences: but so do the social-services departments themselves. If police POSOs, remands, non-school-attendance cases and criminal prosecutions are all left out of account, area differences still remain. Over two thirds of Clayport's remaining villains were received voluntarily, a quarter were removed by social workers on POSOs, and one child was committed to care as in 'moral danger'. By comparison, in Shiptown only 38 per cent were received voluntarily, two in five were removed by social workers on POSOs, and one in five were committed to care through magistrates' and matrimonial courts.

If not entirely masters of their fate, it seems that the departments were not its helpless victims either, and this impression was reinforced by the social workers' own perceptions of where the main responsibility for decision-making rested. Even in relation to compulsory admissions, social-services personnel (alone or in collaboration with others outside and inside the agency) were usually credited with carrying most weight in the decisions that were made. Where voluntary care or rejection of admission was concerned, their role was seen to be of overwhelming importance, and in general this was the way it looked to the families as well.

We have already indicated that some of the differences in patterns of decision-making may be accounted for by the quantity and quality of child-care problems that faced the two departments: that villains, for example, may indeed have been rather more numerous in Shiptown and, just possibly, they were more unruly and in need of firmer control as well. At least that is how they were perceived by some of the main parties to the decision-making - the social workers, police, and the families themselves - and for all practical purposes it is their perceptions which matter.

These perceptions, in their turn, must have been influenced by departmental policies and professional ideologies, and this was a third aspect of the social services' response that we attempted to investigate. Relevant departmental policies were grouped under four headings. There were policies which shaped the departments' organisational structure and determined the procedures for decision-making. Hammering out a departmental role in relation to child care, communicating this to significant referral agents (not to mention potential customers) and seeking mutual agreement on roles, tasks and boundaries with other agencies also seemed to us a vitally important area for policy-making. The provision of resources was obviously crucial; and finally there were policies specifically directed towards shaping admission decisions.

There were common difficulties in identifying what policy actually was, and how it linked with practice in each department and in each of these four areas of inquiry. Official statements of departmental intent were sometimes lacking; or, more usually, there were disjointed or disparate pieces of policy that rarely added up to a coherent whole, because they emanated from a variety of sources and originated from different periods of departmental history. Indeed, the tendency of policies to rise and fall, to be vigorously espoused at first, then modified or neglected and finally perhaps regarded as best forgotten – the embarrassing flotsam of a previous era – was apparent in some of our data. It also seemed clear that, none the less, old policies were rarely publicly discarded and buried, which contributed to the confusion. The status as well as the nature of policy was therefore often ambiguous. Was it policy, or had it ever been so? The answers to such questions were sometimes contradictory. There was apparent difficulty in disseminating policy comprehensively and effectively throughout the departments. Different staff-members at various levels (and not just the social workers on the ground) revealed varying degrees of knowledge or ignorance about its content and even its existence; and, where it *was* understood, compliance was not automatic. Indeed, apart from the very broadest statements concerned with promoting the welfare of children, or endeavouring to support family life, child-care policies did not necessarily command a consensus within the departments, or even within the small teams of social workers at the operational level. Given such uncertainties and complexities, it was scarcely surprising that making the links between policy and practice was as difficult for us as it was for the practitioners.

This is not to say that the two authorities we had chosen to study were exceptional or peculiar, nor that the state of affairs we describe was wholly reprehensible – or indeed avoidable. On the contrary, our observations appear to echo those of other policy analysts who have looked across a wide range of public services. Policies are not, after all, tablets of stone, but evolve and are in *process*; whether emerging or declining, being adapted or discarded, they are bound to present an untidy picture to the observer as well as to those who must implement them. In the words of Michael Hill,

> while it is possible, in the abstract, to treat policies in isolation from other policies, in practice any new policy will be adopted in a context in which there are already many other policies. Some of these other policies will supply precedents for the new policy, others will supply conditions, and some may be in conflict with it.[4]

Furthermore, the various goals to be pursued in child care are not always compatible. Preservation of the family may further a child's best interests or, if family-functioning is severely damaged or damaging, it may actually hamper his development; the best interests of one child in a family may suggest one course of action, but those of his siblings may indicate another; and so on. Added to this, professional opinion is divided on how the various goals may best be achieved. Should all children be provided with care in a family, or is there a role for residential care? In the pursuit of a sense of identity and security for a child, is it better to preserve his or her links with the family, however inadequate they might be, or to sever them and make a fresh start with a substitute family? There is no consensus in the professional literature, and it is therefore not surprising that there is no consensus in departmental policies either.

Moreover, ambiguities are not necessarily accidental, and may in fact be functional. Michael Hill and others have drawn attention to the difficulties of regulating the work of 'implementers', the nature of whose work defies precise codes and categories. We have seen how complicated the task of social workers is in drawing the line between children who 'ought' to come into local-authority care and other, very similar children who need not do so. The factors to be taken into account are so numerous, and the balance of pros and cons is so fine, and so *individual*, that policies, guidelines or 'rules of practice' must leave plenty of room for the exercise of professional judgement. In our view, admission decisions are plainly concerned with judging 'standards' - is the child likely to get 'good enough' care if left at home, or receive it if brought into local-authority care? And, as Jowell has pointed out, 'standards' are not susceptible to precise factual definition: 'the feature of standards that distinguishes them from rules is their flexibility and susceptibility to change over time'.[5]

The exercise of discretion involves the social worker's own beliefs, principles or ideologies, and identifying what these were and where they had originated was often as difficult and complicated as tracing the policies themselves. Discussions in the abstract, before monitoring began, could produce a false impression of consistency, with the emphasis clearly pointing in one direction rather than another: on child protection, on 'permanency' or on the preservation of families, for example. It was at this stage that we sometimes thought we had identified a team 'ethos' - a common belief system, shared and reinforced by the membership, which might lead to a common approach to child-care decisions. When discussions moved on to a case-by-case basis during the monitoring year, such consistency often broke down. Faced with the inherent inconsistencies and conflicting interests within the cases themselves, social workers were forced to adapt and shift their stance: to emphasise family solidarity in one set of circumstances and child protection in another, for example. The area of child-care decision-making seemed to us - as it had to Gilbert Smith and David May in their study of Scottish Children's Panels - one in which a plurality of ideologies overlap and compete.[6] In such circumstances, current *political* ideologies, together with their crucial interpretations of the role of family, state, community and volunteers, are as likely to be influential as any other, more 'professional' belief system.

Discretion also means that social workers are policy-makers in their own right. We were aware throughout our study of their power to ignore or challenge departmental policy and to fill in its broad outlines with their own detailed interpretations: a power that was sanctioned by the departments' stated reliance on 'professional judgement'. What social workers do *becomes* policy if it is done with any consistency and starts to establish a trend. Indeed, if official policies are ambiguous or non-existent, social workers will be obliged to invent their own categories and classifications to bring some order to their deliberations and to avoid the inevitable strain of starting from scratch each time and 'treating every case on its merits'. We suggest that some such process may have been going on in Shiptown, where, though we could find little evidence of an official policy about 'villains', we encountered some telling stock phrases in conversations with social workers. 'This was obviously a "beyond control" type case' was the kind of shorthand used to indicate that the 'need' for intervention was self-evident.

What made most sense to us, in considering the role of the social worker in the decision-making processes that we observed, was in fact the notion of the 'street-level bureaucrat'. Again, Michael Hill usefully summarises the nature of the beast:

> His job is characterised by inadequate resources for the task, by variable and often low public support for his role and by ambiguous and often unrealistic expectations of performance. His concerns are with the actual impact of specific policies upon his relationships with specific individuals; these may lead him to disregard or fail to understand the wider policy issues that concern those 'higher up' in his agency. The 'street level bureaucrat' as a scapegoat for policy failure is a familiar figure.[7]

Further, in Lipsky's words, 'the decisions of street level bureaucrats, the routines they establish, and the devices they invent to cope with uncertainties and work pressures effectively *become* the public policies they carry out'.[8]

Such descriptions seem to encapsulate the essential paradox of the social worker's position. As a 'boundary actor' with direct knowledge of both the agency and its resources and the consumers or clients and their needs, the fieldworker is in a unique position. Many of the departmental procedures and checks upon his performance can only begin to operate if he chooses. His work with the clients in their own homes is private and invisible to the agency; what he tells his superiors about a case, and how he tells it, can determine what happens next: whether a child-abuse conference is convened, whether an adolescent is brought before the court as 'beyond control' and so on, may (so long as no other, powerful agency becomes involved) be substantially within his control. Similarly, his knowledge of and role as gatekeeper to the departmental resources puts him in a powerful position to withhold or give to clients.

Yet the paradox is that he also feels an overwhelming sense of powerlessness - something of which we were made aware time and time again in our discussions with social workers. The inadequacy of resources in the face of unrealistic demands; the ambivalence in public attitudes; the sense of 'never getting it right'; and the structures and procedures that appear to hedge him in - all contribute to this sense of being at the bottom of a heavy hierarchy and in the firing-line so far as the bombardment from clients and community is concerned. To our eyes, the power and the powerlessness are both real enough and were in fact expressed quite vividly by the social workers themselves.

The dilemma for the *managers* is to exercise control while allowing discretion; to endeavour to set standards and supervise the quality of service without its becoming self-defeating. 'Very detailed rule-making is a difficult and time-consuming activity. . . . If the subordinate has to be so elaborately controlled the superior might just as well undertake the task himself.'[9] The tension between social workers and their managers - between the 'ground' and the 'top' - that was evident at times in our study seemed to be analogous to, and even a reflection of, the tension between local and central government. It was another manifestation of the taut and complex relationship between those who set broad policies and those who implement them and, in doing so, adapt, distort, elaborate and develop them.

We have attempted to make sense of our data on policy and practice in general terms, with reference to some broader theories of social policy and decision-making. It remains to try to place this within the context of the different patterns of decisions made in our two sample authorities. What contribution had departmental policies made to the differences which emerged? Once more our evidence is suggestive rather than conclusive, and, given the many other factors involved, this is not really surprising. There were indications that policy, expressed in terms of resources such as day and residential care facilities, may have had considerable impact on what could and could not be done. There was also a hint that the different procedures adopted for overseeing social workers' decision-making may have had some influence on outcomes. But, so far as departmental policies or professional attitudes to the specific issues of admission and the legal means of entry were concerned, we could not discern any striking or consistent difference between the two departments. The same broad issues received their share of departmental emphasis at different times in different places, and the responses of social workers covered a similarly wide spectrum of views. Furthermore, detailed statements on what departmental responsibilities were towards some specific categories of needy children - the villains in particular - were not available, and links between what was said and what was done were sometimes tenuous. Our tentative conclusion would therefore be to echo the words of one wise observer: 'Policy is not what you say when you are thinking: it is what you *do*, when you are not thinking.'[10] On this basis, we assume that policies in Clayport and Shiptown are different because practice differs, rather than the other way round; and we suspect that the same is true for many - perhaps most - social services departments in the country.

PART III

The Follow-Up

9
Six Months On:
The Social Workers' Version

Further information about the children who were considered for care was gathered approximately six months after a decision had been made about them. Our purpose was to learn what the short-term consequences of those decisions had been for the children and their families, and we were specially interested in outcomes for the rarely researched group of children who had been considered but had *not* been admitted. In the process we were concerned to see whether these consequences provided any basis for evaluating the decisions that had been made. Put simply, was there evidence that some decisions were clearly better or wiser than others? Was *not* admitting children (or certain categories of children) a more helpful option than admitting them – or vice versa? Or were there indications that some routes into care had more beneficial consequences than others? These were questions that needed to be asked, though we were not optimistic about our chances of providing unambiguous answers!

Our two main sources – as before – were the social workers and the parents of the children in question. Roughly six months after a decision had been made, they were interviewed again. The questions followed a similar pattern to those in the original interviews, but the emphasis was on detecting what, if anything, had changed.

There were limitations to a follow-up design of this sort. Six months was a very short time in which changes of any significance could be expected to occur. No objective measures of behavioural or attitudinal change had been built into the study, so we were relying – as we had from the outset – upon the subjective impressions of some of the major actors in the decision-making process. Although this has considerable value as a way of describing the basis upon which decisions are reached and carried through, it has weaknesses in terms of being able to evaluate the 'real' effects of different modes of intervention. There *are* some hard facts which can be compared – of which changes and disruptions affecting the children concerned are among the most obvious and important – but for the most part it is social-worker (and subsequently parental) perceptions that are presented once more.

Some other difficulties emerged in practice. The timing of follow-up interviews was more variable than had been anticipated. The state of the case, social-worker availability, and problems of fitting in follow-up interviews on some cases, whilst first interviews were still being conducted on others, meant that the timescale varied from slightly less than six months to over nine months after a first decision. Because of this elasticity, some measures – the number of social-worker visits to families or children, for example – have to be handled with care. Information is also patchy: social workers often knew little about the up-to-date situation in cases which had already been closed (30 per cent in all), and less about children who had *not* been admitted to care than those who had – though their areas of ignorance were to be filled in somewhat by the parental interviews which followed. In the same way, follow-up knowledge was generally more comprehensive for children who had been compelled into care than for those who had been received voluntarily, and all these tendencies meant that rather more detail was available for Shiptown than for Clayport cases.

The admitted and the not admitted

Bearing in mind the gaps and deficiencies, what then was the picture which emerged? We begin by comparing the fate of the children who were admitted with those who were not. The first and most obvious feature was that the line between them had become blurred and they were no longer two discrete groups of 'ins' and 'outs'. On the contrary, there was considerable overlap. Thus of the 200 who were originally refused admission, 45 (22 per cent) had come into care subsequently and half of them (12 per cent) were still in care at the time of the follow-up interviews. Movement across the boundaries in the other direction was even greater, for three out of five of the children originally admitted were no longer in care.[1] For them, admission had been short-lived, though a substantial number were still under departmental surveillance, on supervision orders, or licence from penal establishments to which they had been sent in the intervening period. Table 9.1 summarises the status of the two groups of children at follow-up.

Table 9.1 Status of children at time of follow-up interview

Status	Originally admitted (N = 161) %	Not originally admitted (N = 200) %
In local-authority care	41	12
On supervision order or licence (detention centre and Borstal)	22	9
No strings	36	73
Not known	1	6

The table shows that, despite the many discharges, the majority (63 per cent) of the children who had been admitted were still enmeshed, to some degree, in the care or penal system, six months after the event; whereas an even larger majority (73 per cent) of the not-admitted group remained free of any legal ties to the department. Absence of legal ties did not equate with formal case closure, however, for a majority of both kinds of case remained 'open' (73 per cent of the admitted group and 61 per cent of the not-admitteds), though not all were being actively worked with at the follow-up stage.

So far as the circumstances of the families were concerned, it was no surprise to find that the basic facts of life had changed little in the intervening months. Problems of poverty and unemployment were as much in evidence as before, and well over 40 per cent of families in both groups were without any wage-earner. Financial difficulties beset the majority of families, as they had done six months before, and about a third of the fathers were still said to be unemployed. Again it was the families of the children who were *not* admitted to care who were marginally worse off. There was in fact no evidence that the economic and physical environments of more than a small minority of families had changed dramatically either for the better or for the worse, and this was so whether or not the children had been admitted to care.

Changes in family structure were, however, apparent for both the 'ins' and 'outs' and underlined the continuing significance of family disruption amongst the sample children. A sizable minority of families (one in seven) had experienced changes at their head. For some, a pair had disintegrated, leaving a lone parent; for others, a solitary parent had been joined by a new partner; and, for others again, there was a new combination of partners in the household. Siblings also came and went from the families at much the same rate, and there was an in- and out flow of relatives and lodgers which added to the general fluidity of family units. On balance, the admitted group lost more family members than they gained, and the not-admitteds gained more than they lost. But the differences give only fragile support to the notion that admission itself precipitates further family disintegration; further-more, the impact of new members on a household may be every bit as disruptive as the loss of familiar figures.

The poor health of parents, and in particular of mothers, also remained a prominent though diminishing feature at follow-up, and applied in nearly one in five cases, compared with almost a third six months before. Improvements had therefore come about as some of the crises of acute illness which had led to the original consideration of care had subsided or been overcome.

Crucial family relationships were also credited with a little change, though social workers were often unsure of their facts. Where they ventured an opinion, roughly one in seven 'marital' relationships were said to have improved, and half as many were thought to have deterio-rated. The relationships with maternal kin were believed to be better for 10 per cent of families, but worse for a rather lower proportion of cases. Of more interest, however, were again the *similarities* between accounts of families of admitted children and those of the group who had been kept out of care.

When we turn to *behaviour* (of parents and children), however, the social workers tended to report greater changes – and usually for the better. For example, fewer mothers and fathers were accused of pro-viding poor or inconsistent levels of physical and emotional care at the follow-up stage. There were areas of uncertainty in this data – because some cases were closed, because their focus of concern had shifted, or because some 'only' children were now in care and there was therefore little evidence on which to base a fresh evaluation. However, in the cases where an opinion *could* be expressed, their view was somewhat rosier than at consideration, and their reports indicate a decline in un-satisfactory standards, varying (according to the parent in question and the type of parenting behaviour) between a fifth and a half. This cautiously optimistic view was further reinforced by their comments about changes in the intervening months. In approximately one third of cases they reported a shift, and generally (in roughly a quarter of cases) for the better rather than the worse: only about 5 per cent were thought to have deteriorated. Again, this was so whether the children had been admitted to care or not.

Similar patterns were evident in the reported behaviours of the *children*. The number who were said to exhibit troublesome or worrying behaviour of whatever kind had clearly declined. No less than half of all the children considered originally had been complained about, but a little over a third (37 per cent) were apparently causing concern after six months. By the same token, scores for nearly all the separate items of behaviour that had been categorised were lower at the follow-up stage. Behaviours that were specially likely to alert people outside the family, and other agencies in particular – delinquency, truancy and running away from home – were said to have declined quite markedly. Figures for the first had halved (10 per cent of children, compared with 22 per cent at consideration); truancy had shrunk to a third of its former prominence (6 per cent instead of 17) and runaways now represented only 2 per cent of the children, compared with 12 per cent at the decision-making stage.

Whether this happy outcome was in fact the case remains an open question (though we shall see later that parents told a similar story). The social workers were unable to answer these behaviour questions for approximately one in six of the children, and some problems may well be concealed amongst this group. Perhaps, too, the children's behaviour was no longer regarded as so relevant or noteworthy, once a decision about admission to care had been taken. Nevertheless, as far as the social workers were concerned, behaviour had improved for nearly a third (29 per cent) of all children, and a much smaller minority (6 per cent) were thought to have deteriorated. As with levels of parenting, however, there was little difference between the two groups. From the point of view of the social workers, therefore (and from the parents' perspective as well, as we shall see later), the decision to admit or otherwise had apparently led to very similar outcomes in respect of two of the major issues of concern: the standards of care offered by the parents, and the behaviour of the children themselves.

When we moved from specifics to our more global questions, social-worker optimism, though still cautious, was much more in evidence.

Asked to sum up any changes that had taken place in the overall situation for the child and for his family after six months, they reckoned that there had been some noticeable improvement for a majority of children (58 per cent) and for a substantial minority (42 per cent) of the families from which they came. Only 6 per cent of children were stated to be worse off, compared with one in ten of their families. The circumstances of the rest were either unchanged, ambiguous or unknown. But, again, proportions were almost identical whether the children had been admitted or not.

What sense is to be made of these data? One possible explanation would be that decisions, by and large, were the 'right' ones and that children who would benefit from care were accurately selected out from those whose welfare was best promoted by maintaining them at home. To some extent the social workers seem to have subscribed to this view, for in four out of five cases (82 per cent) their retrospective judgement was that the original decision was the right one, whether it had been for or against admission, and for most of the remainder their answers were complicated or uncertain. For only a tiny minority (3 per cent) did they give an unequivocal 'thumbs down' to the original decision. We shall see later to what extent the families confirmed this perspective.

An alternative conclusion might be that the nature of the decision was immaterial; that the crises which lead to a consideration of admission will subside or resolve themselves one way or another, whether the children are removed from home or not. Certainly the way in which agitation about the children's behaviour declined for both groups by the time of our follow-up interviews suggests something of this kind was happening. The pressure of parents and referral agents upon social-services departments to 'do something' about troublesome children was probably at its height when admission was being actively considered. Once a decision had been reached, the 'case' for care may have been less urgently pressed and/or less sharply perceived by the social workers at the receiving end. Bad behaviour is likely to rest as much in the eye of the beholder as in the activities of the perpetrator, and the same is probably true of other problems in search of a solution. Carried to its logical conclusion, this line of argument would suggest that 'care' could be denied to a large majority of children under consideration without detriment to their future welfare.

Neither explanation is entirely plausible. The first is too naïve and simple, and would elicit hollow laughter from most social workers, struggling with complex cases and difficult decisions. It would also presuppose that children who were to be admitted and those who were not were readily distinguishable from one another at the point of consideration – something which our earlier data do not support.

The second explanation, on the other hand, is too cynical. Examination of the material, case by case rather than in aggregate, indicates that intolerable deprivation, risk and stress would have been caused to many children and to their families if the door to local-authority care had been firmly shut in their faces.

Given that there may nevertheless be *some* substance to both of these interpretations, a third important element could also contribute to much of the apparent similarity in outcome for the two groups. Since our data were based on the subjective impressions of those most intimately concerned in making the original decisions, commitment to those decisions and hope or faith in their efficacy, as well as the social workers' ignorance of many of the 'closed' or dormant cases, may well have concealed some differences of outcome.

What *did* distinguish the admitted children from the rest at follow-up was the care experience itself. The fact of admission set in train a sequence of events involving children, families and social workers which set them apart from the children who were not admitted to care. Most obviously, nearly all the children who were admitted had been separated from familiar faces and places, and in only a handful of cases (4 per cent) was 'admission' used to exert control over a child still at home, or to secure a child's position in an existing substitute placement. Furthermore – and in line with evidence from other research studies – the children who came into care were frequently subjected to moves *within* the care system, thus compounding the original trauma of admission.[2] In contrast, the majority of children who were not admitted stayed in one place and thus avoided the most blatant uncertainties of separation, change and the disruptions of school or day care that were often a consequence.

The contrast is most clearly appreciated if we leave out of account the children who were originally refused care but were subsequently admitted. Those who are left (155 in all) are the children who were 'never admitted' – at least, during the whole of our monitoring and follow-up period of study. Their movements can then be compared with those of children originally admitted (161 children). Table 9.2 summarises these data.

Table 9.2   Children's moves from decision to follow-up (about six months)

	Never admitted (N = 155) %	Admitted (N = 161) %
None	64	4
1	5	14
2	16	43 ✕
3	1	13
4	3	17
5	1	5
6	-	3
7	-	1
Not known	10	-

Nearly two thirds of the former group had stayed in one place, compared with only 4 per cent of the admitted children. Even when moves *had* been made by the stay-at-homes, over half were within the presumably familiar network of family and neighbourhood - to a(nother) parent or relative or, occasionally, to friends. In contrast, admission had obviously involved all but a handful of children in at least one transfer to unfamiliar surroundings, and, for many, other transfers followed. 51 of the admitted children who made a second move were not being returned home, for example, but were moving within the care system - to other residential units, foster homes, boarding-schools and so on; and a quarter of the original 161 had made three or more moves *within* the care system during the follow-up period.

This does not mean that all had gone smoothly for the 'never admitteds'. Roughly half of *their* moves were the result of 'breakdowns' - in relationships, behaviour or child-care arrangements - and a third had moved elsewhere with little preparation. Nevertheless, this compared quite favourably with the experience of the admitted children, all of whose first moves 'into care' were, by definition, breakdowns, and the majority of whose first placements (56 per cent) were said by social workers to have been unplanned, emergency arrangements. Thus, whereas changes at home, in the family structure, affected admitted and not-admitted children to much the same degree, movement for the *child* was a much more striking feature of the admitted group.

With few exceptions, therefore, there was little in the social workers' accounts of outcomes which distinguished the admitted and not-admitted children from one another. The economic and material circumstances of their families remained relatively unchanged. Crises of health and family relationships showed some slight improvement, and parenting-standards and child behaviour had changed rather more – usually for the better. In general, things looked better for over half the children and less than half of their families. Only in the ramifications of the care experience itself, with its initial and continuing disruptions and its inevitably closer entanglements with officialdom, were the two groups in clear contrast with one another.

Voluntary and compulsory admissions

The care experience was not, however, the same for all admitted children, and there were some striking differences between what happened to those who had been received into care on a voluntary basis and those who had been taken into care on a court or magistrates' order. Three quarters (75 per cent) of all children admitted compulsorily, for example, were placed initially in some form of residential care – half of them in observation and assessment centres or in reception homes. By contrast, only just over a third (36 per cent) of the voluntary group went first into residential care, and foster homes were used much more frequently.

Furthermore, for the compulsory group these initial placements were more likely to be unplanned, with no chance of preparation for the child or of pre-placement visits by the child and his or her family. 71 per cent fell into this emergency category, compared with 38 per cent of the voluntary admissions. Not surprisingly social workers were not happy with this state of affairs and expressed mixed feelings, uncertainty or downright disaffection with the first placements of nearly a third of the compulsory cases and one in five of the voluntary admissions.

Visits to and from parents and relatives were more often restricted for the compulsory group. For only a few children (eight) did this amount to an outright ban on one or more members of the family. But for the majority (71 per cent) some restrictions on frequency and timing were enforced, either by the social worker or by the placement itself. In a few cases (4 per cent) the constraints had been proposed by or agreed with the children or the families concerned, but for most they were an unwelcome imposition – as we shall see subsequently from the parents' own accounts. In contrast, restrictions were imposed on only 7 per cent of voluntary cases, though, interestingly, a further 21 per cent themselves favoured restricted access. But for them the *inadvertent* barriers of parental illness, inaccessible placements, travel costs and the less tangible but no less powerful deterrents to visiting that have been explored in detail by the Dartington Research Unit[3] more often applied. In 37 per cent of voluntary cases such unintended barriers were present, so that, for two thirds of the voluntary group, access was in fact restricted. Paradoxically, the inadvertent barriers proved more effective than those that were deliberately imposed, for well over half (58 per cent) of the families of the compulsory group continued to see their offspring, whereas only a third (32 per cent) of the parents of voluntary cases had contact whilst they were in care. The short-term nature of many voluntary admissions may have meant that visiting was seen as less important. A mother in hospital, for instance, would be unable to visit her children and may not always have welcomed their appearance at visiting-times – anticipating their eventual return home. But it was disturbing to see how rarely social workers actually helped parents to establish a pattern of visits: in only 1 per cent of voluntary cases and 2 per cent of compulsory cases did they play an active part in facilitating access.

As time wore on, the patterns of restriction and of visiting achieved changed. A majority (three out of five) of the small number of voluntary cases still in care at six months were by then deliberately restricted – almost half of them with the agreement of the parents, and only two out of five were being visited at all. This parental withdrawal reflects the small number of children who were destined for long-term care and for whom permanent substitute homes were being planned. Changes for the larger group of compulsories who remained in care were much less marked: a few restrictions had been lifted and a rather larger majority were being visited (65 per cent). The imposition of barriers had apparently not deterred the more determined of family members.

The status of the children subject to the two kinds of admission was also in sharp contrast. Only a minority (27 per cent) of the voluntary group were still in care at six months, compared with half of the compulsory group, and most of the remainder were free of any official departmental ties. In contrast, a third of the compulsory group were on supervision orders – to social-services departments or to probation – or on licence from detention centres and Borstals, and only a minority (15 per cent) had no strings attached.

The legal status of those remaining in care was also rather different. For half of the voluntary group, court or administrative orders were now in force. Thus parental rights had been assumed over three children; two were the subjects of full care orders under the 1969 Act, and two more were on interim orders under that Act. Two more were on matrimonial care orders, and two were wards of court. For this small group of ten, voluntary admission had led quite quickly to statutory control. As a proportion of the total group who were admitted voluntarily it is small; but as a proportion of those remaining in care at six months it is of much greater significance. The trend towards treating voluntary care on a strictly short-term basis and of taking control over cases which cannot be quickly rehabilitated seems well illustrated. The fact that eight of the voluntarily admitted group were now in adoptive homes (as were two of the compulsory admissions) also suggests that 'planning for permanence' was playing a small but significant part.

Some children had been readmitted during the six months. 16 of the voluntary cases (22 per cent) came into care for a second time; 10 of the compulsory group (11 per cent) did likewise, and one child came into care three times. Such rapid movements across departmental thresholds give another dimension to the disruptions of care, and mirror the changing placements of many of the children who stayed within its walls.

Frequent moves were in fact part of the care process whatever the legal route of entry, and almost identical proportions of the voluntary and compulsory groups (38 and 39 per cent, respectively) had experienced three or more moves (including the admission itself) by follow-up. However, as we have just seen, for the volunteered this was quite often caused by discharge followed by readmission, so that some changes, at least, were to familiar surroundings. For the compulsories there was more movement within the care system; indeed, an unfortunate minority (16 per cent – 14 children in all) had moved five, six or seven times in the space of six months.

This casts some doubt on an argument that was used by some social workers and their managers against admitting children on a voluntary basis. Voluntary care was said to carry with it the danger of precipitate discharge by parents and the risk of subsequent disruptions for the child through readmission when crises arose again. There was indeed evidence of this happening in some cases, but use of compulsion did not necessarily shield a child from upheaval either, and it is at least debatable whether moving to and fro between familiar (albeit troubled) surroundings and unfamiliar placements is any worse an experience for the child than moving at a great rate between a range of substitute placements, however purposeful and 'planned' some of these transfers may have been.

The facilitation of *planning* through 'control' is indeed one of the major benefits claimed for compulsory removal or detention of children in care, in contrast to the supposed weaknesses of voluntary arrangements, with their inherent dangers of instability through parental interference or the 'drift' caused by social workers' negligence. Statements to this effect have already been quoted in chapter 6 and find support in some of the literature on 'permanence'. It is therefore of interest to explore whether our follow-up data support this contention. The evidence is fragmentary and the timespan brief, but, within these constraints, the short answer seems to be that it does not.

First, by their very nature many decisions to admit compulsorily are made in a hurry. Place of Safety Orders are designed for use in emergencies, and social-services departments may have little advance warning of many remands. Consequently, for the compulsory group as a whole, half of the decisions to. admit were made within 24 hours of first consideration, compared with a third for voluntary cases. Hasty decisions in turn mean there is not time to plan initial placements, either from the point of view of selecting the best from a range of alternatives, or from that of introducing or even preparing parents and children for where they will be going. Allocation of residential resources becomes, perforce, an administrative exercise, out of reach of the social workers who are in touch with the child. Taking control of the situation at admission can therefore actually undermine the chance of planning to ameliorate the effects of that admission. The trauma of separation is thereby increased, as the parents' testimony amplifies in the following chapter. Seven out of ten first placements for compulsorily admitted children were unplanned emergency arrangements of this sort, and for POSOs – the most extreme cases of compulsion – the figure was nine out of ten. So far as managing the process of admission is concerned, compulsion therefore scores badly in comparison with voluntary care.

But is precipitate entry justified by subsequent events? Once *in* care and under 'control', is planning more in evidence? Is there more purpose to the care experience, and are goals set and achieved? Certainly that is frequently the declared intention, with the compulsory route being used more often in order to be *able* to plan. The purpose of a third of such admissions, for example, was said to be 'assessment' - the heavy use of observation and assessment centres confirms this - and the use of compulsion was often justified in terms of ensuring 'long-term control, as an aid to planning'. By comparison, social workers saw assessment as the purpose of only 10 per cent of voluntary admissions, and in the majority of these cases (77 per cent) they were already clear, at the point of entry, that *either* rehabilitation *or* long-term substitute care was their goal. In only a minority of compulsory cases (50 per cent) were goals so clearly in view at the outset. So, for many, the plan was to make a plan.

Those early plans were then reviewed at follow-up, and social workers were asked to look back and to assess whether the outcome of each case, at six months, accorded with the original plan at admission. For four out of five voluntary cases (82 per cent) the answer was an unequivocal 'yes', but in only just over half of the compulsory cases (56 per cent) were they so certain. Indeed, in a quarter of cases (23 per cent) they were sure that outcomes did *not* accord with plans (the equivalent figure for the volunteered was 10 per cent), and for the rest there was a sense of partial achievement or the assertion that plans had never existed in the first place (8 per cent). Perhaps not surprisingly, in view of this, their retrospective evaluation of the original decision to admit was also more negative for the compulsory group. In only three quarters of such cases, as compared with 90 per cent of voluntary admissions, were they prepared to declare that the decision had been the right one.

Nor was there any evidence that second and subsequent *placements* for the compulsory group were any better planned or secured than those for the volunteered. We have already seen the number of changes that were endured by some children in both kinds of care. A similar proportion of these changes came about because of breakdowns in existing care arrangements, and a similar proportion of new placements were arranged in a hurry and were criticised as less than ideal by social workers, whether the children were in compulsory care or not.

In other words, compulsion did not appear to lead to more achievable plans or to greater security for the children, at least in the short term. What it did achieve – and what was so evidently its primary purpose in many cases – was immediate 'control' over children, parents or both, who were regarded as dangerous or disruptive. Here, POSOs are the prime example. Protection of the child from neglect or ill treatment by parents by removal from their care was the justification given for a quarter of all POSOs taken during the monitoring period. But in twice as many cases (52 per cent) it was the child's *own* behaviour that was in question, and it was the child who was being controlled by removal from home. Indeed, there were instances where teenagers were bullying or beating up their parents, so that the protection being offered was to parents rather than children, and the 'safe place' thus created was the home nest, minus the cuckoo! Since most of the juvenile misdemeanours in question were certainly not ones which would have led to a child's remand in custody, we must question the use of 'care' in this context. It was also the case that over half of these children were out of care six months later. A quarter had been in care for no more than a week; and, for approaching one in five, the case had been closed – which raises further doubts about the appropriateness of this mode of admission.

To conclude, therefore, the legal means of entry into care is of considerable importance to child and family, both at the point of admission and in terms of short-term outcomes. The chances of being prepared for the admission itself, of being placed in a non-residential community setting whilst in care, of returning home within days or weeks and of remaining free of legal supervision once at home are all much greater if the child is received into care voluntarily. There is also some evidence that events will more often run 'according to plan'. On the other hand, the compulsory route is more likely to lead to precipitate removal, unplanned residential placements, longer spells in care, closer social-work involvement and statutory supervision on discharge. It also seems that plans may be harder to make and to achieve, and that social workers are more likely to be critical of the outcomes of their intervention. Compulsion may achieve a measure of instant or perhaps even enduring control, but will not automatically promote the welfare of either child or family.

Furthermore, the legal means of entry is not, as some of our respondents suggested, predetermined. Despite the distinctive characteristics of the 'volunteered' on the one hand, and the 'villains' and 'victims', who are generally compelled into care, on the other, we have seen that there is considerable overlap between them and much evidence, both in changing trends over time and in local authorities' different use of compulsion (of which Clayport and Shiptown are prime examples), that points to the scope for choice. Indeed, though social workers claimed that there was no alternative to some decisions, for most they weighed the pros and cons of various courses of action before making their final selection. This being so, when there is a choice to be made between one legal route and another - between reception and a POSO or care order, for example - both policy-makers and decision-makers should be keenly aware of the likely consequences of each course of action.

Clayport and Shiptown

Finally, we turn to compare the picture at follow-up in the two sample authorities. Predictably, there were considerable differences between them - most, but not all, stemming from the original differences in their patterns of decision-making. So Shiptown's higher rate of admissions and its heavier use of compulsion was reflected and even magnified in a range of outcomes - as was Clayport's lower admission rate and its bias towards voluntary care. The legal status of the children in each authority, six months after a decision had been made, provides a clear example. By then, 45 per cent (45) of the children who were originally admitted to the care of Shiptown were still in care, compared with only 29 per cent (18) of their Clayport counterparts. In line with its compulsory emphasis, Shiptown had compounded its high admission rate by retaining a larger proportion of its children in care for at least six months, and the contrast between the two authorities had been exaggerated in consequence. In the main it was the compulsory admissions that had accumulated, and modest differences in admissions of this kind produced marked discrepancies in the totals 'in care' at any one time. In addition, some children who had initially been kept out of care had subsequently been admitted and were in care at follow-up - and, again, the number of such cases was somewhat higher in Shiptown than in Clayport (14, compared with 10). The proportion of the Shiptown cohort in care at follow-up was in fact twice that in Clayport. Furthermore, twice as many Shiptown children were under statutory supervision or on licence from penal institutions (Borstals and detention centres). So Shiptown still held half of its original cohort in some kind of official embrace (and consequently knew a good deal more about what had happened to them); whereas only a third of Clayport's children were still legally attached.

But in another respect the two authorities now looked much more alike. Because, in both, the majority of the voluntarily admitted children had come and gone, those who remained were mostly there under a court order; and even a few (three) voluntary admissions had subsequently been converted into compulsory cases by means of parental-rights resolutions. On this basis, the majority of children in care at follow-up in both authorities were there under compulsion, and *proportionately* (though not numerically) the differences between them had almost disappeared. Inevitably, too, POSOs and remands had all but disappeared, to be replaced in a substantial number of cases by care orders. 19 of Clayport's 28 children in care, and 46 of Shiptown's 59 in care, were by this time on care orders (two and 12 respectively under matrimonial legislation), compared with the handful (five in Clayport and 12 in Shiptown) who had been committed at first decision. Table 9.3 summarises the position.

The same initial emphasis on compulsion in Shiptown meant that the experiences of its admitted children differed somewhat from those in Clayport. Besides remaining longer in care, the Shiptown children suffered rather more disruptions. There were more readmissions; more hastily arranged placements for which they were unprepared; more breakdowns and changes of placement (with consequent changes of school); and a greater use of residential care. Considerably more restrictions were imposed on family contacts from the outset, though this did not prevent the Shiptown parents from visiting more frequently than their Clayport counterparts! (Proximity to residential units, the large number of teenagers involved – doubtless with minds of their own about maintaining contact – and the greater material deprivation of Clayport's parents may all have played some part in creating this anomaly.) Shiptown's children also suffered nearly twice as many changes of social worker – some, but not all, created by its

Table 9.3   Legal status of children at first decision and at follow-up

	Clayport (N = 166) %	Shiptown (N = 195) %
At first decision		
Not admitted to care	63	49
Admitted to care,	37	51
of whom		
compulsory admissions	41	65
voluntary admissions	59	35
At follow-up		
Unknown	7	2
Not in care or under supervision or licence	66	49
Supervision order or licence	9	18
In care,	17	30
of whom		
compulsory[a]	75	81
voluntary	25	19

[a] Including cases under Child Care Act 1980, section 3.

intake system, which automatically passed children on to a long-term team if they lingered in care.

To set against this generally greater degree of turbulence, however, was the fact that Shiptown social workers were consistently more assiduous in visiting both children and their families, whatever the legal status of the case. For example, three quarters of the compulsorily admitted Shiptown children were visited at least eight times in the following-up period (i.e. an average of more than once a month), while for Clayport the proportion was only a third. Moreover, half of the families of Shiptown's 'not-admitteds' also received eight visits or more, whereas less than a third of their Clayport counterparts received as much attention. Clayport's greater 'success' in preventing admissions was thus not easily attributable to more intensive activity on the part of the social workers – at least in so far as direct contact with the families was concerned.

Apart from the intensity of visiting, were strategies for help in the two authorities distinguishable in any way? In theory, when they spelled out the constituents of their plans to assist families and children, there were plenty of similarities. The same mixture of practical and emotional support and advice, similar degrees of surveillance and 'monitoring', similar *intentions* over future visits, and a marshalling of aid from a wide variety of formal and informal sources were evident in both authorities. In practice, Clayport social workers left more to the initiative of the families themselves, and indeed they seemed to have a generally more optimistic view of their capacity to cope with the minimum of intervention. For instance, they more often attributed decisions *not* to admit to care to the capacity of the families to cope, even in the face of quite serious difficulties, and they were more inclined to bow to the wishes of parents or children who were resisting care. They were also readier to close cases, once a decision against admission had been reached. In the same vein (and clearly linked to their proportionately greater use of the voluntary pathway), parents were more often the initiators of a child's discharge in Clayport, whereas Shiptown's social workers had a firmer grip on this aspect of decision-making.

Only in the handful of cases who remained in care at follow-up was there evidence of the exercise of tighter controls in Clayport. Long-term substitute care was the plan for the majority of such children (seven out of the ten children in adoptive homes were Clayport children, for example), whereas Shiptown was more inclined to leave the options open. So 'speedy or eventual rehabilitation' was the goal for one in five of Shiptown's remaining children in care, but for none of those who were still in the care of Clayport.

Impressionistically, therefore, and supported by these fragments of evidence, the Clayport 'style' could be described as both more low-key (even 'laid back'!) in relation to most of the families in its cohort, where admission was prevented or was confined to a brief, voluntary episode; but also as more determinedly controlling in a minority of cases where 'care' was developing into a long-term experience. In contrast, Shiptown was generally more interventionist and paternalistic – readier to take on or to take in cases, but also more open-ended in its commitment once children were in care. In character, Clayport was perhaps the more 'modern' department, reflecting contemporary emphasis on 'prevention' – and, failing that, on care as *either* a very brief episode, *or* as a route to permanent placement in a substitute family. Shiptown, in some respects, adhered to an older model, characteristic of some children's departments of the 1960s where admission was viewed more positively, as a legitimate form of help; where troublesome teenagers were willingly absorbed into the care system; and where indeterminate care was not necessarily seen as a bad thing.[4] However, to complicate the picture, Clayport's 'voluntary' emphasis was more in the old-fashioned, children's department mould, and Shiptown's stress on compulsion had a distinctly contemporary flavour!

Finally, how did the social workers' own evaluations at follow-up compare in the two authorities? To what extent and in what directions had the circumstances of the children and their families changed in the intervening months, and did they share similar views in retrospect, of the wisdom or otherwise of their original decision?

Broadly, the basic facts of life for the children's families had remained untouched in both authorities. Their employment situation, finance, accommodation and the neighbourhoods in which they lived displayed the same drawbacks as before and, not surprisingly, little had changed in the interim. Families in both authorities had continued to fracture and to reformulate to an almost identical degree, and in both the greatest changes were perceived in the behaviour of parents to children and in the behaviour of the children themselves. Social workers in Shiptown and Clayport believed, for example, that standards of maternal care had improved in a quarter of cases and that one father in five was performing his parental role more satisfactorily as well.

They were not, however, equally optimistic about the behaviour of the 'villains' - the group of troublesome youngsters to whom they had reacted so differently in terms of admission decisions. Here both authorities registered a dramatic decline in all categories of troublesome behaviour, despite the fact that Shiptown had taken in a higher proportion of its villains, had more often used compulsion, and had kept more in care, for longer, than Clayport. But, when asked to comment on the changes that had occurred, Shiptown social workers were rather more optimistic. In their view, the behaviour of nearly half (47 per cent) of their villains had improved, whereas Clayport's estimate of improvement in a little over a third of its villains was, by comparison, more modest. But this was not, apparently, a sign of shaky confidence in the low-profile methods that had been adopted in Clayport, for it was in cases where compulsion *had* been used that its social workers expressed most disillusion and their gloomiest predictions. Certainly, Shiptown's apparent faith in robust intervention in such cases was not shared by many of the Clayport social workers.

In general, Clayport's social workers were in fact a shade more pessimistic and self-questioning than their Shiptown counterparts. There were fewer cases in which they were prepared to say that the general situation for child, or family, or both, had improved by follow-up (Shiptown saw improvement in nearly two thirds of their cases; Clayport in only a half). They had also viewed more of their original decisions as difficult, at the time they were made – perhaps because they also claimed greater responsibility than the Shiptown social workers did for making the decisions in the first place. In view of this it was perhaps surprising that Clayport social workers were also more sceptical about the wisdom of those decisions, in retrospect, and felt that only three quarters had been unequivocally 'right', compared with Shiptown's figure of nine out of ten. But Shiptown's greater satisfaction may have been linked with a feeling that many of its decisions were predetermined; that there was, in fact, no 'choice' to be made in a third of all its cases, and that alternatives had not been explored, perhaps because they were assumed not to exist. 'Choice', which the Clayport social workers were readier to own, also enhances the prospect of being wrong.

In conclusion, the picture given by social workers, six months on from the original decisions about admission, is complicated and in many ways ambiguous. No clear conclusions can be drawn about the benefits or otherwise of admission to care or its prevention, beyond the obviously unfortunate disruptions and instabilities that seem to be part and parcel of the care process itself. But the quality and duration of care are strongly associated with the legal gateway through which the child enters. The experiences of the children admitted to care in the two sample authorities therefore differed accordingly, although crucial behaviours and relationships appeared to change to much the same extent and in a similar direction, whatever the precise form of intervention. There are also hints that somewhat different styles of social work predominated in the two authorities and that they gave rise to differing degrees of anxiety and self-criticism. It remains to be seen how far these perceptions were shared by the parents, and it is their views at follow-up which form the subject of the next, and penultimate, chapter.

10

The Family Perspective at Follow-Up

The parents who had been seen around the time decisions about admission were made were approached again, generally after we had seen the social workers for the second time. They had been forewarned that this would happen at our first interview, and they responded generously. We failed to follow through the families of only 18 children out of the original 270 who had been seen previously, and several of these losses were because the family had lost all contact with the department and could not be traced. Refusals were therefore rare, and overall the families of 70 per cent (252) of the cohort were interviewed, compared with 75 per cent at the first stage. There were some discrepancies in the timespan of the follow-up. Most of the Shiptown interviews were achieved between six and eight months after the original decision. In Clayport the pace was slower (there was a considerably larger geographical area to cover), and most family interviews took place at least eight months after the event. For this reason we have not made precise comparisons – of numbers of moves, or visits, social workers or admissions, for example – though in fact the authorities tended to differ *despite* rather than because of these discrepancies in timescale.[1]

The shape and content of the follow-up interviews resembled that of their social-worker equivalents. Parents were asked to describe in some detail the current situation of their family and of the child who had been considered; to reflect on what had changed in the intervening months, and whether it had been for the better or worse; to comment on what the social workers and their departments had or had not been doing in the interim, and to express their feelings about this; to say in what ways they had been helped and what further help they needed;

and to give a retrospective opinion of the original decision and of the events and interventions that were consequent upon it. Again, as at the first interview, mothers were much more frequently respondents than fathers - nearly four times as many were seen - but 64 fathers were interviewed, so the viewpoints that emerge are not exclusively maternal.

In general, the picture drawn by the parents was similar in outline to that given by the social workers. It confirmed, for example, that a large proportion of families continued to experience severe difficulties through inadequate incomes, unsatisfactory accommodation, rough and poorly resourced neighbourhoods, and their own indifferent or bad health. In fact, the account they gave was often bleak and somewhat gloomier than that of the social workers. In a number of instances they reckoned that things had got a great deal worse. Around a third of all families reported a deterioration in their financial situation, for example, and by follow-up nearly 40 per cent of Clayport's fathers were said to be unemployed. In both authorities, a substantial minority of mothers claimed that their health was worse than it had been six months previously. Changes for the better were small by comparison.

A continuing process of family turbulence and disruption was also confirmed by the parents, and was, if anything, on an even larger scale than the social workers had realised. As one example, the parents of no fewer than one in five of the Shiptown children who were not admitted to care had changed partners in the intervening months, and a third had moved house. The fluid family structure and living-conditions that this represents indicate how often social workers need to reassess family situations, and how swiftly their judgements and the plans based upon those judgements can become out of date.

The parental view also reinforced the social workers' contention that it was in relationships and behaviour, rather than in the basic conditions in which they lived, that most changes had taken place and that these changes were more often improvements than the reverse. Between one and two-fifths reported improved relationships between the parents themselves, between them and their children, between the children and their brothers and sisters, and between all of them and their wider network of relatives. By comparison, they claimed that things had got worse in only a small minority of cases - most often between children and their fathers, where discord seemed more widespread and intractable, most especially where the child's own behaviour had been the focus of the original concern.

Their comments convey some of the flavour of these changes and why they thought they had come about. Indeed it was clear that, for a number of families, improvements in one set of relationships had been purchased at some cost to others. Some marriages, for example, were thought to have benefited in this way, when children had been taken into care.

> We've had fewer arguments since Sam went away. Now we always discuss things together.
>
> We were united before and still are, but removal of the tension has meant an improvement.
>
> Our marriage is better since Linda's departure.

For some, improvements were measured against a very unsatisfactory baseline:

> We're communicating better. He doesn't hit me as much. All the women in the group [she was attending a women's support group] blame their husbands but it can't be all their fault . . . [and again, voicing a recurring theme] *children* make or break a marriage.

This conflict between spouse and children, between marital harmony and parental satisfaction was vividly expressed by one depressed mother:

> I feel guilty because the boys are stopping me having what I want. When Jim comes out of the RAF he wants to go abroad. I honestly don't know what will happen. . . . Our relationship would be absolutely wonderful if we never had the children. . . . I think if those children were *his* it would be wonderful . . . if he's had a bad week he can be horrible - he reflects it back on the children. He gets at me by getting at the children. . . . I still feel guilty because I feel I'm depriving the children of what they should have.

But children were not always the losers:

> He's able to talk now and is much happier in himself. We can now have a sane conversation - a vast improvement.

We're not so tense now. We were under a thundercloud before. He doesn't bully his sister as much.

It's nice. He's treating me like a Mum now!

The parents were equally sure that the behaviour of a substantial minority of their children had changed, and, again, it was generally improvements that they saw. In this, their perceptions were in tune with those of the social workers. Table 10.1 compares the incidence of all categories of behaviour amongst the group who were being troublesome at the 'consideration for care' stage with its incidence at follow-up.

Table 10.1 Behavioural change from consideration to follow-up

		At follow-up	
	At consideration (N = 160) %	Admitted children (N = 77) %	Not-admitted children (N = 73) %
Aggression (verbal and physical)	41	24	15
Delinquency	35	12	8
Truancy	24	11	2
Running away	14	6	-
Lying	7	2	2
Sexual problems	10	7	2
Self-injury	6	3	-
Enuresis/encopresis	5	3	1
Unmanageable	61	30	26
Withdrawn	15	6	7
Behaviour better	-	43	30
Behaviour worse	-	11	4

In the parents' eyes there was definite improvement, whether children had been admitted to care or not, but such generalisations conceal a wide variety of responses and some very mixed feelings. Some made clear links between improvements and the admission to care. A mother's comments on her 13 year old, who had been commited to care via a Place of Safety Order after numerous complaints of glue-sniffing, delinquency, aggressive and disruptive behaviour, were

> No complaints. He's good as gold here [on home visits from his Community Home]. He's different altogether . . . much more helpful and understanding and less selfish. . . . the behaviour's improved tremendously, I'll give them their due for that. . . . He's not unhappy there . . . he got away with so much here. I think being away from home's done him good.

For others, the care experienced was appreciated less for its long-term benefits than for the 'short sharp shock' that had been administered. As one father said of his 14 year old son, convicted of burglary and with a record of truancy and disruptive behaviour at school, 'I wanted him to go away – on a temporary basis – more to let him see what it would be like to be taken away from home. . . .' In the event, the boy was remanded but then placed under a supervision order. His father felt the recipe had worked: 'There's a definite improvement. We had a report from school, saying he was fine.'

In another case, removal from home (to an adolescent unit) had improved the 'beyond control' behaviour that had led to a police POSO, but apparently at some cost to the child himself.

> He's on a care order . . . he's very withdrawn, that's all. . . . He's quiet and has a frowning look all the time . . . not bright, a depressed look. He's not as naughty as he was – not going out and staying out. He's a bit easier at home . . . but he looks as if he's got the worries of the world on his shoulders, to me.

Admission was also sometimes unequivocally blamed for deterioration in a child's behaviour. Of a boy at an observation and assessment centre it was said, 'He is being given more freedom. He's not as nice a boy – nowhere near. He's developing some nasty ways. . . .'

Avoidance of admission was also a blessing for some, but not for everybody:

> She's a bit mouthy and arrogant. . . . I was told I was too soft, but I'm not soft any more. Me being firmer and her going to her father's has helped. The problems are not completely gone, but there aren't any *crises* now. Positive action's the thing. Nipping it in the bud. But she has definitely improved.

But for a mother frustrated by departmental refusals, and still threatening her son with being 'put away', the story was different:

> He's a menace now . . . I can't do anything with him. It's murder getting him up because he goes to bed so late. . . . . He won't do anything he's told, he's stealing and he brings back things from town and says he's found them.

Variations on the themes of stability, stagnation or change were almost as numerous as the cases themselves, but in aggregate the picture presented by the parents of the children who had been admitted to care was remarkably like that of the group who had been kept out – just as it had been for the social workers. Where improvement or decline was most marked, it was so whether the children had been admitted or otherwise. In the same way, the parents' retrospective judgements of the original decision and their summary of the situation as a whole at follow-up were almost identical.

Table 10.2 selects a few items for comparison and shows how similar the two versions are. There is a faint suggestion that removal to care may more often exacerbate father–child relationships, and that marriages may more often benefit from a child's removal. It also seems that parents find decisions *against* admission marginally harder to accept than those in its favour. But none of these slight differences negates the overwhelming impression of the similarities in their responses. In fact, like the social workers, the parents provide little evidence that admission to care, *in itself*, leads to identifiably more changes, or to changes in any particular direction, at least in the short term. Rather, what is highlighted is the crudeness and falsity of the distinction between the two kinds of status. As we have seen, 'admission' and 'non-admission' each cover a multitude of responses to a great variety of family situations and, in developmental terms, to a huge age-range of children and young people. There is also considerable overlap as children move in and out of care. Failure to differentiate between these many different situations and the various official responses to them is likely to conceal any differences of outcome that may exist. It also raises considerable doubts about departmental policies and the kind of social-work wisdom which speaks, in global terms, of admission as a 'last resort' – something to be prevented whenever and wherever possible; and about arguments which equate

Table 10.2 Parents' perceptions of change: admitted and not-admitted children compared

	Admitted (N = 125) %	Not admitted (N = 127) %
Child's behaviour better	39	35
Child's behaviour worse	10	9
Mother-child relationship better	36	32
Mother-child relationship worse	6	10
Father-child relationship better	23	20
Father-child relationship worse	18	4
Child-sibling relationship better	24	27
Child-sibling relationship worse	14	7
Marital relationship better	38	20
Marital relationship worse	10	5
Total situation better	59	57
Total situation worse	14	13
Decision was wrong for child	35	38
Decision was wrong for family	32	41

declining admission rates with 'success' and rising numbers in care with 'failure'. The reality is a great deal more complicated - a point to which we shall return.

In contrast, the *mode* of admission - whether it was agreed to voluntarily or whether it was imposed by court or magistrate's order - continued to shape the experiences of parents at follow-up, just as it had at the time the original decisions were made, and their reactions reflect this. First, there was the issue of consultation and related feelings of having some control over events and decisions concerning the child. Parents of children who had been received into care voluntarily were more often consulted and asked for their opinions in advance, when children were to be moved or discharged or when fresh plans were being made for them. A majority (though by no means all of them) claimed to have had discussions and to have felt they had participated in bringing about such changes. Consequently their reactions to the ups and downs of care itself, and to the return home of their children, were at best very positive and at worst neutral. In contrast, parents of children in compulsory care continued to feel that matters had been taken out of their hands. They spoke much more frequently of being *told* what was to happen, rather than being *asked* – or of not having matters discussed at all. Of those whose children had been discharged, for example, a quarter claimed that the matter was never discussed beforehand (many of these were no doubt at the mercy of court decisions which were, in their eyes, unpredictable) and, perhaps not surprisingly, one in five were angry at the discharge. Indignation at having their child removed from their care did not necessarily equate with delight at having him restored unexpectedly! Many also felt impotent to influence social workers' plans for their child, and a third of the compulsory group expressed considerable anger at the nature (or sometimes the lack) of such plans.

Two brief quotations encapsulate this sense of angry impotence. One mother said,

If, after all these years of bringing up Sandra, I wanted to take her on holiday, I'd have to ask their permission now! Because social services are very powerful. The social worker actually said 'I'm very powerful and you must ask my permission'!

And a father declared, 'I don't know any more than when I saw you last year. Our boy could be dead for all we know!' To which his wife responded. 'Oh no – they'd tell us *then*!'

A feeling of helplessness was also engendered by many parents' ignorance and confusion about the law, about official procedures and sometimes the language of law and social work. It was further compounded by their frequent failure to appreciate the significance of what was happening until after the event. A parent of two boys on care orders for being 'beyond control' said,

I felt they possibly needed treatment . . . they saw we couldn't control them. And the social worker said 'put it in writing'. As soon as they had that, it was out of our hands. The child psychiatrist said there was no temporary order. The EWO [Education Welfare Officer] said there *was* a temporary order. The magistrates as good as said they were making an unlimited order. . . . It seems there *is* no temporary order.

Another parent, also with a 'beyond control' teenager, commented,

> We were advised to write and more or less led to believe it was volun-
> tary - he'd be taken away for a while. But after that it was like it was
> taken out of our hands. . . . We agreed to the 28 days but still thought if
> he behaved we could have him home sooner . . . but we didn't have full
> information. . . . I think they should have explained, so you knew what
> you were leading yourself into.

The 'at risk' register was also sometimes a source of confusion:

> Kevin is on a list of a book of kids - the social worker told me that. I
> don't know what it is. He just told me he was on a list of children with
> problems like this - marriage problems or when mothers aren't capable
> enough to look after their kids. I thought, what the hell is going on - it's
> a bit awful. There's other families who don't have to have their children
> on lists but with the same sort of problems. . . . The social worker didn't
> say what the list was for.

Another mother responded,

> When I got her back I had conditions. She should be left with a respons-
> ible baby-sitter and should not be in moral danger - I don't know what
> that is! They said me coming in with a load of friends and she might be
> in danger because of it. I thought the conditions were a bit stupid really,
> but I agreed to them.

Anger and bitterness were also much more in evidence within the
compulsory group, when parents were questioned about the help they
had received and the social worker's part in this. They were more likely to have been visited by social workers since the admission, and to
have been visited 'frequently', according to their own evaluation.
(This confirmed the social workers' claims as well.) Nevertheless, a
third of the compulsory group expressed dissatisfaction with the
pattern of visiting (the voluntary figure was one in ten) and this was
almost always because social workers' visits were regarded as too unpredictable and infrequent. Only a handful of parents complained that
they received too *much* attention from social workers and wanted
fewer visits or no contact at all.

The compulsory group were also much more likely to view their
social worker as unhelpful (38 per cent, compared with 11 per cent)

and to say so in no uncertain terms. Indeed, in our coding of their replies to our question about how social workers had helped them, we had felt obliged to invent both a 'bugger-all' category and one which said they'd 'made things worse', to convey the strength of their feelings! The parents of a third of the compulsories responded in this way (compared with only 4 per cent of the voluntary group), and their hostility had grown during the months since admission, for only 20 per cent had *anticipated* that they would receive merely negative interventions or no help at all, when we first interviewed them. Nor was it a true measure of their feelings of not *wanting* help: the majority of parents still felt they had difficulties, and only 13 per cent were saying they had no need of help and wanted all do-gooders to keep away.

Their exasperation and bitterness were vividly conveyed.

> Never one bit! . . . if the motive behind this was to help us! . . . They have a thankless job but they haven't gone about things the right way. They have had no compassion in the way they have handled things. We've been done an injustice.

> I don't think she has done any thing to help the situation at home at all. . . . I think she *caused* some of the trouble to begin with, more than helped.

> She hasn't been helpful, she's been *unhelpful* - keeping seeing me at work and ringing me at work and not coming to my home. . . . I think she just wanted to say I've had a child put into care.

> It was a mistake to ask for help. . . . Experience has confirmed what papers say about social workers. I'm so disillusioned. They have let us down. . . . I wouldn't ask them to do anything because they would take the other route.

Given such feelings, it was no surprise to learn that half the parents of the compulsory group looked back on the original decision and thought that it had been wrong, both for their child and for the family as a whole. The parents who had agreed to voluntary admission, on the other hand, were much more complacent. Only 5 per cent felt it had been wrong for them, though they acknowledged that for their children (17 per cent) it had more often been a mistake.

Of course, the parents of the compulsory group bear some responsibility for all this aggravation. In some cases it was their truculence and their dangerous behaviour towards their children, their refusal to see blatant problems or to acknowledge their own part in them, even their insistence that awkward children should be removed forthwith, that had led to compulsory removal in the first place. Some of the parents in this group were certainly hard to help, and had come out fighting before the social workers had begun to intervene in any Draconian way. Nearly 10 per cent had, after all, denied that they had any problems, and 17 per cent had said that they wanted no help whatsoever when they were first interviewed.

But compulsory admission had had the effect of reinforcing and even amplifying the angry feelings with which some parents had first tangled with officialdom. For others, a trusting approach and a request for help had quickly turned sour. Anger and confusion at the time of a child's removal were not easily forgotten and were frequently rekindled by the bewildering and seemingly arbitrary way in which subsequent plans were developed and fresh decisions taken. As a means of giving assistance to families, therefore, it clearly creates severe difficulties for both helpers and helped. For this reason alone, the choice of a compulsory route into care is crucial, and its evident drawbacks need to be carefully weighed against any advantages, at the point when admission decisions are made.

The basis for conflict and discontent amongst the parents of children who had been compulsorily removed was already plain to see when we visited them soon after a decision had been made. Our follow-up visits merely confirmed that the uneasy pattern of their interaction with officials had continued and that time had not healed the wounds. With the parents of children who had *not* been admitted to care, the picture was rather different. Although there had certainly been a substantial minority (the ubiquitous third) who expressed dissatisfaction at our first interview, the non-event of a non-admission had given little shape to their complaints at that stage. Rather, there had been a sense of bewilderment and confusion, and sometimes complete ignorance of the fact that admission to care had ever been an option under consideration.

By follow-up, these dissatisfactions had crystallised into some trenchant criticisms which revolved mostly around a feeling of neglect or even abandonment by the 'helpers'. For a considerable number, the decision not to admit their children was seen in purely negative terms. Nothing helpful, in their eyes, had been offered in its place, and some were left with a very real sense of despair.

Criticisms of the infrequency or even complete absence of any visits from social workers (a proportion of cases had, of course, been closed) far outweighed those where it was 'the welfare poking their noses' which was resented: 'I never see her. She always sees the boy on his own in the office. I don't see what she does'; 'Social services didn't want to know. We felt blocked off and shut up.'

But, even when social workers *did* visit, they were sometimes accused of being useless:

> She comes about once a fortnight, usually. She asks, 'How's Pat and how are you feeling?' and that's it. When I say I'm depressed she just says, 'Oh.' She doesn't do anything at all. I was going to be evicted recently – I sorted it out myself, because she was on holiday.

Indeed, our 'bugger-all' and 'made things worse' categories of response were as large for the not-admitteds as for the compulsory admissions, and parental comments were no less pithy:

> Helpful? No way! He didn't have a clue!
>
> Helpful? No – you must be joking! That's the joke of the year!
>
> *One* day I'll find a way of making the system work! The social worker's been a pain in the arse!

Thus, in the parents' eyes, two of the chief sins of social workers and their departments were high-handed intrusion and 'take-over', which was generally linked with compulsory admission and was evident from the beginning; and ineffectual intervention or downright neglect, which emerged only gradually and was often most vociferously asserted where there was no admission to care. Inevitably, patterns of response in the two sample authorities reflect this dichotomy. Shiptown parents, many of whose children had been compulsorily removed, were originally the more discontented and angry group. By follow-up, however, exasperation had spread amongst the Clayport parents (so many of whose children had been kept out of care) and, in extent if not in intensity, it had even outstripped levels of disaffection in Shiptown. Proportionately more Clayport parents reckoned they still had problems; more declared their social worker unhelpful and said that nothing whatsoever had been done to help them, and more disputed the wisdom of the original decision.

But this turn-around was not solely because of obvious differences in the pattern of the original decisions that had been taken. It affected all kinds of cases, and seemed to be linked to the generally lower level of social-work visiting in Clayport which both social workers and parents reported. Whether children were admitted or not, and whether they entered care by the compulsory or voluntary routes, Shiptown social workers were more likely to remain in touch with the parents on a regular and even frequent basis. For this reason perhaps, the Shiptown parents also claimed to have had considerably more help of both a practical and an emotional kind than their Clayport counterparts did.

Thus, at follow-up, there was something of a paradox. Shiptown maintained its image as the more intrusive, paternalistic and controlling department and provoked considerable parental hostility on this account. But, to offset this, its busyness and capacity to marshal help of various kinds was appreciated. Clayport, on the other hand, was consistent in its greater stress on consultation and collaboration with parents – even, in some cases, where compulsion had been used – and this certainly gave satisfaction. But, to offset *this*, its lower intensity of social-work visiting and the apparently sparser amounts of identifiable 'help' that were offered stimulated considerable parental resentment and disillusion. Indeed, there was nothing in the *parents'* account to suggest that Clayport's higher 'success' rate in preventing admissions was due to more vigorous efforts on the part of social services, but rather the reverse. Shiptown may have prevented fewer admissions, but, in those cases where it had prevented them, levels of satisfaction with help received were a good deal higher.

On the other issue of practice on which the two authorities differed most sharply – the taking in of troublesome teenagers – the parents provided no evidence that *either* authority's policy was markedly the more successful. Broadly, improvements in the child's behaviour and attainments were registered in a substantial minority of cases in both authorities – with the Shiptown parents seeing marginally more changes for the better amongst those of their villains who had been taken into care; and the Clayport parents perceiving slightly more improvement amongst *their* villains, who had stayed at home! In other words, parental approval tended to endorse whatever line of practice their particular authority favoured – another very small indication perhaps, that parents *can* play a part in shaping that practice at a local level.

We have dwelt at some length on the complaints and criticisms made by parents at the follow-up stage, but it would do parents, social workers and their departments no justice if we failed to point out that the majority of families expressed some degree of satisfaction with what had happened. To most of our questions about the helpfulness of social workers and the rightness of the original decision, roughly a third gave a very positive response (as many, in fact, as were fiercely critical), and the rest found some good things to say or were at the very least neutral in their comments.

The reasons for their satisfaction were very similiar to those given at the decision-making stage. They felt involved and were consulted; the social worker listened and appreciated their point of view; the social worker visited frequently and was able to offer tangible help as well as emotional support; the social worker was honest and a 'real' person, and not a faceless official. We even had to invent a small but poignant category for responses which conveyed warmth and appreciation for a socal worker's efforts on their behalf, even though they failed and brought no obvious benefits. This we called 'No help – but not for want of trying!' and in essence it seemed to echo the responses of some of the Family Service Unit's clients in Eric Sainsbury's study, who clearly distinguished between the moral worth of a social worker's trying hard on their account, and his 'success' in terms of actual help received.[2]

A sample of quotations gives some idea of the range of positive responses – from lukewarm to very appreciative, and from the mixed to the unequivocal.

> Yes, the social worker helped. I think it sorted out my mind . . . what I could and couldn't do. But I could have done with social-work involvement before . . . and there's too much talk and not enough action.

> My only regret is that the placement didn't come earlier. It's wrong to have it as a last resort.

(Both interesting comments on what parents perceive as delays and prevarication.)

> Yes, the children seemed to enjoy it [a voluntary admission]. I felt that the children were in good hands and my mind was eased.

He's all right. He is very abrupt. Says what he has to say. But he has helped. He is the only one who has taken an interest.

She has been very helpful. She got our furniture and a gas fire. Helped when food was pinched and also helped to keep Jessie at home.

Yes. I had mixed feelings at the time, but the social worker knows how to talk to me. On my level and my nature.

I definitely couldn't have got better help. You couldn't get better help than the social-services department. It's nice when they come to the house. They're good to the kids. I wouldn't be without the social worker.

But there was another side to this particular coin: 'A few months ago I was getting too much help, too much kindness and I wasn't able to cope with it.'

But, again: 'Extremely helpful. Their help gave me peace of mind. I wanted the best for him and I realised that I wasn't giving it to him. It [admission to care] was the only solution.'

And, finally, one of our 'not for want of trying' group: 'Jerry is no better, but everyone has tried to be helpful. I've met an enormous number of nice people through Jerry.'

As we have already indicated, such levels of satisfaction were unevenly spread throughout our sample – to some extent, as between our two local authorities, but more especially amongst the different categories of case. The fewest bouquets came from the parents whose children had been removed compulsorily, though there were nevertheless a sizable number who had good things to say. Those whose children had been kept out of care were a little more contented, but the strength of feeling amongst the disaffected was no less intense, and we have seen how abandoned and neglected some of them felt. Indeed, some of the saddest situations we encountered were where families with seemingly insuperable problems were apparently struggling with little or no assistance, with no idea of where to turn for help, and with no belief that anything could be done to make things better.

In contrast, as the summary table 10.3 indicates, a much more satisfied group – or, to be more accurate, the least *dissatisfied* group – were the parents of children admitted to care voluntarily. Here was a group of parents who had received a service, which many of them had actually requested and which most of them valued. It had apparently met a need – usually at a time of family crisis – and little of the anger and

Table 10.3   Satisfaction and dissatisfaction with help received and family situation at follow-up: three categories of case compared

	Voluntary admissions (N = 54) %	Compulsory admissions (N = 70) %	Not admitted (N = 127) %
Satisfied responses			
Social worker helpful	42	37	42
Practical help given	61	33	43
Emotional help given	34	27	41
Decision right for child	70	30	30
Decision right for family	72	33	32
Dissatisfied responses			
Social-work visiting pattern			
resented	11	31	14
Social worker unhelpful	11	38	26
No help or made things worse	4	34	30
Wrong decision for child	17	50	38
Wrong decision for family	5	53	41
Family situation at follow-up			
Better	68	51	58
The same	7	13	15
Mixed (changes for better *and*			
worse)	5	20	10
Worse	17	13	15

NB: Where two opposite statements do not add up to 100 per cent, the missing percentages are composed of mixed or neutral answers and a few where parents were unable to comment.

frustration felt by other parents was apparent amongst these families. Moreover, it was valued not only because it apparently related to more favourable outcomes (more of the parents of the volunteered believed that things were unequivocally 'better' at follow-up), but also because the style of intervention was generally more acceptable.

This is a particularly interesting finding because it goes against the tide of policy and practice. Voluntary care has diminished over recent years and we saw how often social workers, their managers and advisers referred to it in cautious or ambivalent terms. Recent trends have moved more towards the extremes of compulsory admission with departmental 'control', or of no admission at all; yet it is within these two positions that parental dissatisfaction is at its height - sometimes, it seems, *regardless* of any improvements that may have come about. Once again, it seems it is the *way* in which help had been offered, rather than its effectiveness, which is often at issue and which is so fiercely resented. What the professionals have pursued is not necessarily, therefore, what the families want or appreciate, and this should surely be a factor to be borne in mind when determining the future directions of child care.

Finally, social workers and their departments were not the only 'helpers' that the families had had, and others had contributed to the predominantly favourable changes in their problems and their circumstances that they perceived. Relatives and a few friends had rallied round and provided assistance for a quarter of the families whose children were kept out of care, and also for a quarter of those where the children had been removed. Only the parents of the volunteered had had little support from kin or neighbours (5 per cent) - perhaps a measure of their isolation and therefore of their *need* for an official child-care 'service', as well as a reason for their appreciation of it.

A few parents had had to look for support from informal and unlikely sources. One lone father confessed, 'It may sound ridiculous, but the man who has kept me going more than anyone else has been my insurance man.' For many more, a variety of statutory and voluntary agencies had played a part, most notably for the not-admitteds and the volunteered. With the compulsories, however (that is, the 'villains' and the 'victims'), the role of other officials was more often simply to pass them on to social services! In fact, despite all the formal and informal sources of support which had been tapped, the social-services departments were likely to be involved in a whole range of cases for some time to come. More than half the parents, regardless of whether their children had come into care or not, said they were still in need of help; and most of them hoped that the social-services departments would be able to offer at least some of the assistance they required.

The picture of past events and present circumstances given by parents some months on from the original decision is therefore a mixture - with a fair measure of light, but not a little shade. In many respects it confirms what social workers say and reinforces the finding that changes for the better or worse occur in the crucial areas of behaviour and relationships, whether children are admitted to care or not. It also shows most families to be appreciative of help received and fairly optimistic about the developments that have taken place. But it also provides some new and less happy insights. Conflict and anger over a child's removal from home do not diminish with time, and may even be magnified by a continuing sense of powerlessness. Feelings of neglect and of being *un*helped are not uncommon, and preventing an admission to care may simply look like a failure to help in a desperate parent's eyes. Voluntary admission to care is, from a parental point of view, by far the most acceptable form of child-care service on offer, yet professionally it is unfashionable and in decline.

In the final chapter we shall review these and the other major themes that have emerged, and shall look at their implications for policy and practice.

11

Conclusions

Our study has yielded a complex tangle of findings which we have attempted to unravel as we have gone along, and which will not be reiterated here. On the way, interpretations of these findings and their implications for practice at all levels have been touched upon – although sometimes, of necessity, in tentative or ambiguous terms; the lessons to be learned are by no means always clear.

The limits of the design and focus of the study also need to be taken into account before conclusions are drawn. We have looked at child-care decision-making in only two English local authorities. Details of policy and practice, organisation and style, even perhaps of parental response, almost certainly differ widely across the country, and not necessarily in ways which were apparent in Shiptown and Clayport. Nor does time stand still, and what was true at the beginning of the eighties may not be quite the case today. Indeed, since then a House of Commons Committee on Children in Care has reported, and in its wake a major review of child care law has been instituted. Further sections of the Children Act 1975 have been implemented, and new legal procedures and a code of practice on parental access have been introduced. Furthermore, many local authorities, including Shiptown and Clayport, have changed departmental structures yet again and have articulated new and more detailed child-care policies. Some of our observations must therefore seem either obvious or out of date.

We have also chosen to rely heavily upon the subjective judgements of two sets of participants who were central to the decision-making process – the social workers, and the parents of the children who were being considered for care. The strengths and weaknesses of this approach have already been rehearsed, and we would merely stress again the value of exploring and comparing such perceptions, because they have such a powerful influence on the decisions taken and the actions which follow from them. What they do not provide is any objective measure of the scale or intensity of the problems which troubled the families and challenged the social workers, nor of the degree of change that took place over time. Also missing are the perceptions and reactions of the children themselves; and, in some cases at least, they would almost certainly have differed from those of either the social workers or their parents. We wish that we had had the time and resources to add this dimension to our study. As it is, we have colluded with the adults who make crucial decisions on their behalf.

Nevertheless, despite the limitations, and beneath the plethora of local detail, three fundamental themes emerge which are to some degree echoed and amplified in parallel research studies conducted in other areas of the country.[1] They concern child-care and family problems and the official responses they elicit, which would be recognisable anywhere and, perhaps, at any time. So our discussion has a relevance that stretches wider than the two authorities, and beyond the immediate period under scrutiny.

Main themes

First, there are important issues around the decision to admit or not to admit to care. This was, of course, the focal point of our study and it is clearly regarded as a matter of concern both nationally and locally, which was why the research was mounted in the first place. Providing full-time public care for children is a costly business, and shrinking social-service budgets at central and local government level are strained by supporting children 'on the rates'. There is also much evidence that separating children from parents or other caring adults, and from familiar surroundings, can do them harm, and that the physical, psychological and educational development of children in public care leaves a lot to be desired.[2] Furthermore, much public care has been shown to be insecure and unstable, subjecting children to repeated changes of placement and caretakers, or to institutional environments where emotional links are hard to forge - points which this study has merely reinforced.[3] Long stays in care have also been blamed on lack of planning and a directionless, reactive style of work which can leave a child isolated, without any close ties to others, and grossly unprepared for adult life.[4]

For all these reasons, the decision to admit a child to care is seen as crucial by policy-makers at all levels, and not least by the social workers who act as gatekeepers to the local-authority care system. Yet, despite the fact that our own study has contributed to this emphasis, we have found it a limiting and at times unhelpful focus in several ways.

From our own point of view, it has led us to neglect areas of work with families and children where admission to care is not (or not yet) considered a serious possibility. We do not know, therefore, how much assistance in the form of day or domiciliary care, advice or guidance, practical help, or the more fundamental processes of forging and supporting community networks of aid are being offered to how many families in this position – assistance which could have considerable significance for an authority's admission rates. There may be a great deal (though we have to point out that, even where admission was considered, a substantial minority of families claimed they had had no help at all), but we simply do not know. Nor do we know whether these unreached families are alike in character and circumstance to those whose children were considered for care. We suspect they are, but their inclusion in the study might have rounded out our picture of the 'not-admitteds' – and the factors which maintained them in that state – in a more satisfactory way. It might also have put the decision 'to admit or not' in better perspective: not *the* child-care decision, but one amongst many other crucial decisions about how to help families with children. Concentration on the gateway to care induces a kind of tunnel vision in researchers and, we suspect, in policy-makers and practitioners as well.

The focus has also had its limitations, because it tends to ignore the fact that the public child-care system is permeable. Its boundaries are not a Rubicon that is crossed in only one direction. The majority of children (three out of five in the study) return from care within a short time – some of them within days or weeks. On the other hand, children whose admission is prevented at one point in time may well come in later – one in five of our original group of not-admitteds had done so by follow-up. Some children even cross and recross the boundaries several times (a third of our admitteds had already been in care at least once before). So sharp distinctions between 'admitted' and 'not-admitted' status are false, and turn a situation that is actually grey and fluid into a misleadingly static picture in black and white.

For the social-services departments, too sharp a focus on the gateway to care can narrow and distort notions of 'prevention'. Rather than seeking to prevent disruption, stress and harm to children and their families - to which admission to care *may*, in some cases, be a positive and appropriate response - the term becomes equated simply with prevention of *admissions*. This, in turn, leads to the 'goalkeeping' mode of child care, identified by David Donnison as long ago as the fifties, when success is measured by how many children can be kept out of the public child-care system. The faults and failings of that system have been well documented - here, as elsewhere - but, again, rather than placing emphasis on improving poor standards of public care - a form of secondary or even tertiary prevention - the temptation is to strive to keep the children out 'at all costs'.

A further difficulty is that admission to care is not a unitary concept: it clearly has several purposes, and is a response to a wide range of different problems and situations, as this study has underlined. At its simplest, there are at least three distinct sorts of public child care on offer. One is for families who are beset by difficulties or handicaps which interrupt or interfere with their capacity to look after their children. Their problems may be acute or chronic, one-dimensional or, more usually, multifaceted and interconnected, and they are likely to be short on supportive networks of relatives or friends to help out, and without the means to pay for child-care services outside these networks. For such families the local authority can provide - and, indeed, is legally obliged to provide (under the old 1948 Act and its 1980 successor) - a child-care service. Provided that it is judged to be in the interests of the child's welfare, no limits are set on the circumstances in which an admission can take place, nor (apart from an upper age limit) to the time the child may spend in care. Parents can and do request such admissions (more properly, 'receptions' into care), though they can also be effected in their absence. In the words of one commentator, it 'does not imply any criticism of parents who may seek care for their child as a solution to a crisis. It can be a very constructive move by the parents.'[5] It is therefore a type of admission that responds to parents as unfortunate rather than blameworthy, and casts the local authority in the role of the child's caretaker, acting on the parents' behalf. As such, it can be seen to be at one end of a continuum of services which includes domiciliary help and day care for children. It therefore forms, in our view, part of a range of child-care services for *families* and not, as the narrower interpretations of 'care' and 'prevention' would imply, a stark alternative to such services. Given the severity of poverty and disruption in most of the families with whom social-services departments come into contact, and the undoubted increase in their number through rising rates of unemployment and divorce, it is disturbing that the provision of such a service seems to be shrinking, relative to other forms of public child care.

A second type of admission provides a protection and rescue service for children who are thought to be in danger, whether it be physical, sexual, moral, emotional or developmental. Here the emphasis is on parental faults and failings and on the child as a victim of inadequate or inappropriate parenting. The local authority intervenes on the child's behalf, and, more often than not, if an admission is arranged (and even if it is requested by the parents) the local authority itself takes over parental rights as well as duties. In essence, the child-care service offered is protection for very vulnerable *children*.

The third type of admission relates to the child whose own behaviour is causing problems. Children whose behaviour troubles no one but their own families, or who behave in ways which adults too easily overlook – depressed and withdrawn children, for example – are unlikely candidates for care. But children whose disruptive and anti-social behaviour spreads beyond the family, and is visible to schools, police, neighbours and strangers, may well be so. For them, admission to care has a more ambiguous meaning. The intentions of the 1969 Children and Young Persons Act were to cast admitted 'villains' in the role of 'victims' of another sort – vulnerable youngsters from difficult backgrounds who had succumbed to family, neighbourhood and societal pressures, and were in need of care or control not otherwise available to them. In practice, familiar elements of punishment, containment and deterrence are also in the minds of decision-makers and, it must be said, the parents themselves. In the event, the child-care service offered to this group is as much a retributive and protective service for the *public* as it is a 'care' service for the young people themselves.

Admission to care is therefore a shorthand term for a variety of responses to a range of problem situations, whose significance to the child, the child's family and the child-care system itself is equally varied. It follows that practice wisdom or explicit policies that take no account of these complexities and ambiguities are of little use in day to day decision-making. Statements that assert that 'admission to care should be a last resort' or that 'it is to be prevented at all costs', and policies which equate low admission rates with good child care, for example, seem to us to be singularly unhelpful – yet they were much in evidence in departmental documents and in discussions with staff at many levels. Detailed guidance as to what kinds of admission are best avoided and how prevention might be achieved, and suggestions about which admissions may actually be beneficial, and why, might be of more use.

There is also a sense in which a defensive 'last resort' stance – much the most common reaction, in our experience, though it is based in part on obvious faults in the child-care system itself – actually contrives to *reinforce* these failings, ensuring that public care is indeed something to be avoided. Some of the precipitate entrances into care, with their distressing lack of preparation, hastily arranged placements, and all the attendant risks of breakdown and further disruptions to follow, seemed to be directly attributable to such negative attitudes. A 'rule of pessimism'[6] operated about the care system, which meant that admission was sometimes almost unthinkable, until it became too late to think at all. 'Last resorts' are, after all, seldom desirable or constructive places to be.

Social-services departments also need to take account of the parents' views. They were apparently as likely to find admission helpful as otherwise, not only for their own sakes, but for their children's as well. On the other hand, their assessments of 'prevention' were by no means always positive, and professionals who insist that it is always preferable should listen to what is valued and appreciated about some admissions and should honestly examine the help that is actually offered when admission is denied. 'To admit, or not to admit' has therefore seemed to us an oversimplistic and even dangerous question to pose.

In contrast, whether to admit by voluntary or compulsory means seems a highly relevant question and brings us to our second theme. It is a question that individual social workers and their departments and even the DHSS need to address, because the consequences for the child, the parents and for the social workers who seek to help are considerable. We have seen that, for the children concerned, being *compelled* into care carries a high risk that the admission itself will be hasty, ill prepared and even traumatic. Place of Safety Orders are the extreme case, where entry is so managed that children rarely have the comfort of familiar adults around them, or any foreknowledge of where they are to go, as they make the transition from home to 'care'. Indeed, for some it will mean literally being carried off, protesting, and for a few it can apparently involve a dramatic entrance to a 'safe place' in handcuffs! And though POSOs *are* the extreme case, they are also so much a part of normal child-care practice that they formed over a *third* of all admissions and 60 per cent of all compulsory admissions in the monitoring year. For most children, compulsion is also likely to mean placement in *residential* care (as distinct from fostering) and the imposition of restrictions on contact with family members. It also increases the chances that the children will remain in care for a long time. (Half the compulsory admissions were still in care at follow-up, compared with less than a third of the voluntary group.)

For parents, compulsory removal has other implications. The majority will experience loss of control over decisions which affect their children's lives – not only at the point of entry, but throughout the time their children remain in care. They may be 'told' rather than consulted about plans for their children's future, or may even be kept in ignorance of what such plans are, or whether they exist at all. Many are likely to feel angry, frustrated and resentful at this perceived takeover, and to interpret events as a betrayal.

For social workers, compulsion also has its drawbacks. They too experience some loss of control over decision-making to others within their own organisations, and to professionals from other disciplines and in agencies outside the social-services departments. They are also likely to feel less satisfaction with the decisions, the placements and the plans that are made for this group of admitted children. Further, it is they, in the main, who have to face and attempt to deal with the hostility of the parents. Thus the compulsory mode of entry, and the sense of outrage which it often creates, present considerable difficulties for both the helpers and the helped.

By comparison, voluntary reception into care is generally better managed and much more acceptable to parents. For some, (though by no means all) there is planning and preparation. Children are more likely to be introduced to placements in advance and to be accompanied to them by familiar adults, and they are more likely to go into foster homes. Most will return home fairly swiftly. Parents are much more likely to be consulted, to feel involved and to have a sense of sharing in plans and decisions for their child. Social workers are similarly happier with these admissions and more often judge them to be appropriate and beneficial.

There seems every reason, therefore, to think very carefully before the legal means of entry is chosen; for there is certainly a choice to be made. Despite the evident differences in emphasis in the child and family problems with which alternative routes into care have become associated – the *behavioural* focus of many compulsory removals and the large number of teenagers amongst their ranks, compared with the *situational* stress to which much voluntary care is a response, and the younger age group that is usually involved – there is much overlap. 'Victims' and 'volunteered' share very similar deprivations and disadvantages, and official concern over standards of parental care is manifest for both. Even the older 'villains', for all the *relative* stability and comfort of their home base, have been, and usually remain, subject to stressful family relationships. Children who enter care therefore form another continuum – of age and family circumstance – and where they are placed on that continuum, and what is therefore considered to be the best means of effecting their admission, is a matter of interpretation and emphasis. In fact, we saw that such interpretations differed in our two sample authorities. Clayport, for instance, was just as likely to admit its villains by the voluntary route as to remove them compulsorily, whereas Shiptown much preferred to take control. On the other hand, Clayport was more likely to take protective action over its victims.

When choices are to be made, therefore, our data suggest that voluntary care should be the preferred mode of entry and not, as it appears at present, a course to be taken reluctantly or apologetically. There is clear evidence that the admission process and the care experience itself are likely to be less distressing for the child or young person and certainly less upsetting for his parents. The research data cannot take us beyond this, to a point where we can assert that outcomes will also be better – that children will be better cared for, better protected, or their behaviour modified more successfully if voluntary rather than compulsory admission· is arranged. But neither is there evidence in this study which points in the opposite direction, and it seems to us that decisions in which parents (and, one hopes, the young people themselves) can participate, care which is in some sense shared, and separations which can be planned and managed with some degree of sensitivity, are in themselves sufficient reason for choosing the voluntary route wherever possible. This, in our view, applies to awkward teenagers as much as to younger children, since separation from familiar people and places is an anxious and stressful experience for people of any age, especially when there is tension and difficulty in the home they leave behind. It may also apply more often to young children at risk than current practice allows. The fact that POSOs and care orders were generally the recommended course in such cases, that several parents expressed a desperate fear of harming their children and were asking for rescue and a breathing-space, but that, nevertheless, departments showed some resistance to admitting neglected and abused children to care, suggests that opening the voluntary door a little wider might introduce more flexibility and responsiveness into this difficult and delicate area of child care.

We would therefore recommend that decisions to remove children from their families compulsorily should always be supported by explicit reasons why the voluntary route was inappropriate or inadequate. In this, we merely reiterate a basic tenet of the 1969 Children and Young Persons Act, which supports intervention *only* if the child 'is in need of care or control which he is unlikely to receive *unless* the court makes an order' (emphasis added).[7]

Such a change requires a considerable reorientation in attitude amongst the decision-makers, and some social-work trainers as well. Voluntary receptions into care have not been popular in recent years, and arguments against them centre on the power they leave in the hands of unpredictable parents. Accordingly, it is alleged, they should be avoided in order 'to protect children from the "in and out of care at parental whim syndrome"', as one of a clutch of like-minded students recently phrased it. Although this is obviously a serious consideration where the child's welfare is threatened, our research demonstrates not only the risks of exercising compulsion, but also parents' perceptions that its use is sometimes at the whim of the social workers!

So far as Place of Safety Orders are concerned, we would urge that police and social services co-operate in keeping comprehensive records of all orders made and that, despite their ambiguous 'non-admission' status, they be included in the published annual returns of children in care. In this way their *real* scale and significance may be better appreciated, for it is our strong impression that the apparently dramatic growth in their use has occurred rather by accident than by design, and is not always fully recognised. The high ratio of such precipitate removals to other forms of admission compares most unfavourably with, for example, the use of emergency compulsory procedures for adults under the Mental Health Act.[8] So, although the protection offered to vulnerable children in these circumstances must be of over-riding importance, the widespread use of such drastic action warrants much closer investigation. We would especially urge, therefore, that authorities carefully examine the justification for, and consequences of, their decisions in this respect.[9]

Our third theme concerns the role of policy and its relationship to the discretion exercised by social workers. In chapters 6 and 8 we set out our understanding of that relationship and found that child-care policies were not always useful, clear or unambiguous and that their dissemination was a rather hit-or-miss affair. The social workers were not rule-bound, and, although they were caught between the pressure of referrals and the limitations of departmental resources, they had some room for manoeuvre and the exercise of choice in how they responded to family problems. But it was a choice that sometimes went unrecognised, or was informed by only partial knowledge of the available options.

In our view, the conditions in which child-care decisions are made could be improved in several ways. We see, first, a need for clear, comprehensive and much more detailed and specific statements of departmental child-care policy, which should be reviewed and updated on a regular basis.[10] Their dissemination is also important. Codes of practice and memoranda have their value, but will be quickly regarded as so much waste paper unless policies are also *talked about* - explained, argued, defended and modified in the light of experience. For social workers, who play a major role in admission decisions, their most im-mediate and potentially influential reference point is likely to be their team-leader. Departments that wish to get their policy messages across must, above all, persuade their senior social workers. They occupy a crucial position in the organisation, being in daily contact with social workers, familiar with the particular problems of their own localities, and often involved in face-to-face work with clients, which, in the social workers' eyes, gives them a credibility that those further up the hierarchy sometimes lack.

We are not arguing for policies which tie the social workers' hands, or erode their discretion to find solutions to fit the particular case. On the contrary, we see just as much danger in rigid policies which reduce people to categories and departmental responses to a set of formulae as we do in unbridled and poorly informed freedom of action on the part of social workers. Discretion for those who operate at the boundaries of the organisation and who actually meet the families it serves is vital if the service offered is to be truly personal and genuinely in tune with community needs.

However, discretion, in our view, cannot be well exercised in a policy vacuum. The decision-makers need to know, in some detail, what the child-care goals of their organisation are and what facilities are available to achieve those goals; and bland, rhetorical statements that smack of a United Nations Charter are of no help here. They also need the challenge of testing their decisions against specific policy and practice guidelines; especially so since individual generic social workers are not likely to have to make decisions about child-care admissions in more than a handful of cases in any one year. The discipline of showing how any particular course of action fits in with accepted views of good practice and, if it does not, of arguing out its justification seems essential if professional discretion is not to degenerate into professional whim.[11] This kind of interchange and testing-out was well demonstrated in the Children's Panel which met weekly in Clayport. Social workers attending were made aware of departmental policies, but they also had freedom to challenge and persuade, in their turn, if the circumstances of a particular family did not fit neatly into the normal departmental solutions. Thus existing policies, the extent of their own discretionary powers, and their evident responsibility to help shape policy themselves were all underlined.

Social workers will also be helped to a better exercise of discretion if they have access to as much information as their department can muster. It was our experience that the social-services departments accumulated a mass of valuable material on referrals made, decisions taken and some of the consequences that followed, but that this was rarely presented in a form which related to the social workers' immediate working-group – the team. Rather, information was aggregated for districts or for large areas of the authority, and crucial differences in the pressures on, and responses from, different teams were obscured. Indeed, one of the valuable spin-offs of research feedback sessions with participants in the study was that it enabled them to appreciate what their particular team did, in relation to others within the same authority; and comparisons can engender reflection and reappraisal.

Policies also need to be addressed not only to the personnel within the organisation, but also to those agencies who regularly refer children and families to them. It seemed to us that definitions of which sort of referrals could reasonably be considered, and which services were properly on offer, were not always worked out sufficiently clearly, or at a high-enough level to be genuinely 'departmental'. In consequence, coherent statements of what the department could or could not, or perhaps should or should not, be asked to do, were rare. We therefore had the impression that what departments actually did was sometimes shaped more by referral agents who knew what they wanted than by the departments themselves.

Issues of practice

We turn finally, and briefly, to some specific issues of practice which were highlighted in the study. The first concerns the assessments on which social workers base their decisions to arrange or prevent the admission of a child to care. We saw that in many ways they accurately reflected the facts of each family situation and also shared some parental perceptions of what the problems were. Where they were sometimes weak was in their exploration of kin and neighbourhood networks as potential sources of help; and in their recognition of the strengths and positives within families – including the somewhat neglected fathers, whether resident or not. What this suggests is that a wider perspective is sometimes needed, one which avoids an exclusively problem-focused approach and which, in looking well beyond the nuclear family unit, may produce better assessments and a broader range of possible solutions. We do not hold out hopes that kin and neighbours can solve everything, and thereby divest the authorities of their responsibility for providing substitute care. On the contrary, they had their own share of difficulties and deprivations, added to which strained and fractured relationships with relatives and friends were sometimes part of the problem; it was also clear that a number of families had already approached these networks without success, or regarded the help on offer as inappropriate or inferior. But a thoroughgoing investigation which places a family assessment within a wider context is none the less obviously important. Assessments also need to take account of the changing state of families. The fluidity of family structures and the speed with which they fragment and re-form is striking, and means that plans to assist, and the assumptions on which they are based, need to be regularly updated.

A second crucial area of practice concerns the admission process itself. Too often this was conducted in a way calculated to reinforce rather than reduce the shock and damage of separation for the children and young people involved. Long-established lessons of good child-care practice, which emphasise careful preparation of child, parents and caretakers, the presence of familiar people (and things) when moves are made, and the reassurance of regular contact with home, were honoured more in the breach than in the observance. We have indicated that this was specially so in the case of compulsory admissions, and this is one of the reasons why we favour the voluntary route. But improvements do not depend solely on statutes, or on the efforts of social workers alone. They rely heavily upon providing placements that are actually in excess of demand, on having sufficient residential and foster care, for example, to make it possible to reserve placements in advance and to make choices between them; and they require methods of allocation which do not merely respond to last-minute crises. If the economic imperative rules out such provision, it becomes all the more important that the admission itself be handled sensitively, with at the very minimum the reassurance of familiar adults around to ease the transition to an alien environment.

The importance of maintaining contact between the admitted child and his family has also been stressed. The Dartington Research Unit has looked at this in much more detail, and our data merely reinforce their findings.[12] Perhaps the most important lesson is that, besides imposed restrictions on access, there are a whole range of unintended or inadvertent barriers which deter parents from visiting, and very little is done by social-services personnel to help them overcome these barriers. Yet departments have power to give financial assistance to help parents keep in touch, though this seems rarely to be used.[13] It would seem an urgent matter to exploit these powers to the full, not only for the comfort they might bring to parents and children alike, but also because the maintenance of links makes a child's return to his family a much more likely prospect.[14]

The study has also emphasised the conflicts which arise between parents and social workers when children are removed from home under compulsion. The exercise of such powers cannot of course be avoided entirely, though we have suggested that it might with benefit be reduced. No practice wisdom will make this an easy task for social workers, and parents will naturally feel angry and aggrieved however it is handled. But, from the parents' own accounts, there were some clues as to how it might sometimes be managed better.

There is obviously a need to make sure that parents understand what the legal powers really mean, and why they are being used; and to ensure that they are properly advised of their legal rights. These are not easy tasks, and information in writing will usually need to be supplemented by verbal explanations - even translations - if they are to appreciate the full implications of the action taken. It also seems clear that social workers need to spell out, at an early stage in negotiations, their own ultimate legal powers and responsibilities for children's welfare, rather than producing them like an unpleasant rabbit out of a hat once all their efforts to help in other ways have failed. The sense of treachery - of having been betrayed by social workers who appeared to shift suddenly from a helping to a controlling and even punitive role without warning - was very strong in some families, and fuelled their sense of outrage. Sharing the less acceptable face of social work with families from the outset is an aspect of communication that was much appreciated by parents; though *how* it is done, as with all social work, is of crucial importance. Presented as a threat, or as sanctimonious moralising, it is unlikely to be either effective or appreciated. Frankly and honestly presented in the context of a genuine concern to help, and as an integral part of that concern - the ultimate safety net - the power to control and compel can be both understandable and even helpful to some parents. Social workers can offer their own skills and their department's resources (including voluntary care) to work with parents for the sake of children; they can also clarify that they, and other professionals, have a duty to safeguard standards of care and, in the last resort, to intervene compulsorily to protect children if those standards are not met.

Facing the anger that is engendered by compulsion is also likely to be more constructive than leaving it simmering. Parents frequently felt that attention switched quite sharply away from them once children entered care, and if they were angry about the admission this looked to them like evasion and retreat. As one father said, 'I'm bloody angry with him - but I'd feel better if only he'd have the guts to visit, so I can *tell* him how angry I feel!'

We have seen, too, that social workers are frequently called in to 'do something' about a child at a time of crisis, when his behaviour appears intolerable and when the reactions of others to him are at fever pitch. Yet, in a sizable proportion of such cases, both the behaviour and the reactions will subside, and the bad patch will be overcome within a relatively short space of time. This tells us not that social workers should therefore keep away or do nothing; but that their most useful role might be to keep this hope alive, and to try to help the children and all the involved adults (teachers and policemen, as well as parents) to *survive*, without taking drastic and irreversible action or applying immovable labels. The task is an active and strenuous one, albeit dogged rather than dramatic. The research, and our knowledge of adolescent development, suggest it may be a more rewarding approach than extremes either of studied passivity or of Draconian intervention.

The instability of the care experience itself has also been highlighted, and again we merely reinforce what has emerged from other studies. Our focus was not primarily on how placements were chosen or maintained, so we can make only a few tentative comments. An obvious one is that admission to an observation and assessment centre inevitably adds an extra placement to the experience of most of the children involved, so developments in non-residential assessment could be of benefit in this respect.[15] Interim admissions of all kinds also contribute to the chain of disruptions in caretaking and education for children, so reduction in the number of remands and POSOs would also help. In addition, and linked with this, admissions which are planned and prepared before they are affected may ensure that more first placements are satisfactory and last for as long as is necessary.[16]

Lastly, if parents are not to feel unheard or neglected, decisions to prevent an admission - especially where that is what the parents actually want - need to be taken and followed up with as much detailed attention as those where an admission is arranged. In other words, preventing admissions to care means - or should mean - a great deal more than saying 'No'.

In conclusion, we have suggested that it is field social workers who bear the most responsibility for deciding whether or not children are admitted to care. This has meant that they have been at the centre of the stage in this study, and the critical spotlight has therefore fallen most directly upon them. However, the decisions they make and the ways in which they are implemented can only be as good as the policies, the resources, the support and the guidance that are available to them. Gaps and inadequacies in any of these areas will adversely affect practice. The social-services departments, local authorities and central government are jointly responsible for standards of prevention and care, and any failures at ground level are quite clearly their failure as well.

We therefore believe there are policies and practices that need to be challenged, but at the same time it would be wrong to convey the impression that child care in Shiptown and Clayport – or indeed elsewhere – is a wilderness, ripe for the researcher's scythe. We are aware of numerous examples of work that was sensitive, committed and brave. This we found especially admirable in the face of the more depressing features of the contemporary social-work scene: mounting pressure on local-authority budgets, public scepticism, ubiquitous internal reorganisations, unflagging demand – and contradictory research-findings! Research, like social work, carries with it the risk of betrayal. Social workers and their managers have entrusted us with much that is intimate and compelling. We hope that, in arguing for change, we have betrayed neither them nor the families they seek to serve.

Notes

Abbreviations: BAAF-British Agencies for Adoption and Fostering;
DHSS-Department of Health and Social Security;
HMSO-Her Majesty's Stationery Office;
NCB-National Children's Bureau;
OPCS-Office of Population Censuses and Surveys.

Chapter 1   The Background

1 *Report of the Committee of Inquiry into the Care and Supervision provided in relation to Maria Colwell* (DHSS-HMSO, 1974).
2 N. Parton, 'The natural history of child abuse: a study in social problem definition', *British Journal of Social Work*, 9 (1979).
3 For example, R. A. Parker, 'Planning for Deprived Children', (National Children's Home, 1971); J. Rowe and L. Lambert, *Children Who Wait* (Association of British Adoption Agencies, 1973).
4 *Report of the Care of Children Committee (Curtis)*, Cmnd 6922 (HMSO, 1946); R. A. Parker (ed.), *Caring for Separated Children* (NCB-Macmillan, 1980); *Second Report from the Social Services Committee on Children in Care, Session 1983-4*, House of Commons Paper 360-1 (March 1984).
5 All figures are taken from the HMSO Command Papers *Annual Returns of Children in Local Authority Care*, issued by the Home Office until 1970, and thereafter by the DHSS and the Welsh Office.
6 *Personal Social Services Local Authority Statistics: fostering and Place of Safety, financial assistance* (Statistics and Research Division, DHSS).
7 J. Packman, *Child Care: needs and numbers* (Allen and Unwin, 1968).
8 See, for example, J. Bradshaw, 'The concept of social need', *New Society*, 19 (1972); and G. Smith, *Social Need* (Routledge and Kegan Paul, 1980).

9 Some data on this were collected in Packman, *Child Care: needs and numbers*, and in a small unpublished thesis: Peter Leonard, 'A Study of the Admission of Children into Care in an English Industrial Town', 1956. Other, local studies by the research sections of social-services departments may also have looked at this group, but there have been no recent, large-scale studies which have done so.

10 See, for example, B. Davies, *Social Needs and Resources in Local Services* (Michael Joseph, 1968); B. Davies, A. Barton and I. McMillan, *Variations in Children's Services among British Urban Authorities*, Occasional Papers in Social Administration (Bell, 1972); R. Webber and J. Craig, 'Which local authorities are alike', *Population Trends*, no. 5 (OPCS, 1976); M. Carley, *Social Measurement and Social Indicators* (Allen and Unwin, 1981); P. Townsend and N. Davidson, *Inequalities in Health* (Penguin, 1982).

11 J. M. Prottas, 'The power of the street level bureaucrat in public service bureaucracies', *Urban Affairs Quarterly*, 13 (March 1978); M. Lipsky, *Street-level Bureaucracy: dilemmas of the individual in public services* (Russell Sage Foundation, 1980).

12 A. Webb and G. Wistow, 'Implementation: central-local relations in the personal social services', in G. W. Jones (ed.), *New Approaches to the Study of Central-Local Government Relationships* (Social Science Research Council, 1980).

Chapter 2   The Shape of the Study

1 C. A. Moser and W. Scott, *British Towns* (Oliver and Boyd, 1961); H. F. Andrews, 'Cluster analysis of British towns', *Urban Studies*, 8 (1971); D. M. Greve and C. A. Roberts, 'Principal component and cluster analysis of 185 large towns in England and Wales', *Urban Studies*, 17 (1980); and Webber and Craig, 'Which local authorities are alike', *Population Trends*, no. 5. The two ports are 'commercial centres with some industry' in Moser and Scott's terminology, and 'regional service centres' according to Craig and Webber. They also belong to a broad 'family' of towns which deviate least from the national mean on the major dimensions of measurement, so in this sense they resemble a lot of *other* towns, giving our small study a wider relevance.

2 See R. Rowbottom, A. Hey and D. Billis, *Social Services Departments* (Heinemann, 1974); and D. Billis, G. Bromley, A. Hey and R. Rowbottom *Organising Social Services Departments* (Heinemann, 1980).

3 Ibid.

4 *Report of the Committee on Local Authority and Allied Personal Social Services*, Cmnd 3703 (HMSO, July 1968).

5 *Annual Returns of Children in Local Authority Care*, published in summary as Command Papers, but issued in detailed form by the DHSS and the Welsh Office to the local authorities who contribute the data.

6 Copies of all the interview schedules used in the study are available on request from Dr Jean Packman, Department of Sociology, University of Exeter.

Chapter 3   The Children and their Families: The Social Workers' View

1 The unit of information was the *child*, a schedule being completed on each of the 361, even when there were children from the same household. Comparison with national data, which are frequently based on *households*, must therefore be made with caution. The 'families' described were those in which the children were normally resident at the time of consideration, and the 'parents' were their current adult caretakers.

2 For example, Packman, *Child Care: needs and numbers*; *Who Are They?*, a study of 2,283 children received into public care between May 1978 and May 1979 Strathclyde Social Work Department; and S. Millham, R. Bullock, K. Hosie and M. Haak, *Lost in Care. the problems of maintaining links between children in care and their families* (Gower 1986).

3 'Households and families', ch. 2 of *Social Trends*, no. 12, HMSO 1982.

4 Ibid.

5 From Kathleen E. Kiernan, 'The Structure of Families Today: continuity or change?', in *The Family* British Society for Population Studies, Occasional Paper no. 31 (OPCS, 1983).

6 6 per cent of fathers of children whose births were registered in the June quarter of 1979 were classified as unskilled manual workers. See G. Boston, 'Classification of occupations', *Population Trends*, no. 20 (OPCS, 1980).

7 See, for example, M. P. M. Richards and M. Dyson, *Separation, Divorce and the Development of Children: a review* Child Care and Development Group, University of Cambridge (Report to DHSS, 1982).

8 Packman, *Child Care: needs and numbers*.

9 C. Gibson, 'The association between divorce and social class in England and Wales', *British Journal of Sociology*, 25 (1974), quoted in Richards and Dyson, *Separation, Divorce and the Development of Children*.

10 The proportion of adopted children in the child population as a whole is not recorded and estimates are difficult to make because the death rates of adopted children are unknown. However, according to L. Lambert and J. Streather, *Children in Changing Families* (Macmillan, 1980), between 1 and 2 per cent of the National Child Development Study cohort of children were recorded as adopted, at the age of 11, in 1969. Annual adoption rates have, of course, declined quite substantially since then.

11 The role of social workers and social-services departments as the recipients of referrals from other often universalist services is well brought out in R. Dingwall, J. Eekelaar and T. Murray, *The Protection of Children* (Basil Blackwell, 1983).

12 For example, M. Rutter, 'Why are London children so disturbed?', *Proceedings of the Royal Society of Medicine*, no. 66 (1975); M. Rutter and D. Quinton, 'Psychiatric disorder - ecological factors and concepts of causation', in H. McGurk (ed.), *Ecological Factors in Human Development* (North Holland, 1977); Michael Rutter, 'Family, area and school influences in the genesis of conduct disorders' in L. A. Hersov, M. Berger and D. Shaffer (eds), *Aggression and Anti-Social Behaviour in Childhood and Adolescence* (Pergamon, 1978).

Chapter 4   The Decisions

1 $\chi^2 = 7.2$; n = 361; df = 1; p < .01.
2 $\chi^2 = 9.3$; n = 361; df = 1; p < .01.
3 $\chi^2 = 4.9$; n = 287; df = 1; p < .05.
4 $\chi^2 = 7.9$; n = 279; df = 1; p < .01.
5 $\chi^2 = 15.3$; n = 289; df = 1; p < .001.
6 $\chi^2 = 14.3$; n = 361; df = 1; p < .001.
7 $\chi^2 = 9.0$; n = 358; df = 1; p < .01.
8 $\chi^2 = 7.5$; n = 361; df = 1; p < .01.
9 $\chi^2 = 10.8$; n = 355; df = 1; p < .001.

10 See for example, Allison Morris, Henri Giller, Elizabeth Szwed and Hugh Geach, *Justice for Children* (Macmillan, 1980).

11 Until 1977, social-services departments were only required to inform the DHSS of the number of Place of Safety Orders in operation on one day in each year (31 March). Because POSOs last for no more than 28 days, this greatly underestimates the number of orders taken in any year. Even the annual figures that have been collected since 1977, which are generally in excess of 6,000 per year, may be underestimates. Enquiries made in the sample authorities, to the DHSS and to the Select Committee on Children in Care (authors of the Short Report, who were taking evidence at that time and initiated a question in the House) all failed to clarify whether police POSOs and those involving a non-social-services department resource (a hospital, for example) are included in the relevant local-authority returns. The likelihood is that they are not, which would in part explain why numbers in the sample authorities appear so high: a ratio of one to every two other admissions in Shiptown and Clayport compared with a ratio of one to six admissions nationally, according to the published statistics for 1980.

12 Paradoxically, Shiptown had an emergency duty team of social workers which operated out of office hours, whereas Clayport did not, and the latter's social workers were in dispute with management throughout the monitoring year and were doing no out-of-hours duties at all. On this basis, we might have expected the Clayport police to be the more active force. A publicly expressed philosophy in favour of 'community policing' in Clayport may therefore be significant. We were also informed, at a feedback meeting with Shiptown social workers, that the prominence of police POSOs in their city may have owed something to the preference of the Clerk to the Magistrates. It was alleged that he liked to be present to advise any magistrate who was asked to sign a POSO and that, rather than be on self-imposed call for all out-of-hours emergencies, he recommended that the police should use their own powers in this respect wherever possible.

13 Children and Young Persons Act 1969, section 28(1).

14 Children and Young Persons Act 1969, section 28(2).

15 Children and Young Persons Act 1969, section 29(1).

16 This, along with other research evidence on POSOs, was considered by the Short Report on Children in Care in 1984, and has contributed to the review of child-care law being undertaken in 1985.

Chapter 5   The Decision-Making Process

1 See for example, Dingwall, Eekelaar and Murray, *The Protection of Children*.

2 $\chi^2 = 16.8$; n = 131; df = 1; p < .001.

3 $\chi^2 = 8.0$; n = 131; df = 1; p < .01.

4 $\chi^2 = 16.6$; n = 131; df = 1; p < .001.

5 $\chi^2 = 9.2$; n = 297; df = 3; p < .05.

6 $\chi^2 = 9.5$; n = 224; df = 1; p < .01.

7 $\chi^2 = 36.8$; n = 220; df = 2; p < .001.

8 Child Care Act 1980, section 18(1).

9 For example, Dingwall, Eekelaar and Murray, *The Protection of Children*; and R. Bacon and I. Farquhar, *Child Abuse in an English Local Authority*, unpublished research report to DHSS (1983).

Chapter 6   In Search of Policy

1 R. A. W. Rhodes, *Public Administration and Public Policy: Recent Developments in Britain and America* (Saxon House, 1979).

2 A. Webb and G. Wistow, *Whither State Welfare?* (Royal Institute of Public Administration, 1982).

3 Ibid.

4 There were other departmental resources which were clearly relevant, which we would have liked to explore more fully. Section 1, monies under the Children and Young Persons Act 1963, was one area where we failed to obtain sufficient information. County's published budget was much more generous than Shire's (though modest in comparison with other county authorities of similar size), but Shire's exceptionally low figure was dismissed as erroneous and an artefact of computer error, and the correct sum was never tracked down. Nor was County's budget necessarily a good guide to what was actually spent, for team budgets in Clayport were reputedly often underspent. Nevertheless, it may be of some significance that of the 17 children whose admission to care was said to have been averted by financial assistance (not necessarily always Children and Young Persons' money), 15 were from Clayport.

Intermediate-treatment schemes were also of relevance to the admission rate of 'villains'. County's budget for intermediate treatment was again somewhat more generous than Shire's in relation to its child population, but accessible schemes in both Clayport and Shiptown were said to be sparse.

5 Shiptown's four day nurseries made available details of the 776 children who were on their books in the middle of our monitoring year. (Many children attend part-time, and numbers therefore outstrip places available.) They were categorised according to the reason for their admission, and the breakdown was as follows:

	No.	%
Children of single parents	207	27
Children in need of intellectual stimulation	192	25
Children in need of good physical care	63	8
Children from very poor housing conditions	61	8
Children subject to or at risk of non-accidental injury	53	7
Children with behaviour problems	49	6
Children whose parents are mentally ill/subnormal	37	5
Children who are physically handicapped	34	4
Children of very young parents	27	3
Children who might otherwise be in residential care (including one home on trial on care order, and one in private foster care)	23	3
Children who are mentally handicapped	16	2
Children who have physically disabled parent	14	2

Although only a small proportion (3 per cent) were regarded as being candidates for residential care, were it not for day provision, the similarity between their home circumstances and those of the children considered for care is striking.

6 Drawn from R. Titmuss *Essays on the Welfare State* (Allen and Unwin, 1958) and used in *Introduction to Welfare: iron fist and velvet glove* (Open University Press, 1978).

7 M. Adcock, R. White and O. Rowlands, *The Administrative Parent*, BAAF research report to DHSS (1982).

Chapter 8   Weaving Threads or Tying Knots?

1 Delinquency data were derived from the criminal statistics for England and Wales, 1980; C. Lupton and G. Roberts, *On Record* (Social Services Research and Intelligence Unit, 1982); and Devon County Social Services Department, *Children in Trouble 1980*.

2 Ibid.

3 See, for instance, R. Hadley and M. McGrath (eds), *Going Local - Neighbourhood Social Services*, National Council for Voluntary Organisations Occasional Paper no. 1 (Bedford Square Press, 1980); and the Barclay Report, *Social Workers: their role and tasks* Bedford Square Press (1982).

4 Michael Hill, *Understanding Social Policy*, 2nd edn (Basil Blackwell and Martin Robertson, 1983), p. 88.

5 Quoted ibid., p. 90.

6 G. Smith and D. May, 'Executing "Decisions" in the Children's Hearings', paper prepared for Social Science Research Council Seminar on Monitoring Child-Care Legislation, Exeter University, 1978.

7 Hill, *Understanding Social Policy*, p. 99.

8 Lipsky, *Street Level Bureaucracy*, p. xii.

9 Hill, *Understanding Social Policy*, p. 98.

10 Dalziel, personal communication.

Chapter 9   Six Months On: The Social Workers' Version

1 Only a half of the cohort of admitted children studied by the Dartington Research Unit in their work on links between children in care and their families (Millham et al, *Lost in Care*) had been discharged at six months. However, they excluded remands from their sample, whereas in the present study remands would account for a considerable proportion of early discharges. Our own more elastic timescale of follow-up interviews would also tend to boost the discharge figures.

2 Millham et al., *Lost in Care.*

3 Ibid.

4 See, for example, J. Packman, *The Child's Generation*, 2nd edn (Basil Blackwell, 1981).

Chapter 10   The Family Perspective at Follow-Up

1 For example, fewer Clayport children had been readmitted to care or had had changes of social worker, despite the longer timespan between family visits in this authority.

2 See E. Sainsbury, *Social Work with Families: perceptions of social casework among clients of a Family Service Unit*, (Routledge and Kegan Paul, 1975).

Chapter 11   Conclusions

1 For example, the DHSS-financed studies by D. Fruin and J. Vernon for the NCB, *Social Work Decision-Making and its Effect on the Length of Time which Children Spend in Care* (1983); by the Dartington Social Research Unit Millham et al., *Lost in Care* (1986) and by P. Marsh, D. Phillips and M. Fisher, for the ESRC, *In and Out of Care* (1985).

2 See, for example, J. Bowlby, *Attachment and Loss*, vol. I: *Attachment* (Penguin, 1971); M. Rutter, *Maternal Deprivation Reassessed* (Penguin, 1972); S. Wolkind and M. Rutter, 'Children who have been in care - an epidemiological study', *Journal of Child Psychology and Psychiatry*, 14 (1973); J. Essen, L. Lambert and J. Head, 'School attainment of children who have been in care', *Child Care, Health and Development*, 11, no. 6 (1976); L. Lambert, J. Essen and J. Head, 'Variations in behaviour ratings of children who have been in care', *Journal of Child Psychology and Psychiatry*, 18, no. 4 (1977).

3 See, for example, Rowe and Lambert, *Children Who Wait*; and Millham et al., *Lost in Care.*

4 See for example, Parker, 'Planning for Deprived Children'; Rowe and Lambert, *Children Who Wait*; and the studies by the NCB on the length of time children remain in care (Fruin and Vernon, *Social Work Decision-Making*) and by the Dartington Social Research Unit on links (Millham et al., *Lost in Care*).

5 A. S. Holden, *Children in Care* (Comyn, 1980) p. 31.

6 Dingwall, Eekelaar and Murray, in *The Protection of Children*, argue that a 'rule of optimism' operates in relation to cases of child abuse, whereby social workers are hopeful that care will improve and children will be protected without recourse to care-proceedings. We would see a 'rule of

pessimism' concerning the *value* of admission to local-authority care as the other side of this particular coin.

7 Children and Young Persons Act 1969, section 1.

8 According to the *Review of the Mental Health Act, 1959*, Cmnd 7320 (HMSO, 1978), compulsory admissions under section 29 represented between 6 and 7 per cent of all admissions in the 1970s.

9 The *Second Report from the Social Services Committee on Children in Care, Session 1983-84*, para. 129, recommends further detailed research on Place of Safety Orders.

10 Para. 233 (ibid.) recommends an extension of the practice of written statements of policy, 'so long as they are couched in terms which can guide social workers in their daily duties, and only to the extent that they are followed up in practice'.

11 Roy Parker used similar arguments in defending the use of prediction instruments as a tool to aid professional judgement, and not as a replacement for it. See R. A. Parker, *Decision in Child Care* (Allen and Unwin, 1966).

12 See Millham et al., *Lost in Care*.

13 Child Care Act 1980, section 26 (previously Children Act 1948, section 22).

14 See, for instance, J. Aldgate, 'Identification of factors influencing children's length of stay in care', in J. Triseliotis (ed.), *New Developments in Foster Care and Adoption* (Routledge and Kegan Paul, 1980).

15 See the DHSS Working Party Report on *Observation and Assessment* (1981).

16 Nearly 20 years ago Roy Parker observed, 'An important step in improving the standard of child care work will be made when the urgency or "immediacy" of decisions is reduced' (*Decision in Child Care*, pp. 83-4).

Suggestions for Further Reading

For abbreviations see beginning of Notes.

Related research studies

Adcock, M., and White, R., *The Administrative Parent*, BAAF, 1982.
Millham, S., Bullock, R., Hosie, K., and Haak, M., *Lost in Care: the Problems of Maintaining Links between Children in Care and their Families*, Gower 1986.
Dingwall, R., Eekelaar, J., and Murray, T., *The Protection of Children*, Basil Blackwell, 1983.
Fruin, D., and Vernon, J., *Social Work Decision-Making and its Effect on the Length of Time which Children Spend in Care*, NCB-DHSS, 1983.
Marsh, P., Phillips, D., and Fisher, M., *In and Out of Care*, ESRC, 1985.
Rowe, J., *Long Term Foster Care*, Batsford-BAAF, 1984.
Sinclair, R., and Webb, A., *Decision-Making in Statutory Reviews on Children in Care*, DHSS, 1984.

Variations in services for children

Davies, B., Barton, A., and McMillan, I., *Variations in Children's Services among British Urban Authorities*, Occasional Papers in Social Administration, Bell, 1972.
Packman, J., *Child Care: needs and numbers*, Allen and Unwin, 1968.
Parker, H., Casburn, M., and Turnbull, D., *Receiving Juvenile Justice*, Basil Blackwell, 1981.
Roberts, G., Reinach, E., and Lovelock, R., *Children on the Rates*, Social Services Research and Intelligence Unit, Portsmouth Polytechnic and Hampshire Social Services Department, 1977.

Social need

Burgoyne, J., and Clark, D., *Changing Patterns of Child Bearing and Child Rearing*, Academic Press, 1981.
Carley, M., *Social Measurement and Social Indicators*, Allen and Unwin, 1981.
Imber, V., *A Classification of the English Personal Social Services Authorities*, HMSO, 1977.
Rimmer, L., *Families in Focus: marriage, divorce and family patterns*, Study Commission on the Family, 1981.
Smith, G., *Social Need: policy, practice and research*, Routledge and Kegan Paul, 1980.

Social policy

Hill, M., *Understanding Social Policy*, 2nd edn, Basil Blackwell, 1983.
Packman, J., *The Child's Generation*, 2nd edn, Basil Blackwell, 1981.
Parker, R. A. (ed.), *Caring for Separated Children*, NCB-Macmillan, 1980.
House of Commons Social Services Committee (chaired by Renée Short), *Second Report on Children in Care*, House of Commons Paper 360-1, March 1984.

Social-services organisations

Billis, D., Bromley, G., Hey, A., and Rowbottom, R., *Organising Social Services Departments*, Heinemann, 1980.
Hadley, R., and McGrath, M., *Going Local: neighbourhood social services*, Bedford Square Press, National Council for Voluntary Organisations, 1981.
Lipsky, M., *Street-level Bureaucracy: dilemmas of the individual in public services*, Russell Sage Foundation, 1980.
Parsloe, P., *Social Services Area Teams*, Allen and Unwin, 1981.
Satyamurti, C., *Occupational Survival*, Basil Blackwell, 1981.

Consumer studies

Page, R., and Clarke, G. (eds), *Who Cares? Young People in Care Speak Out*, NCB, 1977.
Rees, S., *Social Work Face to Face*, Edward Arnold, 1978.
Sainsbury, E., *Social Work with Families: perceptions of social casework among clients of Family Service Unit*, Routledge and Kegan Paul, 1975.
Sainsbury, E., Nixon, S., and Phillips, D., *Social Work in Focus*, Routledge and Kegan Paul, 1982.
Thoburn, J., *Captive Clients: social work with families of children home on trial*, Routledge and Kegan Paul, 1980.

Index